PERSIST and PURSUE

★ A MEMOIR ★

PERSIST and PURSUE

Breaking Barriers to Achieve a Dream

Pierre Nzuah

Bloated Toe Publishing
Peru, NY

Library of Congress Control Number: 2020903004

ISBN-13: 978-1-939216-67-0   ISBN-10: 1-939216-67-2

Visit the author at
www.pierrenzuah.com

Visit the Bloated Toe Publishing website:
www.bloatedtoe.com   info@bloatedtoe.com

Front cover photo by Gregory E. Kie, SUNY Canton
Senior Media Relations Manager

Back cover photo by Richard McCants

Covers designed by Pierre Nzuah,
created by Jill C. Jones and Lawrence P. Gooley of Bloated Toe Publishing

Printed and bound by
Versa Press, 1465 Spring Bay Road, East Peoria, IL 61611-9788

Manufactured in the United States of America

Contents

(continued)

Contents

Foreword

The story about to unfold is one of dogged persistence and gleeful pursuit. It is also a story of hope, of hard work, of the realization of dreams, of the strength to be found in humility and, finally, of the power of love to make the improbable happen. More than anything, Pierre's is a story about respect for opportunity. It is this, in particular, which makes his journey so compelling and instructive. Each person we encounter on our path of days through this world offers us the gift of lessons to learn. Pierre's gift to you, the reader, and to those of us who are blessed to know him, is a reminder about profound, resilient, and daring respect for the opportunities which abound, quite literally, in every moment.

In our culture these days, there seems to be a regrettable lack of appreciation for the opportunities we do enjoy, and for the breadth and depth of the opportunities we might enjoy. There is a sense that when we talk of "opportunity," what we really mean is easy opportunity, or obvious opportunity, or legislated opportunity, or an opportunity that is granted or given, or an opportunity that is just the same as everyone else's opportunity; opportunity which needs to be boundless and broad, and worthy of its own mobile phone app. As if opportunity were only ever to be found on an eight-lane superhighway streaming toward an inevitable, positive outcome with controls set on cruise and nary a concern or doubt about arriving at the destination; and, that anything less than an equal opportunity is really no opportunity at all.

Paradoxically, we also live in a culture where, already in possession of so much, we sense little headroom left for more; that any remaining opportunity is capped from the onset. We carry an assumption that opportunities are in scarce abundance, found in isolation, meted out sparingly, and reserved for the lucky or privileged, and only epic in nature; something akin to winning the lottery and with the same chances. As if opportunity is only ever swinging for the fences and scoring a grand slam every time we come to the plate. We fail to appreciate the virtue of simply having our chance at bat to get on base or advance the runner. We further assume that opportunity manifests as a permanent event rather than an ephemeral process.

Pierre's story runs counter to all of this. Reading this book—the story of his life—it becomes clear that Pierre finds every decision, action, conversation, and "chance" occurrence an opportunity on his pathway to the future. True, taken in isolation, such small moments don't seem to carry very far, but each one carries just far enough to arrive at the next. Pierre understands opportunity to be a function of cause and effect, but also sees opportunity as a tipping point of critical mass—a series of little changes until there is nothing but change. While it is true that hard work is required to bring any opportunity to fruition, more often than not it is through those seemingly small acts of kindness, given by others, leading to another, and combined with those which ensue, which ultimately gift us with the tools necessary to allow us to bring our hard work to bear. Pierre Nzuah's whole outlook on life, and the incredible journey he has already traveled, is guided by a profound respect for opportunity everywhere and all the time. May Pierre's story be such an opportunity for you!

Rev. Michael P. Catanzaro, Pastor
First Presbyterian Church on the Park in Canton, NY

About Cameroon

The Republic of Cameroon, the author's homeland, is a Central African country bordered by Chad to the northeast, the Central African Republic to the east, Equatorial Guinea, Gabon, and the Republic of the Congo to the south, and Nigeria to the west. The country's coast, on the Bight of Bonny, is part of the Gulf of Guinea and the Atlantic Ocean. Due to its geological and cultural diversity, it is often referred to as "Africa in miniature." Cameroon has beaches, deserts, mountains, savannas, and rainforests. Mount Cameroon is the highest point at almost 4,100 meters (13,500 feet) in the Southwest Region of the country. Douala, Yaounde, and Garoua are the

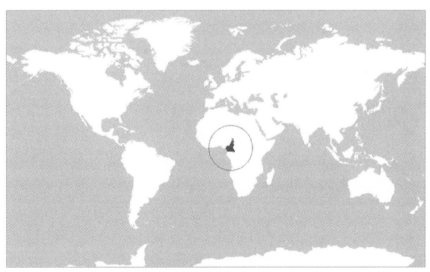

The location of Cameroon highlighted on the world map.
(Source: www.freeworldmaps.net/africa/cameroon/location)

largest cities. (Source: africa.com/heres-what-you-need-to-know-about-cameroon)

In primary school, children are taught to visualize Cameroon as a country sitting on the ambit of the African map.

Cameroon is a land of more than 250 distinct tribes and over 200 different languages. Native music includes makossa, bikutsi, new rumba, and bend-skin, to name but a few. Official languages, taken from the country's colonizers, are English and French.

With such great diversity among a population of more than twenty-five million, almost every Cameroonian has a different experience and a different story to tell about growing up in the country.

Introduction

From Dust to Snow

All trees were dead.

Everywhere I looked, I saw white.

It was extremely windy and the temperature was twenty degrees below zero. I was wearing a brand-new suit and a pair of pointy dress shoes. I carried no winter coat, no boots, and no mittens to keep my fingers warm. When I stepped outside of the building at Hancock International Airport in Syracuse, New York, my face went numb and I ran back inside. I couldn't handle the brutal cold. .

That was January 21, 2011, and that's how I arrived in the United States to pursue my American dream.

But my dream actually began many years earlier when I was still a boy in Central Africa, in my native country of Cameroon.

PART I

OVERCOMING DAUNTING
ODDS IN CAMEROON

1

My Family and Village

I was born (in March 1985) and raised in Baligham village in the Northwest Region of Cameroon. Our family compound was comprised of several mud-brick houses grouped around an open courtyard.

In our tradition, newborns receive a last name to honor a family relative. That is how I got my last name, Nzuah. The first name can be anything, usually a Western name. My mother was pregnant with me for more than nine months and had some medical complications. My uncle Pierre, a motorcycle mechanic, always gave her rides to the hospital on his motorcycle. When I was born, he wanted me to be his namesake, but my last name had already been chosen to honor a deceased great aunt. As a result, my first name honors Uncle Pierre.

I'm one of the children in my family who does not have my father's last name. My father, Pa Jean Mofor, added his last name on a child's birth certificate only if pronouncing those three names all together transitioned smoothly. The order of the names does not matter. The family name can be placed first, second, or last. In any of these arrangements, adding my father's last name, Mofor, to Pierre Nzuah didn't have a smooth transition. Why did he care about that? My father was a great believer in attending ceremonies at the end of each primary-school term to listen to the class standings being read out loud on the assembly ground. He developed a habit of arranging the names of his children in an order that could be read smoothly.

My family is polygamous—two wives and one husband. My parents were subsistence farmers, and the farm work was mainly done by my mother and "stepmother." My mother, Odette Ngegang (aka Mama Bar), has seven children—six boys and one girl. My stepmother, Mboying Suzanne (aka Mami Suzanne), has eight children—two boys and six girls.

Apparently two wives weren't enough for my father because he had a couple of extramarital affairs that produced two daughters, one from each of his mistresses. Instead of getting angry with my father about his infidelities, my mom and stepmom dared him to get married to those mistresses. As a child, I was usually my father's messenger to his mistresses, delivering packages to them and never breathing a single word to my mom or stepmom. The mistresses rewarded me with goodies, and sometimes money for beignets.

In our family compound, my mom and stepmom each had mud-brick houses. A separate, four-bedroom, mud-brick building housed grown-up male children, with more than three of them often sharing the same bedroom and bed. In my family, we refer to each other as brother or sister—to us there is no such thing as stepmother, stepbrother, stepsister, or "half siblings." Despite occasional fights, we children got along well with each other. A stranger visiting our family compound would have had a hard time telling which child belonged to which woman.

A tailor by profession, my father lived in another four-bedroom, mud-brick house along the roadside, right at the entrance to our compound. My dad lived in one of the rooms and used the rest of the house for his tailoring workshop, which had about five sewing machines. He also had a marking machine that he used to make special designs on fabrics. At the beginning of every school year, he sewed and sold school uniforms for nursery, primary, secondary, and high school students. He also "recycled" sandbags and rice bags to make hundreds of school bags for elementary school children.

In addition to tailoring, my dad maintained an Arabica coffee farm and plantain farm on the land adjacent to our family compound. He also kept free-range chickens—he loved scrambled eggs.

He would let some of his hens set in order to hatch and expand the chicken flock. When I was growing up, my father always kept at least five goats. Each of the older boys was assigned one to raise. We tied long ropes around their necks, pulled them each morning to new areas with fresh grass, and staked them out with the ropes to graze for the day. In the evening, the goats were brought back to a room where they were kept overnight. We didn't have a big barn for animals like farms had elsewhere in the world. Usually, my father kept the female goats for reproduction and sold the castrated males when they were over a year old. The money generated from the goats—and coffee and plantains—paid his children's school fees and bought beer.

When I was about five or six years old, I didn't have a goat to take care of yet, but I wanted one. Early one morning, I went into the room where they were kept at night and got one of the biggest goats, one assigned to my elder brother, Kenne Avent Innocent. Our goats were usually hungry in the morning, so they rushed to get to the fields of fresh grass. As soon as I got this stupid goat outdoors, she made a loop around me, and I was wrapped tight by a rope that was made from several strands of twine. Before I knew it, I was on the ground being pulled by the goat over a long distance. By the time I freed myself, my elbow was bleeding like crazy.

My dad took me to a traditional doctor, who stopped the bleeding with some kind of black herbal medicine, and my elbow was wrapped around with a white gauze bandage. Nothing else was done for the next two weeks, and the injury got infected. The odor from this festering wound was indescribable, and kids were keeping their distance from me. Luckily, my namesake, Uncle Pierre, noticed that I couldn't bend my arm. After I explained everything to him, he boiled water and used it to wash the wound. God bless him. With his motorcycle, he took me to the Baligham Health Center where I was treated with western medicine.

Later in the evening, Uncle Pierre came to our family compound and yelled at my father, after which he gave him the schedule to take me back to the hospital for treatment. Thanks to Uncle Pierre, my wound healed, but it left an everlasting scar on my elbow.

5

On the farm plots we owned, my mom and stepmom cultivated corn, cassava, beans, peanuts, yams, and other food crops. Besides the farm plots on the compound land, they had other pieces of farmland spread around the village. Some of these plots were more than four miles away from home, and we got to them on foot.

My mom and stepmom were completely independent women and didn't rely on their husband for anything. They processed cassava—the agricultural mainstay for farmers in Baligham village—turning the root into *garri* (a powdery foodstuff), which they sold at the weekly village market. The profit from selling garri was used to purchase cooking oil, salt, dry fish, and other kitchen staples not grown on the farm. Different crops do well in different parts of the village, so not all farmers grow the same crops. As a result, villagers buy from other farmers what doesn't do well on their own farms.

My father, Pa Jean, attempted to get an education when he was a young boy. Missionaries were forcing children to attend school—free of charge. My father told me he began attending an English-language institution in the village and loved going to school. However, his father, Pa Mayoka Mofor, didn't want him to go to school. Instead, Pa Mayoka wanted my father to stay home and take care of the goats, chickens, and other farm animals. He only managed to get through first grade—"Standard One," as it was known at that time—before my grandfather took him out of school completely.

My father was very angry at his father for not letting him go to school. Instead of watching out for the chickens, he just watched the hawks as they got the baby chicks one after the other. This was his way of getting back at his father. He said leaving school was what made him a delinquent young man. My grandmother, however, told us that my father was always stubborn. For example, whenever he was sent to fetch water, he would return home and then intentionally drop the full calabash as he approached the door. Because of this behavior, his parents sent him to stay with his grandparents—my great-grandparents—in the Western Region of Cameroon, a French region. At his grandparents' village, my father was enrolled in a French-language academic institution, where he started school

6

at the standard-one level again. His stubborn attitude got him sent back to his parents' home in Baligham village, and that was the end of his educational career. How he managed to speak, read, and write in both English and French remains a mystery to me.

In contrast, my mother had no interest in education. She told us that whenever missionaries came to the village and family compounds to take kids to school, she ran and hid herself in the bushes. All she wanted to do was help her mother on the farm. One day, while she was hiding under an Arabica coffee tree waiting for the missionaries to leave, she fell asleep. When she woke up, she saw a poisonous black mamba snake wrapped around the top of the tree. She got up and ran quickly to the house, crying. Her mother consoled her and then took her to the farm, so she never saw the inside of a classroom.

When my mother got married, my grandmother sent her second-younger sister, Aunt Manyi Jacqueline, to live with her so she wouldn't be lonely. To my father, Aunt Manyi was like his first daughter and he vowed to make sure she had an education. Like my father, Aunt Manyi enjoyed attending school. She completed sixth grade, but with only one year left to finish primary school, her parents chose a husband for her and she was forced to drop out and get married. To this day, Aunt Manyi laments the fact that she was forced to give up school for marriage.

When Aunt Manyi had her firstborn—my cousin Yimely Samuel—my mother sent my elder sister, Philomin, to live with her and take care of the baby. I never knew that Philomin was my sister until I was about fifteen years old. I always thought she was Aunt Manyi's first-born child and so did my younger siblings.

In the village, we had no access to basic necessities such as pipe-borne water. We fetched our drinking water from streams running across the neighborhood, and didn't think about human activities upstream, such as bathing or clothes washing. If the water we got from a running stream was dirty, we just let it stand to allow the dirt particles to settle before we drank it. We could have attempted to purify this dirty water before drinking, but nobody had time for that.

There was no electricity. Almost everyone in the village used kerosene lanterns. Some bar owners had diesel generators that powered televisions for special events. Whenever there was an important soccer competition, such as the African Cup of Nations or the Champions League, elderly people buying beer were allowed to get into these bars for free. However, anybody not drinking beer had to pay something like 100 FCFA or 20 cents to watch a soccer game. In my neighborhood, only Mr. Albert had a TV. Since most of us didn't have money to pay for TV time, we created small peepholes into his bar house to look through during games.

I can't remember ever having a single room or bed to myself. I always shared a bamboo bed with two or more brothers. The mattress on the bed was made up of several sandbags sewn together and stuffed with grass. When my brothers living in the city visited the village, five of us shared the same bed. While it was okay for the girls to live in their mommy's house, my father wasn't a fan of any teenage boy living in the same house as his mom. As soon as a boy turned about twelve years old, my father repeatedly mocked and teased him, calling him a mommy's boy until he left his mother's house to join his brothers in the big boys' house.

One of my responsibilities as a child was to run errands for my father. At an age when I could barely speak, he started sending me to the bar to buy beer and cigarettes. I still remember that his favorite beer was 33 Export and his favorite cigarette brand was Red Club. Since I was brought up only speaking the dialect Ngemba, I didn't know how to pronounce the brand names of the beer and cigarettes he wanted, so my father wrote the name of what he wanted on a piece of paper and wrapped the money in it. I took this to the bar and handed it over to the bartender, who read the order and gave me what my father had written. When there was change, it was put in my pocket or wrapped up in the same piece of paper to take back to my dad. As a little kid, I never missed an opportunity to sip his beer whenever he stepped away. Unlike some of my older and younger siblings who thought beer had a nasty taste, I loved the bitter taste of my father's beer, though I didn't know why.

Life in the village—then and today—is very different than in the cities. Cooking with meat or fresh fish was a luxury for my family. My mother didn't cook meat except for special occasions, such as Christmas, New Year's, and our annual family reunion. Since my father considered hunting dangerous, he prohibited us from hunting the way other villagers did to get meat. My brothers and I settled on trapping small animals and birds for our "bushmeat." Most frequently, we trapped giant rats and small ostriches.

These ostriches were not the type you find in zoos. They were slightly smaller than a chicken and could fly long distances. In the evening, before dark, we went to nearby bushes to set the traps (usually four), using corn and peanuts as bait, and returned early the next morning to check them. On a lucky day we could catch two giant rats, but sometimes we went for months without getting a single one. Out of frustration, we would stop trapping for a while.

Whenever we caught a giant rat, my mother would use it to prepare a delicious *fufu* corn meal, or sometimes a plantains meal. Giant rats were actually considered a problem during the growing season because they dig up groundnuts. Villagers were subsistence farmers and would not allow any wild animal to eat their farm products. Many people became hunters and trappers, which drastically diminished the giant-rat population.

In our village, most of the young people move to cities after their primary-school education to look for work, or move to larger nearby towns to pursue further education. Young people who are unable to succeed in the cities usually return to the village, where there is free housing, and where various relatives are willing to provide them with free food if they are lazy or unable to fend for themselves.

This was the way it was in my family and village when I was a child.

2

Fighting for My Place in School

When I was a child, there were no nursery or kindergarten schools in my village. In any case, my father believed these kindergarten classes were a waste of money. However, I was sure to attend primary school because my father loved education more than anyone else I knew.

Being raised by parents who have no formal education, I grew up without knowing about books or fancy toys. My brothers and sisters and I were never told bedtime stories. We either fell asleep when we were tired from the day's work or play, or we were forced to go to sleep when our mother turned off the kerosene lantern and asked everyone to go to bed. Unlike my mother, my dad was harsh when he wanted us to go to bed. When it was getting late and we kids were still up, he would make sure we had taken showers and then used his authoritarian voice to order us to bed. No child had the guts to oppose my father. Anything he said was final.

At the age of six, when I was ready to start Class One, my younger brother Ntinwa Job was diagnosed with spinal meningitis and was treated at a hospital in a nearby town. A few weeks after he was discharged, the area on his spinal cord where he had been treated started to pop out. At this time, my mother had some money from her palm-oil business, so she took Job to several hospitals, but nothing was done to stop his spinal cord from getting worse.

11

After spending all her capital and borrowing more from family and friends, she reluctantly returned home without results. Most hospitals in Cameroon are not adequately equipped or staffed. There is no such thing as a health-care system. My mother had to pay for everything out of pocket.

A few private hospitals could have provided better treatment for Job, but they were very expensive and my parents could not afford it. Most of them require upfront payment, or patients are not allowed to leave at the end of their treatment until the bills are paid—and they are charged for those additional days in the hospital. For this reason, most people in villages seek treatment from traditional (sometimes quack) doctors, and only go to the hospital when a situation becomes life-threatening. I have no idea how people like my grandfather lived beyond one hundred years of age in a village that had only a simple public health center.

Job's condition never improved. As his spinal cord continued to push out, his chest started popping out, too. His growth was stunted. Just like that, my brother quickly became handicapped. When the school year started, I was forced to stay home and babysit him while my mother worked on her farm acreage. I was sad to see my friends going to school while I was left at home, caring for Job and other little children in my neighborhood. A year passed and he still needed close attention, but my next-younger brother, Mbohlang Festus, wasn't old enough to take care of him. I was stuck at home again, unable to attend school.

In 1993, at the age of eight, I could not take it anymore. I was fed up being a babysitter while all my age mates and friends were at school. My father told me I had to wait one more year—which is what he had been telling me for the past two years. I was desperate to attend school, but I was too young and afraid to oppose his decision. While I didn't understand the broader importance of getting an education, I had the drive to go to school and learn just like other kids. I cried and turned to my mother for help, but she couldn't convince my father. Cameroon had no free education at the time. Each child had to buy a uniform and pay a fee to attend. Though it costs less than twenty dollars a year to put a child through primary school, that is a lot of money for a large, rural family. By the time I was pushing to go to school, my father had become discouraged with the outcome of educating his children: my older siblings who had graduated from high school were not finding jobs or opportunities to advance their education.

I thought my father just hated me when he refused to send me to school. I looked up to him as a role model. As a little kid, I fantasied about going to school in order to get a high-paying job that would enable me to marry many wives and have many children—all to make my father proud.

So in September 1993, about one week before the start of the school year, I decided to break any barriers in my way, even though I knew this would upset my father. My plan was to sneak out of the compound every morning to attend school without his knowledge. I could not go to my father for help with school supplies; I had to find alternatives.

One of my older brothers, Kenne Avent Innocent, had just graduated from primary school and was on his way to secondary school. I washed his primary-school uniform, which was much too big for me, and used twine as a belt to hold up his big khaki shorts, which were more like long pants on me. I buttoned up and tied the edges of his short-sleeve blue shirt to make it fit better.

Paper and books are rarely used during the first year of primary school. Children bring small slates or blackboards with them to class, which they use to learn to write. My half sister, Euphrasia, helped me find a blackboard. She got it from Fidelis, the son of one of my grandmothers on my mother's side. It was very large but I was glad to have it. I bought chalk with the money I saved from selling mushrooms, plums, and mangoes along the roadside during village market days that occurred once a week.

When I began attending Government School (G.S.) Mificat, Euphrasia would look to make sure my father wasn't around, and then she'd whistle for me to come along. This went on for more than two weeks before he found out.

One morning on my way to school, I ran into him as he was coming back from somewhere outside the compound. I was terrified that he was going to whip me before sending me back home. However, he just stared at me and then walked on without saying a single word. I wished my father had said something because I spent the whole day at school scared to death, knowing I was going to be in deep trouble when I got back home.

That evening, we all sat around the fireplace in my mother's house, eating dinner. My father started yelling and asking a series of questions.

"What did I tell you?"

"Didn't I say I was going to send you to school next year?"

"Who is going to take care of your brother now?"

"Do you ever listen?"

"Who is going to pay for your school fees?"

I couldn't answer any of his questions. I was scared, and shivered as he went on and on. He was angry at my mother for not telling him I was sneaking to school behind his back. He stomped out of my mother's house that night without finishing his food, and I could hear him talking to himself as he walked away. My dad was really angry, but at least he didn't get physical. He would have crushed me because he was in his prime and very strong.

The next morning, he showed up when I was dressed in my oversized uniform, ready for school. He told me he would pay for my school fees only if I was first in my class.

In Cameroon, the academic year is divided into three terms. At the end of each term, students are tested and ranked from first to last based on their final examination scores. The end-of-term results are read at a general assembly that parents and other villagers attend to find out how children have performed. This makes it very difficult for students to lie to their parents about their academic standing.

It was prestigious to be among the top five students in a class. Despite all the hard work during my first term, I was fifth in my class. My father wasn't impressed with my performance. After the assembly, he asked me the same question over and over again.

"Who was the small boy standing in front of you?" He was trying to remind me about Jojo Charlen, the student who ranked ahead of me.

My father succeeded in getting under my skin. I wanted to work harder in the second term so Jojo Charlen wouldn't rank in a better position than me. A man of his word, my father didn't pay for my school fees because I wasn't first in my class. He also didn't get me a school uniform, even though he sewed and sold more uniforms than anyone else in the village. I continued to wear my older brother's stained, oversized uniform.

During the second term, I worked much harder but only managed to improve my position to second, ranking behind Nzem-ecock Glory. After the assembly, I cried all the way home. Besides knowing my father wouldn't pay my fees, I was angry at myself because a girl had beaten me to the top position in my class. As a child growing up in a male-dominated society, I was infected with the myth that men had to be superior to women in every aspect of life. Girls also grew up thinking their male counterparts were superior.

My dad was surprised when he got home and saw me crying. I'm sure he was happy that I was taking school seriously. He consoled me by promising to pay for my school fees even though I hadn't yet made it to first place. At the conclusion of the year, I finally achieved first place in my class, and my father was there when the results were read. When I handed my report card to him, I could tell he was very proud of me, even though he didn't say it. He rarely praised his children. But I could tell he was proud by the smile on his face and his offer of a bonbon. It is still hard for me to believe that my father, perhaps the most famous tailor in our village, allowed me to wear an oversized uniform throughout my first year in primary school.

* * * * *

I was very pleased with the things I learned in Class One. My parents always made sure we washed up before going to bed, but cleaning our teeth was not a priority. Our teacher, Mr. Youmbi Richard, taught us how to brush our teeth using a chewing stick.

15

As a class activity, we went out with our teacher to find eucalyptus branches, which were used to fashion chewing sticks. Back in the classroom, he taught us how to brush our teeth through a song and demonstration. The song went like this:

> This is the way we brush our teeth with chewing sticks
> Up and down with chewing sticks
> Early in the morning (2X)

Our teacher, who was in his fifties, taught us the importance of respecting elderly people, emphasizing that they are a source of wisdom in society. In particular, children in my village are obliged to be the first to extend greetings to their elders. We were taught to always be polite and to greet anyone we met on our way, whether we knew the person or not.

The foundation of my love for mathematics goes back to the teaching methods in my first year of school. We were taught how to solve arithmetic problems using counting sticks—a simple calculator. We began with ten sticks and only did problems with solutions of ten or less. If we were doing addition, our teacher told us to think of our sticks as mangoes, which happened to be my favorite fruit. For two plus three, I put two sticks on one side and three on the other side. I brought them together and counted to get my answer. As we got to higher numbers, we started imagining a counting stick representing five or ten mangoes. Learning math this way worked well for visual learners like me. I was surprised when others complained that math had no application outside of the classroom. Sometimes I visualized my counting sticks as money, which made it difficult for me to get a problem wrong.

Our classroom was in a mud-brick building with window and door openings that lacked glass or doors. Class One and Class Two pupils shared the same room, with first-year students on one side and second-year students on the other. Although we had different teachers, we shared the same blackboard, which was divided into two equal parts by a thick chalk line. At the front of the room, the teachers shared a bamboo table constructed by students.

Our teachers also divided the time when each would talk to their students. Because of a shortage of instructors, our first-year teacher also served as headmaster. Although Class One and Class Two shared the same room and sat on the same bamboo benches, the Class Two students were proud of being one year ahead of the first-year pupils and prohibited us from ever stepping onto their side of the classroom. We hoped to treat Class One students the same way when we moved up to Class Two.

3

Getting to Class Five with Poor Reading Skills, and Through Primary School with as Few Lashings as Possible

After my top ranking at the end of Class One, I vowed to work as hard as possible to be the top student each year. There was stiff competition all through Class Two to Class Five from my main rivals: Foncham Eric, Seying Rudolf, Samgwa Ernest, and Ntinwa Maurice. Most of the time I outperformed these students, but I hit a serious obstacle after Class Four.

Beginning in Class Five, when I was twelve, testing changed from mostly oral exams to written exams. Each student was charged 300 FCFA for printed tests, but the money was not my main problem. It may seem incredible to those schooled in America or Europe, but I had succeeded through four grades without being able to read adeptly. Lessons at that level were taught aloud by the teachers, and I was able to listen and remember. My parents never read to me. I had no access to children's books.

As a result, I had a hard time learning how to speak, read, and write proper English all at the same time. I finished third at the end of the first term in Class Five, my poorest performance in a long time. My father wasn't happy. I wasn't happy either—I had become comfortable outperforming my peers.

I knew that my poor reading skills were the problem. When I was asked the questions verbally rather than having to read them, I was much better at answering correctly. My half sister Euphrasia helped me learn to write through dictation, guided me through reading passages, and helped me complete assignments through make-up quizzes. Thanks to her, I was back in the first position during the second term, but Samgwa Ernest beat me to the top spot during the third term by three points.

*   *   *   *   *

Besides paying for printed exams, we had to contribute to the school through labor. All our classroom buildings were of mud-brick construction, with corrugated iron or zinc roofing. Seating for eight or more was provided on long bamboo benches that were usually built by students.

Primary-school classrooms had open windows—no glass. The wind blew dust into the rooms, coating the benches and floors. At the end of each school day, teachers would announce: "Tomorrow, everybody should bring to class a vessel filled with water."

This was a daily routine. In order to keep the dust down, we had to water the floor every morning before we swept. In fact, in the early classes, it was a general knowledge question on exams: "When do we water the floor?" The answer: "Before sweeping."

Being first in our examinations earned me the position of class "Head Boy." As such, I did not have to bring a water vessel. Instead, my duty was to oversee the watering and sweeping of the class-room, including keeping a list of students who did not bring their water vessels or failed to help sweep. Penalties for repeat offenders included a beating on the palms or buttocks. Usually, teachers pun-ished the culprits by making them fetch water three times from the closest stream using a standard water bottle, while their fellow stu-dents were in class studying.

Corporal punishment was common at my school—and it wasn't just the teachers who dished it out. In Class Three, if only one student correctly answered a question, our teacher, Ms. Maureen, would have that student go around the classroom and whip each of his or her classmates on the palms. "Go around the classroom and give everyone one stroke," Ms. Maureen would say.

On multiple occasions, I had the opportunity to go around the classroom and whip my classmates. This was a good chance for me to get back at the bigger students whom I would never dare face in a one-on-one fight. I would go easy on my closest friends. However, I later changed my mind when one of my best friends, Ntinwa Maurice, had his own turn and didn't take it easy on me. He hit my palm with a cane as if I were a stranger to him.

For the most part, I detested corporal punishment. It was one of the reasons I went to school early and always made sure I had my homework done on time. If you missed a day of school or came late without an acceptable excuse, the consequence was corporal punishment—and you were responsible for catching up on missed work. Most teachers rarely listened to excuses from students. In cases where there was illness or an accident, smart parents brought their children back to school so they could explain the situation to the teachers. This helped spare them from lashings.

A typical school day began at 8 a.m., but we had to be on campus at 7:30 for morning assembly. All students lined up according to their class. The flag was hoisted, the Cameroonian national anthem sung, the Lord's Prayer said, and general announcements made. Then, we sang as we marched to our respective classrooms:

> Oh when the saints, oh when the saints,
> Oh when the saints go marching in,
> Oh Lord I want to be in that number,
> Oh when the saints go marching in.

Students who arrived late had to kneel down at the school entrance. Depending on the teacher presiding over morning assembly, the punishment might be a whipping on the palms or buttocks, or weeding in the school's garden. Since my school had no gate, not every latecomer was caught. The times I came late, especially during the farming season when the corn stalks were high enough to hide me, I would sneak onto the school grounds and hide behind the classroom. Then, as my classmates marched into the room, I joined the line and walked in. Or, I might jump into the classroom through the back windows. A student caught sneaking in would receive severe punishment. Luckily, I was never caught and none of my classmates ever betrayed me.

When I began primary school, I was already familiar with corporal punishment—from my father. If we did something wrong, such as steal a neighbor's mangoes or pawpaws, my father would beat us with his tailoring tape measure. If he caught two of us fighting, he ended the fight by lashing both of us repeatedly without asking who started the fight. My father was too athletic to run away from. Getting whipped with a tape measure was more painful than the eucalyptus canes used by primary-school teachers.

I didn't like being whipped—and I know most people detest the use of corporal punishment in schools—but I have to admit I think it helped me. Fear of whipping kept me from falling back to sleep in the morning. It was the reason I did my homework on time and correctly; two wrong answers meant two lashes on my buttocks. It was the reason I never dared to fight on campus. I believe moderate corporal punishment combined with merit ranking helps to get the best out of every student.

*　*　*　*　*

Being a student didn't spare me from doing morning chores and farm work. I was assigned to take care of one of my father's goats, which meant I had to find fresh grass for it each morning. I also fetched water for my mother to use for cooking and made my own lunch by frying corn and groundnuts.

In my village—and across the country as far as I know—there were no public-school buses. Most students walked to school. My primary school was about two kilometers away, and I was responsible for waking up early enough to fetch water for my mother before walking to school. Some students and teachers had more than twice that distance to walk. Sometimes I walked barefoot because I didn't own any shoes, but it wasn't too bad—except during dry season, when the dusty dirt roads were burning hot.

One tradition in our school was for two or more students to get together during lunch break to share food. This act of eating in a group is called *njangi*. Some days, members of my group would all bring similar food. The best days were when we all brought different things to share, like Irish potatoes, rice and beans, or yams. In Class One I was in a njangi group that included my distant uncle Fidelis, who was already in Class Seven. Fidelis never brought any food to the group. Instead, he would buy five donuts made from cassava, which cost 10 FCFA. While this was not equal in value to what the others contributed, we were glad for the donuts because we did not have money to buy any special foods.

Before we left for school each morning, my mother would tell us kids what chores to do when we came home, such as fetching water or firewood. All tap water in my village had become purely "decorative" long ago, so I had to walk a long way with other children in search of drinkable water. For firewood, we trekked quite far with our machetes to cut dead trees or bamboo that belonged to our families. We'd tie the firewood into big bundles and transport them home on top of our heads. The bundles were so heavy that we had to help each other lift them into place. For long distances, we would stop along the way to relax our necks.

On other days after school, I would meet my mother on the farm plot. If I knew I was going to meet her there, I would put work clothes in my school bag so I could change out of my uniform after classes, and then walk the few kilometers to help her. Once on the farm, my mother would give me something to eat that she had brought from home, and for a few hours I'd help with whatever farm work she was doing. At the end of the day, she prepared a bag of raw food for me to carry home on my head. We would bring yams, sweet potatoes, corn, beans, plantains, and other farm crops.

Even after a long day of school and work, I had to do my homework at night. There was no electricity in the village, so several of us would sit around the table doing homework by a kerosene lantern. Because of my father's love of education, he would usually provide the kerosene for his children and neighboring kids to study together.

However, this had to happen in our compound, where he could make sure we weren't doing something other than studying.

My primary school had no library, and most parents had no money to buy textbooks. We had to pay close attention in class because the teacher was our only source of information. Most teachers understood this and helped us by writing lessons and homework on the chalkboard, which we copied into our exercise books.

*   *   *   *   *

At school, I was known as "Mr. Book" because of my competitiveness and dedication to schoolwork. At home, though, I was known as a fast-tempered kid. I was easily irritated by little things and never accepted defeat in any argument. My parents didn't like this behavior.

I recall on one occasion coming home from school, and my mother had cooked two different dishes: rice with groundnut soup, and fufu corn with *njama njama*. She took some of the food to a death celebration that was being held in the neighborhood. Unlike fufu corn, rice was a rare dish in our home because it had to be bought at the market. As a result, most children preferred rice over fufu. On this day, my brothers had eaten all the rice before I got home, and I was the only one who had to eat fufu corn. I lost my temper and yelled at my mother for favoring my brothers over me. She yelled at me to stop behaving like a baby. I was so angry at her, I told her I wasn't going to eat her food anymore. She thought I was kidding, but I went on a hunger strike—sort of. After about a week of me not eating at home, my mother told my dad about what was going on.

"Don't worry, he can't go on like that forever," my father said.

Hearing this from my room, I was even more aggravated and vowed to continue with my so-called hunger strike. After a while, my mom wondered if I was eating at the homes of relatives. She asked everyone, but was told they hadn't seen me for some time. What was I really doing? Living on mangoes, pawpaws, and other fruit. During one lunch break at school, I climbed to the top of a nearby mango tree and was caught. The woman who owned the tree was standing underneath with a big stick in her hand, ordering me to come down. I climbed higher, planning to wait until she left. Unfortunately, she looked for a nice spot under the tree and sat there waiting. When the school bell rang to end lunch break, students were running back to their classrooms. I was stranded at the top of the mango tree. In order to get the woman to leave, I started cutting and throwing down her mangoes, both ripe and unripe.

"If you don't leave, I'm going to keep cutting your mangoes," I said.

"You're a bad child," she said, and left.

I didn't have any money, so I wasn't able to buy bread or other food from the store, and fruit alone wasn't enough to sustain me. After about two weeks, I had lost a lot of weight and started to have blackouts on a regular basis. I wasn't backing down, though.

The news of my food boycott spread across the neighborhood, and everyone was pleading for me to give it up. My mother urged me to eat, but that didn't work either. One evening when I came home, she had gathered people from the neighborhood to help her beg me to eat. Unexpectedly, my father also pleaded for me to eat. This was the first time my father had begged me to do anything.

After all the talking, my mother handed me some groundnut soup and a plate of rice topped with a piece of fried fish. Without saying a word, I joined everyone in eating. It felt so good to eat real food again. And as I thought about what I had been through, I vowed never to do such a thing again.

* * * * *

Children in my village experience growing up much differently than children in cities or in other countries. Without fancy toys or playgrounds, kids find ways to have fun. Like other parents, mine did not buy playthings; we had to make our own. We learned how to make soccer balls by collecting plastic bags and tying them together with pieces of string. These "balls" fell apart rather easily, so we retied them over and over again. I made airplanes by using mango-tree leaves because they are longer and make a better-designed craft. After building one from a tree leaf, I would plug a small stick into the middle section and run around with it as fast as possible. It was the most fun on windy days. I made small vehicles out of bamboo, peeling the hard outside layer away and cutting the soft middle into small pieces to construct a toy car. The hard back was used to pin the soft pieces together. The only tool I needed was a knife. The tires were created from pieces of old rubber slippers. The CV shaft was a piece of stick passed through a pipe, which was made from the branches of a pawpaw tree because they have a hollow interior. My favorite vehicle was a truck that I could use to transport small amounts of groundnut. The most durable toy vehicles were made from motorcycle or car tires. My namesake, Uncle Pierre, owned a mechanic repair workshop. We would frequently search his trash can for abandoned tires.

Growing up, I had a lot of responsibilities. My village has a rolling weekly market day. Some people went there to sell their surplus farm products, but my father went to sew and sell school uniforms and bags. On market day, I had to wake up very early in the morning, usually at 4 a.m., to join my siblings in transporting my father's sewing machine and tailoring tools to the site, while still allowing enough time to prepare for school. Sometimes I woke up grumpy but had to pretend I was happy; my father would be very upset if he knew I didn't want to help. In thinking back, I guess having a strict father was a good balance to having a laid-back mother. Someone had to be the tough parent.

During my years in primary school, I sold sugar cane to make money. Once or twice a week, I bought large quantities— usually 200 FCFA worth—from different growers in the village, and retailed it at school in 10 FCFA and 25 FCFA amounts during lunch breaks. From a good week of business—when I didn't eat too much of the sugar cane myself—I could make a profit of up to 100 FCFA. My father always convinced me to give him my earnings to save for me, and I didn't have the guts to refuse. Whenever I asked to use some of the money on big occasions like Christmas or New Year's, my father would ask; "Should I give you the money to spend on Christmas, or should I use it to pay for your school fees?"

Deep inside, the voices in my head said that it was his responsibility as my father to pay my school fees, but I couldn't say this to his face. Because of my passion for education, I had to give him the answer he wanted to hear: use the money for my school fees. I can still see myself walking away disappointed each time this happened.

Christmas and New Year's were the two biggest celebrations in the village, which is why I was angry at my father for keeping my earnings. This was a unique time of year when parents were obliged to buy news shoes and clothes for their children. My mother always waited until the last market day before the holidays to buy our festive clothing. My siblings and I would wait anxiously for her return to find out what she had gotten for us. One year on Christmas Eve, she came back and told me there was nothing left that was my size anywhere in the market. I thought she was kidding—until she distributed clothes to everyone but me. I burst into tears and stomped outside. When I realized no one was paying attention to me, I rolled in the dust, crying loudly until my mother came up with a solution.

That year, Christmas Day was also market day in neighboring Bagham village. My mother arranged for me to travel there with my older brother Innocent to buy holiday clothes. Before the rooster crowed on Christmas Day, he and I had begun the long walk, and after several hours we arrived at Bagham village. I got my new holiday clothes. Yes, acting like a monster paid off, but I sometimes blush at my headstrong behavior as a child.

4

Class Six Ends with a Bang

The most important celebration in Cameroon, aside from Christmas and New Year's, is the National Day. May 20 commemorates the day Cameroon passed a referendum to change from a federal system of government to a unitary state. In my primary school, students in Classes Five through Seven were given the privilege of representing the school in marches and traditional dances at the celebration held in Santa, the town closest to my village, about sixteen kilometers away. Primary-school students would leave the village a day early to spend the night with students from the village who were already attending secondary and high schools in Santa. Each one there might host eight primary-school students in his or her small, one-room quarters.

The second time I attended the National Day celebrations in Santa was in 1999, when I was in Class Six (at age fourteen). In preparation, I accumulated 4,000 FCFA—the most money I had ever raised—by making and selling bamboo chairs at the village market. At the time, my brother Innocent, who is five years older than me, was attending secondary school in Awing, a neighboring village. He came home on May 18 so we could travel together the next day. On the morning of May 19, we left at about nine o'clock. Some other students had headed to Santa as much as two hours earlier. Most of us couldn't wait for this day to come—it was a chance for us to get out of the village and to spend money on "luxury" items without the watchful eyes of our parents upon us.

After hours of trekking up and down steep hills, we arrived in Santa at around two in the afternoon, only to hear the news that a war had broken out between my village, Baligham, and the neighboring village of Awing. The dispute was over a contested piece of land. Some students were lucky enough to have relatives in other nearby towns, like Bamenda and Mbouda, where they went to stay for as long as the war lasted. But the rest of us had no such relatives nearby, so we had to stay in Santa, surviving on the little money we had and hoping the war would end soon.

With my 4,000 FCFA in hand, I decided to live on a 200 FCFA daily ration and pray that the war wouldn't outlast my budget. In Santa, we heard rumors about the number of people killed or taken hostage by both sides, the number of houses burned, and so on. At one point, someone told us that houses were burned right to the center of the market, which was located in the heart of our village. And we heard that the attackers planned to burn down our entire village by the end of the next day. We were very worried about our family's safety. The population of Awing was more than twice that of Baligham, and it was hard to believe they wouldn't crush the people in my village in a matter of days. However, this particular story turned out to be a lie. Some buildings were burned, but the rumor was a wild exaggeration.

During the war, the men were at the front—the land located between Baligham and Awing. Women were responsible for cooking for the fighters. Only children were allowed to flee to safety in neighboring villages that were on good terms with ours. According to orders issued by the village Chief from his palace, any adult who left during the war would be severely punished or completely banished after the war.

After a week of fighting, the government intervened with military forces deployed at the border to end the conflict. The Senior Divisional Office (SDO) of the Northwest Region of Cameroon visited the palaces of the two villages to enforce a cease-fire. The two chiefs and their representatives then arranged to meet with the SDO in Bamenda, the capital of the Northwest Region, to resolve the dispute through dialogue.

A day after the war ended, Napoleon, a young man from my neighborhood, was sent to Santa to bring us back to the village. When he brought the good news to us, the first question I asked was whether my parents were still alive. Almost everybody asked him the same question about their parents. He told us that only two people from my village were killed in the war. It was sad to hear of the deaths, but I was relieved to know that all my family members were still alive. We packed our bags and trekked with him back to the village.

When Innocent and I arrived at our compound, my family was patiently waiting for us. Most were sitting in the compound yard, talking about the war and drinking palm wine. My mother was overjoyed we were alive because they had been told that, on the day the war began, some students had been abducted by a neighboring village. This rumor and others could not be verified because cell phones were nonexistent in the village at that time.

We joined the others and sat outside to eat food my mother and stepmother had prepared to celebrate life. This was the first time Innocent and I had eaten a real meal in a long time. On our way back from Santa, we had pooled our remaining money to buy bread and sardines, luxuries that we now shared with our family. The bread was spiced up with sardines cut into small pieces, and my niece Kebun-jion Gillian passed the treat around to everyone.

As we ate, my father and others who were in the village during the war recounted stories about what had happened. Some villagers who lived closer to the warfront had lost their homes and belongings. They were safe because they ran to the center of the village to seek shelter. Losing a home and all it contained was serious: villagers kept all their farm harvests in their homes.

At this time, we were worried that my brother Innocent wouldn't be allowed to go back to complete his last term of school in our rival village, Awing. Despite the tension, the two villages worked things out after the cease-fire, and Innocent joined other students in going back to Awing to complete the academic year.

In my village, we also went back to school and took the third-term promotion exam. I finished first, as I had in the first two terms of Class Six. It was in this class that I became a well-rounded student—strong in all subjects and outperforming my academic rivals.

5

"What Is It With You and School?"

At the end of the academic year in Class Seven, students must take the national exit exam—the First School Leaving Certificate (FSLC). Failure means repeating the entire academic year and taking the exam again, but by Class Seven my math and reading skills were the strongest in the school. In my neighborhood, several people depended on me to read and write letters for them. Phones were rare and generally unavailable. If someone received a letter written in English from a relative living in the city, I would read it, translate it into our tribal dialect, listen to the reply in dialect, and write the return letter in English. Finally, I would read back what I had written—translating back into dialect—to make sure I had it right.

Class Seven was exciting, a decisive year in my academic career. When my father came to listen to the end-of-term results read publicly on the assembly ground, he was certain that at least one of his kids would be ranked first in their class. I remember one term when at least one of my siblings was ranked among the top three students across all the seven primary-school classes. By Class Seven, I was known throughout the school as a top student. When our Class Seven teacher—one of my very best primary-school teachers—began reading the results, he said: "Number of students who sat for this examination, 37. Number passed, 20. Number failed, 17. And the first in this class is?"

Then, he paused a few seconds and the students chanted, "Pierre Nzuah, Pierre Nzuah, ..." before he called out my name. I stood in front of the whole school to receive applause from students and spectators. The top three students in each class were usually recognized; others stayed in line, and those who had failed did not hear their names read, which signaled to their families and spectators that they hadn't passed the class.

Every Class Seven student had to pass the national exit exam (known as the FSLC) in order to graduate from primary school. Preparatory study was intense. We attended special classes every weekday from seven to eight in the morning before the regular school day began, and when that ended at 2:45 p.m., we were given a thirty-minute break before attending evening classes until about six o'clock. Many teachers at the school worked with us during these prep classes. However, it was not free. We paid an extra cost of 1,000 FCFA, in addition to the 3,000 FCFA school fee and 8,400 FCFA for the national exams. Having a child in Class Seven was a serious liability for parents struggling to take care of large families.

Attending the special prep classes was a burden on me. I had to leave home before six thirty in the morning, and returned home more than twelve hours later. During the third term of Class Seven, when the national exam date was looming closer, we attended Saturday classes as well. I wasn't a fan of waking up early, and I didn't like having to make food for myself. Sometimes I woke up after my mother had prepared some food, and would take that with me. Since I was lazy about making my own food and didn't like carrying the additional weight in my already heavy backpack, an alternative food supply was necessary to make it through the long school days. The solution was definitely not getting up early to cook. By this time, I was the go-to person in my class for help with every subject, and I thought of the saying, "Use what you have to get what you want."

I told my classmates that I needed food in order to continue helping them with homework or answering their questions about our studies. I was optimistic this plan would succeed because many students relied on me both at school and in home-study groups.

My plan worked! Before every evening session, my classmates offered more food than I could eat, providing a variety of choices. This helped me, but it also meant that I couldn't deny study help to someone who had given me food, so I had to pay even more attention in class to ensure I was able to answer questions brought to me by other students.

*   *   *   *   *

Class Seven was a pivotal point in my academic career since it wasn't clear if I would have the opportunity to attain further education beyond primary school. My father had no intention of sending me to secondary school because of the lack of opportunity in Cameroon for young people with academic degrees. The system had failed him: some of my siblings graduated from high school and couldn't get into any higher institution because of widespread corruption and bribery. Before I was born, the government had provided scholarships to students who graduated with distinction from high school. My father's hope was that my eldest brother, Yemeli Vincent, would benefit from a scholarship to study abroad. Unfortunately, scholarships were no longer available when he graduated from high school in 1992. This is where my father's plan collapsed, and he lost intereest in sending his children for education beyond primary school.

Growing up on the farm, and considering the work and financial situation of my parents, I knew it wasn't going to be easy for me to find a way to attend high school. But that didn't stop me from pushing on. The education system in Cameroon is actually very rigorous. Besides the national exam, students who want to attend secondary school must take the Common Entrance exam. Those who pass with high scores are placed on List A; those who receive average scores are placed on List B. Students with failing scores have no chance to attend high school, so passing the Common Entrance exam was a challenge—but convincing my father to register me for it was an even bigger obstacle.

When I discovered from my teacher that I had only been registered for the national exit exam, I knew my father had no intention of helping me attend high school. It was one of the saddest days of my life. I couldn't confront him because I knew that would do no good. Instead, I turned to my mother, crying as I talked to her.

"What is it with you and school?" My mother asked. "I need you to help me on the farm."

"Mama, you know that's not going to happen," I said.

As a child in a polygamous family, the odds were against me. My father had the habit of sending the child of one wife to secondary school only if the child of equivalent age from the other wife was going to attend school as well. My chances of going beyond primary school were slim because even though my half sister Euphrasia had been a very smart student, she was not sent to secondary school. Being female didn't help her case. Her failure to attend secondary school hurt my chances of leaving the village to further my education.

For months, I tried to persuade my father to register me for the Common Entrance exam, to no avail. I devised all kinds of simple strategies to try to convince him. I helped tap his palm wine; I made sure there was water for him to take evening showers. My father was unmoved. About a week before the deadline for exam registration, someone in the family died and my eldest brother, Vincent, came back to the village for the burial. He was the one man in the family who could have a fierce, man-to-man conversation with our father. I had no other choice but to use Vincent as a tool to get through to our dad. During my brother's second day in the village, I ran into him late in the evening as I was returning from school.

"Aleko'oh Pierre?" Vincent asked in dialect. How are you Pierre?

"Apouh," I replied. All is well, in other words. "I've always sent my results to you at the end of every term, right?" I asked.

"Right."

"You know I always take my studies seriously, right?"

"Right," Vincent replied, "but why are you asking me these questions?"

"Because I want to go to secondary school, but our father has refused to register me for the Common Entrance exam," I explained.

"Don't you worry," he assured me. "I am going to talk to him."

"Thank you." You can imagine how elated I was with my brother's response.

Very early in the morning on the day my brother planned to leave the village, he had a long talk with our father. I cracked open the window to eavesdrop on their conversation. Vincent didn't even bother to ask why he didn't want to send me to secondary school. He told our father that he didn't want me to attend a general educational institution as he had. Instead, he said, he'd like for me to attend a technical institution, where I could learn a hands-on trade so I wouldn't end up jobless after graduation as he had.

When my brother broke the news to me (I pretended to be surprised), I was so excited that I wasn't going to end my education at the primary school level! I thanked him over and over again. This may have been the first time I was overjoyed to the point of shedding tears. I was excited to continue my education—whether it was at a general or technical institution didn't matter to me. I wanted more education, and I wanted to get away—from my village, from working on the farm, and from living with my parents.

Although my father agreed to let me attend secondary school, he told my brother that he didn't have the money to pay the Common Entrance examination fee. My brother Vincent paid it on his way back to Douala, stopping at the school campus to register me for the exam. Our teacher, Mr. Peter, broke the news to me in front of the whole class: my brother had just registered me and had selected the Government Technical College (G.T.C.) Santa as a first-choice institution for me to attend.

Out of my primary-school class of thirty-seven, I was one of only five students to register for the entrance examination. Among the remaining thirty-two of my classmates, some had no other option but to remain in the village and work on their family's farm. Others planned to learn trades such as carpentry in workshops, and some intended to seek business opportunities in various cities. Most of the girls in my class had no plans at all. They would end up on farms with their parents and get married soon after leaving school. In fact, one girl in our class had a husband and was ready to settle down right after primary school. After a hard Class Seven school year, my entire class passed the national exit examination, and all five of us who took the Common Entrance exam also passed.

* * * * *

While looking forward to the next step in my academic journey, I was thankful to God that I was born a boy. I don't think my brother Vincent could have convinced my father to send me to secondary school if I had been a girl. In my village, parents preferred to send only male children beyond primary school. Furthering a girl's education was seen as a waste of money, for they could easily become pregnant and get expelled. And, as we used to debate in my family, some thought sending a girl for higher education would benefit her future husband, not the family. My father never participated in these debates, but I'm sure he had something like that on his mind.

Out of the nine girls in my family, my eldest half sister, Mofor Marie, was the only one to attend secondary school. Why only her? She was the firstborn of my stepmother, and when she completed elementary school, my father didn't have a lot of children yet. He was still in his prime and had the energy to make money through his tailoring work and his Arabica coffee-growing business. Also, Marie was one of his first two children to complete elementary school, and it would have been a family disaster for him to send my brother Vincent to secondary school while leaving Marie in the village. My father wanted to maintain some kind of balance to keep his two wives happy. And, finally, he simply loved Marie since she was his first daughter.

I recall the day we were helping my father harvest his Arabica coffee and he talked about one of the reasons he couldn't keep Marie at home. His plan was to have her become a nurse.

"When I'm sick and dying in my hospital bed, I want her to be there in her white scrubs. She will close my eyes when I'm dead and put me in the mortuary. Then she will hire an ambulance to take my body to the village."

My mom and stepmom yelled at him before he could complete the story, telling him there was no chance he was going to die and leave them with the children. For a while, they debated who was going to die first and who was going to be stranded with the children.

In any case, when Marie was done with high school, she came back to the village. To the great surprise of all, she decided to marry her boyfriend, a butcher and farmer. In my village, a woman can be considered married when she leaves her parents' home and starts living with a man. The traditional marriage rites can be done years later. In the village, my father was known as nonconfrontational, but we children knew him as strict, particularly when it came to the family. When he found out that Marie had suddenly decided to get married, he took his revolver, went to the compound where she was, and—with gun in hand—grabbed her and brought her back home. The next day, before the roosters crowed, my father took Marie to Bamenda and registered her for the nursing exam in a private institution. She took and passed the exam, did the training, and became a nurse, just as my father had envisaged. Even though she couldn't find a lucrative civil-service job, she found employment at a private clinic. I've got to hand it to my father for this one!

The story was different for the other girls in the family. Upon completion of primary school, they were forced to stay at home to cook for the family and help out on the farm. Like Euphrasia, most of them really wanted to further their education, but tradition was against them. As they got older, they married, and my father collected some financial reward in the form of bride price and goats. Parents in the village don't feel compelled to send their female children to get more education because they will eventually marry and leave home.

6

Getting Into Secondary School

After passing the entrance exam, I had to prepare for placement tests at my new school. These included mathematics, English language, and a face-to-face interview. My first choice for secondary school, G.T.C. Santa, was located in Njong village in the township of Santa, about twenty kilometers from my home village of Baligham.

Of the five students from my primary school who were hoping to enter secondary school, Bulla Irene, one of the two girls among us, was able to travel to Santa by car, but the rest of us made the journey on foot. On the day before the test, we left the village very early in the morning and took several shortcuts, climbing hills straight up rather than following the switchbacking road. We took a few breaks to catch our breath and share the food we brought for the long walk. Unfortunately, it rained during most of the trip, so we arrived in Santa soaking wet.

Nevertheless, it was an interesting journey because we knew each other well. We talked about how excited we were to finally have an opportunity to get away from our parents. For me, leaving the village meant no one was going to order me to fetch firewood or water or to take care of goats. No more working on the farm after school, and I was going to be respected by primary-school students whenever I was back in the village for breaks. At this point, I didn't see any downside to leaving the village to attend secondary school.

The next day, interviews and testing took place at Mile-12, in a large cooperative building that could accommodate about two hundred candidates vying for admission. We began with math, followed by an English-language test.

After the placement tests, which I was confident I had aced, we each had to go through the face-to-face interview. I was very nervous about it, having never done one before, and had no one to help me prepare. Fortunately, it was shorter than I had anticipated.

After asking questions about why I wanted to attend secondary school, one of the interviewers requested my primary-school report card. I handed it to him with all my records, Classes One through Seven.

"You did an excellent job in primary school," the interviewer said.

I can't remember saying thank you, but I certainly remember that his laudation made me feel more at ease.

In Cameroon, more than half the students tested and interviewed would not be accepted into secondary school. I don't understand why the government can't make an effort to build more public schools to accommodate the needs of our country's growing population. By the time I completed primary school, there was no secondary school in my village; the nearest were about twenty kilometers away. This shortage of schools has made the common entrance examinations, placement tests, and interviews the collective sieve through which only a fraction of prospective students can pass.

When Patrick (my future roommate) and I had finished our interviews, we met up with our classmates, who were very optimistic about their chances of being accepted. The next day we trekked back to the village.

The lists of selected students were published in August 2000, and all five of us from my primary school were accepted into secondary school. Successful candidates had to pay their school fee before classes began or risked losing their spots to students on the waiting list. This worked out well for me: for the first time, my father paid my school fees in one installment, and did so before classes started.

The cost was 15,000 FCFA, a huge increase over my primary-school fee and a big liability on my father. In addition to that expense, I now had to pay house rent.

All four of my classmates accepted into secondary school had paid their school fees, too. However, a few weeks before the start of the academic year, Bertine decided she was going to get married instead of continuing her education. Despite every effort by her single mother to convince her to go to school, Bertine stood her ground and our group was reduced to four.

* * * * *

Attending secondary school away from home meant making substantial changes in my daily life. I had always believed that cooking was a woman's job, so I never bothered to watch my mother or ask her to explain how she made food. Now that I was going to live far away from her, I would be responsible for my own meals. Nonetheless, I assumed that if other students were able to survive, I could, too.

To prepare for this new adventure in feeding myself, I put together a collection of raw food from our big farm, picking fresh plantains and bananas, and digging up sweet potatoes, white yams, and Irish potatoes. Back at our family compound, I added a half bucket of dry corn, some beans, and groundnuts. In other families, parents put together basic household supplies for children going off to secondary school. Not in my family. We were responsible for putting together everything we might need. Since this was my first time, it was difficult deciding what supplies were important to bring.

I also needed to provide my own money for transportation and basic kitchen supplies, like cooking oil and salt. My father made money from his tailoring work, but I was only one of many children he supported. He also had commitments that obliged him to make payments on a weekly or monthly basis to many *njangi* contribution groups in the village. Njangi is a social group of two or more individuals who meet weekly, biweekly, or monthly to contribute money for the benefit of one member of the group. (My njangi back in primary school shared food, not money.) In the cash njangi groups my dad belonged to, each person contributed a certain amount of money that was given to one member. At the next meeting, contributions went to someone else. That process went on until everyone had benefitted. Sometimes a lottery determined the order in which members would receive funds. If someone picked a higher number but had an urgent need for money, they could improve their position by offering cash or some other incentive to a member with a lower number.

My mother, on the other hand, depended on her self-sufficient farming to take care of the family and had no other source of money to help me. The norm in my family was that the women took care of food and whatever the children wore each day; the man was responsible for most of the education costs. My father had already paid my school fees. His remaining responsibilities were to sew a school uniform and provide money for my house rent.

In order to come up with the money to live on my own, I had to produce garri from my mother's cassava farm. She and some of my siblings helped me process it, after which I would sell it during the village market day when people from Douala, Yaoundé, and other larger towns came to buy bulk garri to retail it in the city.

In my village, the method of producing garri was simply known as "grinding cassava," a tedious process that begins with harvesting. The cassava plants are pulled from the ground; the roots are peeled with sharp knives and then washed; the cassava is loaded into small bags that are carried on one's head to the roadside; and the small bags are loaded into large bags for transporting home from the farm on a special hand truck. Considering the condition of the village roads—deeply rutted and muddy—it takes a lot of energy to get the cassava from the farm to our home compound.

At home, we pay someone with a diesel-powered machine to grind the cassava into what's call "grained" cassava, which is then put into bags. Each bag is placed between two large sticks to squeeze out all the liquid. While the grained cassava is drying, we spend a day fetching firewood to be used for frying it.

After two or three days of drying, the grained cassava is sifted, turning it into white cassava powder that is fried with palm oil, which transforms the powder into a yellowish product known as garri—ready to be eaten or taken to the market for sale. The price of a bucket of garri varies depending on weather conditions. Whenever it rained on market day, the price dropped because buyers from the cities couldn't make it through on the muddy, messy roads.

Two of my brothers, Daniel and Innocent, make a living by buying garri from the village and selling it in Douala. I used to help them buy it during village market days. Whenever it started to rain, we would stop buying garri and wait for the cheaper prices once the rain stopped. Aside from drying grain, there is no preservation of food in the village. Products harvested from the farms have to be consumed or sold as soon as possible.

* * * * *

In September 2000, the academic year started the day after our village market day. I had six and a half buckets of garri that was produced with the help of my mother and younger brother Festus. I sold six buckets to raise my transportation and spending money, and kept a half bucket to take with me to school.

You should have seen me—I was so ready to leave the village once I had some money in my pocket. But then I walked down to my father's tailoring workshop at the market to collect my school uniform and the rest of my school supplies.

"Papa, I'm ready to leave now. The last car will be leaving soon."

"I started sewing your uniform but I didn't have time to finish it."

For a moment I thought he was joking. "What about my drawing instruments?" I asked.

"I'll buy them during my trip to Bamenda," he replied.

I was so angry that my father was busy sewing uniforms for other people's children and had forgotten to take care of his own son, and was afraid that maybe it was a scheme to keep me in the village. As he tried to give me reasons for the delay, I stomped out of his workshop because I was too outraged to talk. So many terrible thoughts were going through my mind, but I didn't have the guts to say them to my father.

I ran through the crowded market and into the building where my mother was buying garri for my brother Daniel. Tears ran down my face—I couldn't control myself. In the crowded room, other people tried to console me, but when I told my mother my grievances, she got angry.

"What is it with you and school?" she asked. "This child, you can kill someone because of school."

Although she looked angry, I knew she was on my side, but couldn't condemn my father in front of me and the other people. Even my father rarely criticized his wives in front of the children. Several people in the room urged me to stop crying, assuring me that my father, with his love of education, wouldn't make me stay in the village. I wasn't so sure. It seemed to me his love of education was gradually fading away.

It was very sad watching my friends leaving the village without me, but I promised to do everything possible to join them. I was so angry, I didn't want to see my father's face again. But I gave in and joined him and some of my siblings to transport his sewing equipment back to our compound from the market.

At home, my father didn't tell me if he had finished sewing my uniform and when I might be able to leave for school. He even tried to avoid me. But I kept tracking him down, asking the same question over and over: "Papa, when am I going back to school?"

He kept assuring me that I would be going very soon, but wouldn't give me a specific date. I was scared to ask him too many questions at once, so I often turned to my mother, who was much easier to talk to. One evening when I started talking to her, it angered me when I noticed my father was eavesdropping. I took the opportunity to air some of my frustrations.

"If I wasn't born into this family, I could have been born to rich parents who would be happy to send me to school. Papa only knows how to sew uniforms for other people's children." I continued with my rant, and father couldn't take it. He walked into the compound and began asking questions that I couldn't answer.

"What did you say? Say it again," he dared me. I tried to get away from him because I knew I had gotten myself into deep trouble, but he kept walking toward me. As he continued daring me to repeat my comments, I stupidly fell into his trap.

"You heard what I said."

He got very mad and started chasing me around the compound with his metal tailoring tape. With the harvesting season over and the corn stalks cut down, there was no place to hide. My father was athletic, while I was a fat kid running as fast as I could. He caught me on our second run around the compound and gave me the beating of my life.

"You don't talk to me like that. Am I your friend? Who are you to tell me what to do? You will be going back to school on market day," my father said after he had beaten the stuffing out of me.

The next market day was on Monday, a week after the academic year had begun. Instead of crying or being sad from the beating, I was relieved and happy that my delinquent behavior towards my father had paid off.

On Sunday night, my dad called me into his workshop and gave me my school uniform—a khaki shirt and a pair of khaki pants. He promised to buy my drawing board, T-square, set of squares, and a set of math instruments and drop them off for me in Santa.

On Monday, using a hand truck, I helped transport his sewing machine and other equipment to the village market. Returning home with the truck, I used it to carry my luggage back to the market, where cars were available to drive me to Santa.

When I arrived there, students were still in school, but I soon saw Seying Rudolf on his way back from classes.

"Singing," I yelled repeatedly to my primary-school classmate. That was his nickname … and it drove him nuts.

"Nzuah!" Rudolf yelled back, because he knew I hated being called by my last name. "We were talking about you yesterday," Rudolf said. "We were afraid you wouldn't be coming to Santa."

I told him that my father finally decided to let me go because I drove him crazy until he finally agreed.

"Nzuah, you haven't changed," Rudolf said.

Having now arrived in Santa, I started worrying about a place to live. Luckily, Rudolf was staying in a small studio apartment that he shared with Mr. Moses, who was away. Rudolf said I could stay with him until I found my own studio apartment, and helped move my stuff into his room. Later that evening, I met my other classmate, Mofor Patrick, who had planned to share a place with me. We agreed to go room hunting that weekend.

But first I had some catching up to do because classwork had begun a week earlier.

7

Finally! Form One, Secondary School

Very early on the morning of September 19, 2000, I put on my uniform and realized I had no backpack, notebooks, or textbooks for my first day of secondary school in Form One. Throughout primary school, it was my father's responsibility to buy books and hand them out to us before the first day. Here I was, about to start secondary school, and I didn't even have a pen or pencil.

I bought a few twenty-sheet notebooks before Patrick and I began our four-mile walk to school. I had thought the trek to primary school was a long journey, but walking four miles each way was harder than farm work. I was exhausted after just two days of school. When classes were done, we started the long walk back, arriving home late in the evening—and I still had to do homework.

I was tired, but things were fine—until I came home on Thursday under heavy rain, soaking wet. Mr. Moses had returned and was very angry that Rudolf had allowed me into the room without his knowledge. I looked past him and saw Rudolf crying. Mr. Moses had beaten him severely for giving me a place to stay.

"Why did your father allow you to come to Santa without looking for a room first?" Mr. Moses asked me. "There is no place for you to sleep here tonight," he added.

I just stared at him and couldn't think of anything to say. Turning back towards Rudolf, he said, "Didn't I tell you not to accept strangers into this room?" and then struck him a few times on the forehead.

I was so sorry that my best friend had gone through this because of me. We were longtime friends from way back in primary school. The saddest thing was that Mr. Moses moved my bag of raw food out into the rain. As soon as I saw it, I knew the food in it was wet. Yes, I had myself to blame for leaving the village without finding a place to stay in Santa, but I felt Mr. Moses—my fellow villager—should have handled this situation differently.

As night fell, I stood outside, crying. Mr. Moses hadn't even given me a chance to change out of my wet uniform. Then, like a miracle, I saw a guy who looked like someone I knew from the village.

"Philemon?"

"Pierre," he said back. "What are you doing here?"

I told him what had transpired. Luckily for me, Philemon was renting a room nearby and helped me move into his place. I hung my uniform up to dry overnight because I had to wear it the next day. Opening my food bag confirmed that the garri was soaked and had to be thrown away. Garri is an important food for students because it is filling, can be prepared in a number of different ways, and stores well if kept dry. Philemon put some sheets on the floor, and we spread out the beans, corn, and other food items to dry. He really came to my rescue and I feel indebted to him.

I had to look for a place to stay, but there were also other things to be done. Having been so focused on leaving the village and getting into secondary school, I hadn't prepared for living away from home. Lacking among my belongings were many daily necessities, like cooking utensils and bedding. On the way to school, Patrick and I decided to return to the village for the weekend and gather the basic items we needed to live on our own.

When classes ended on Friday, we took a crowded taxi to get back quickly to downtown Santa. Then we started the long walk to the village. My parents were stunned to see me just four days after I'd left. I told them everything I had been through during my first week of secondary school. My mother said it was time for me to give up, which sounded like a great idea—but I had come too far.

On Saturday, I helped my mother on the farm and gathered some food items to take back to school. She tried to convince me that going back wasn't going to make my future any better than that of my siblings, but knew everything she said was going in one ear and out the other. In the evening, I met with my father in his workshop to estimate my rent. On Sunday morning he gave me ten notebooks and the amount we had calculated. I thanked him. Patrick joined me, and we began trekking back to Santa. Atop our heads, both of us had heavy bags containing food and household utensils. After several hours of walking and resting, we arrived in Santa, where I spent the night in Philemon's room again. Even though he said I could stay for as long as I wanted, I was eager to live in a place closer to school. The long walk was tiring me out and taking up too much time.

While we were in the village, Patrick's father, Pa Elias, took it upon himself to find us a cheap, mud-brick room owned by one of his friends. Having hoped for an upgrade from the mud-brick houses we grew up in, Patrick and I were both disappointed, but out of respect for him, we did not argue. It was cheaper than what my father and I had expected.

Pa Elias provided us with a small bed and mattress, about the size of a standard dorm-room bed—but two of us had to share it. The mattress was locally made from empty rice bags sewn together and stuffed with grass. When we moved into our room, it had no ceiling. We joked that we could read at night by moonlight, but living in a room without a ceiling was troubling because Santa is one of the coldest places in the Northwest Region of Cameroon.

Unlike our homes in the village, our room did have electricity—but it had no switch, and the landlady refused to buy us one. We turned on the light bulb in our room by hooking two cables together. Patrick and I were each shocked many times. At night when we returned from visiting a friend, I developed a habit of letting Patrick lead the way into the room—so he would turn on the light and risk the shock. He soon realized my trick and started doing the same thing. After several weeks of being shocked, we combined our money to buy a switch for 200 FCFA.

As freshmen in secondary school (I was fifteen at the time), we knew it would take us a long time to get the basic things we needed for our room. Until we had enough money to buy a used cooking stove, we prepared our food on the open fireplace and fetched firewood each evening after school. We had no tables or chairs, either. Constructing some out of bamboo was easy because I had been making them since my early days in primary school.

Cooking was never my forte, nor was it Patrick's. In the early weeks of school, neither of us would cook unless we were really famished, and often we went to school hungry. There was raw food, but we didn't have the motivation to turn it into a real meal. We left for school at about seven in the morning and returned at four in the afternoon—tired and facing homework. We decided it was necessary to take turns cooking.

The solution we came up with was this: each of us would cook enough food to last for two days. This was good for me since I was cooking food items brought from my family's farm. Patrick, on the other hand, wasn't good at putting together food from the village. When it was his turn to cook and he was out of food, he would visit his father in downtown Santa, get some money from him, and buy things such as rice. This brought a good mix to our diet because rice wasn't among the crops cultivated in the village. As teenagers from different homes, sharing the same bed and a lot of household responsibilities, Patrick and I went through many ups and downs in order to get along. Luckily, we found ways to resolve our differences without getting our parents involved.

* * * * *

Being away from my parents gave me a lot of freedom, but without being told what to do by them, I had to manage my time and get past several temptations.

There was a movie theater located just a few meters from where we lived. At the beginning of the first term, I watched an average of one movie per week. Then I got carried away and started watching at least three every week. The cost of three movies was the same as three cups of rice, which we could have cooked and eaten for days.

Because my village didn't have a theater, movies were a big treat for me and I became addicted to watching them. On my way back from classes each day, I'd stop to see what was playing at the theater that evening. School was gradually becoming my second priority.

Besides movies, soccer was also a distraction. In the village, we used to have to pay to watch important soccer games. In Santa, there were several bars where watching soccer was free. My after-school plans became watching TV or going to the movie theater, or both. To make things worse, the Sydney 2000 Olympic Games took place during my first year in secondary school, and following the Olympics became a huge part of my schedule, especially when the Cameroonian men's soccer team was playing. Because of the time difference, we would stay up late to watch the games instead of studying. I was having fun at the expense of my education.

Before starting secondary school, I loved to play foosball when we were in Santa for the National Day celebration. Now, living there, it was available 24/7—but it cost to play a round. I became experienced, started playing opponents for money, and won bets quite often, but found it difficult to go home before losing what I had won.

I stupidly got carried away by all the distractions, to the point that I forgot about why I had come to Santa, including every effort I had made to force my father to give me this opportunity. Instead of studying after school, I went to the movies. At times I wished my father was there to scare me into studying. Even if I had a test the next day, I often went to the theater, and sometimes even forgot about the test. When it was too late to study at night, I'd set my alarm to get up early. But because my room was so cold, I'd usually wake up and go right back under the covers. As a result, I studied for tests on the way to school.

Despite neglecting my schoolwork, I wasn't failing in any of my classes. This was mostly because I always sat in the front row, paid very close attention to my instructors, and took good notes. However, when the first sequence tests were over, I had performed way below my ability, and started to think about what I would tell my parents—especially my father—if the term ended at this point.

I remembered how I had always lifted my family name high when I was in primary school. It seemed unlikely that I would replicate that honor in secondary school if I didn't change my behavior. With my conscience judging me, I gave up some of my newfound hobbies and started paying more attention to schoolwork. During the second part of the term I did exceptionally well. However, it was too late to bring my ranking up to what would make my father proud. At the end of the first term, when every score was combined and averaged, I was ranked second in a class of fifty-one students. Some of my classmates who narrowly missed failing were very happy to go home and tell their parents the good news that they had passed. But I was disappointed in myself. Ranking second to a classmate wasn't where I wanted to be. I was in no mood to make conversation after receiving my report card. As we left campus, my friends asked what was wrong, and I responded with one word: "Nothing."

Trekking back to the village for Christmas break, I wondered how I could convince my father that finishing second was the best I could do. My mother didn't worry me—she was always okay with whatever ranking her children achieved. She felt my father was obsessed with the idea of seeing his children rated at the top of their classes.

My plan was to head straight to my mom's kitchen for food, but when I arrived home, my father was in his workshop, which was located at the entrance to our compound. After we exchanged greetings, he wanted to see my report card.

"You came in second?" he asked, staring at me.

"There was a big boy called Peter in my classes. He is like a second teacher in our class and knows everything, so no one can compete with him."

Whether my father bought it or not, I was happy that he didn't make me cry. Instead, he told me to get something to eat in my stepmother's house if I didn't find anything in my mother's house. This was an honor because my father was always served special dishes that kids weren't allowed to have, often including an extra piece of meat or fish.

At the end of the Christmas and New Year celebrations, I gathered some food from the farm and left for the second term. But I went back to my bad habits, spending most of my free time hanging out with friends, playing soccer, and watching games from different European leagues. I had favorite teams in the English, French, Spanish, German, and other European top leagues. Because my father hadn't complained about my first-term results, I felt no pressure to work harder. I became contented with my standing and did not topple Peter from the first position during the second term. When I got back to the village for a week's break, my father again seemed satisfied with my results. My eldest brother Vincent was in the village during the break and asked to see my report card.

"You were ranked second in your class? Why not first?" He asked.

"There is this big boy in my class. He is older and smarter than everyone," I replied.

"Age and size don't make him smarter than you," Vincent said. "You just need to study harder."

He then told me about how he used to outshine older and bigger guys in his high school class, which earned him a lot of respect among his classmates. Now that my father had taken a break from criticizing my results, here was my brother taking his place! I didn't understand why I was the only child in my family whose results were given a lot of attention. Was it because I had a history of setting the bar high?

When I was back in school for the third term of the academic year, I vowed to make a complete change in my daily routine. There was no more playing soccer or foosball and going to the movies. I reduced my time spent watching European soccer and hanging out with friends. The goal was to emerge first in the class, and I knew I had to make a lot of adjustments to get there. Ranking for the third and last term was based on the cumulative average of the three terms, and Peter had a huge lead over me from the first two terms.

After cutting down on my social activities, I studied every night before going to bed, even when there was no test the next day. I dedicated more time to studying subjects with higher weight, like math, English, drawing, and French. One of my strategies for dethroning my rival was capitalizing on his weakest area, which was math and other calculation-based subjects. In the evening, I would go over topics I hadn't understood in class. Each time I felt like giving up, I recalled my brother asking, "Why not first?" That single phrase motivated me and helped me change my study habits.

Extra studying paid off; I was doing well in all my subjects. But while everything was going well academically, I was hungrier than I'd ever been. In order to study more, I cut down on the time spent working on people's farms in exchange for food and cash. During our second sequence tests, we ran out of food in the middle of the week. Some days we survived by convincing our landlady's grand-kids to get us some sweet potatoes from their farm, which we peeled and ate raw.

On one Thursday, my roommate, Mofor Patrick, decided to go back to the village because our situation wasn't getting any better. I promised to help him catch up on any schoolwork he missed. On Friday, our math teacher noticed a lot of students were missing. It seemed as though many of our classmates were in the same situation as Patrick and me. The teacher decided to give a surprise math test. Luckily, math was one of my favorite subjects and I could do well on a test at any time. After finishing the test, I couldn't stop thinking about Patrick, who had gone to the village to get food for both of us. Using another sheet of paper, I took the test for him in a differ-ent handwriting—and without a few of the answers—so the teacher wouldn't discover what happened.

That was the most unacceptable thing I did in secondary school. But I knew Patrick hadn't done well on the first sequence test, and having a zero on the second sequence test would jeopardize his chance of advancing to the next class. At my school, it wasn't easy for a student to justify absences. Being hungry and needing to return to the village for food was not a good enough excuse. If a student claimed sickness, a school administrator would demand medical records to prove it. So it seemed unlikely that my roommate would be given a chance to make up the test, and it would have been terrible if I moved on to the next class, leaving him behind. I had mixed feelings after the test. I wondered what my roommate would think about me having a higher score than he did, and what would happen if the teacher found out what I had done. I kept these concerns to myself, and when Patrick came back from the village, I didn't tell him I'd taken the test on his behalf. But I told him a math test had been given while he was away.

"I'm dead," he said. "My father is going to kill me."

When we got our test papers back, I scored 18/20. Patrick was surprised that he received a test paper back on which he scored 14/20. After class, he asked if I was the one who took the test for him. I said I was, but warned him to tell no one. Patrick was so excited that he didn't care if I had a higher score, and said he didn't think he could have done any better if he'd taken the test himself. This particular episode helped improve my relationship with Patrick. Although I did something wrong, he was very grateful that I had taken the risk. As far as I know, he never told anyone about what I did, and neither did I—until now.

For the rest of the term, I continued to work hard but didn't bring it to the attention of my main rival. I didn't want him to know I was trying to displace him from first position, and was afraid that if he discovered my plan, he might put more effort into his studies. Thanks to intense studying, I was acing all my tests—and keeping my results secret. I knew I was doing well because I also kept track of Peter's results. When I got all my final examination papers back, I was sure I was ahead of him for the third term, but didn't know if I had done enough to offset his performance when all three terms were averaged together.

Before report cards were distributed on the last day of school, my heart was beating faster than the time I watched the Cameroonian men's soccer team overcome a two goal deficit against Spain at the Sydney 2000 Olympic Games to win gold, the only medal for my country that year. When I opened my report card, it showed I was ranked first position in my class. In primary school, results were read out loud, but in secondary school, report cards were given to the students without fanfare. Still, Peter's face told the story. I beat him only by a tiny margin, but I was ecstatic.

Back home after the third term, I handed the results to my father, knowing it would shock him. When he opened my report card, he was speechless. Then he said, "You came in first!" I smiled. In most families, I'd receive congratulations and hugs, but this wasn't the tradition in my family. Still, I knew my father was pleased because he went around the entire neighborhood bragging to his friends about my results. Finally, I had made him proud again.

8

Third Term Holiday, 2001

The holiday after third term was long, June to September. I spent it helping my father tap his palm wine, or *matango*, as it is commonly known in Cameroon. Special palm wine is produced from the same palm trees that produce palm oil for cooking. A more common form of palm wine consumed in my village is produced from the raffia plant, which is also used to make bamboo chairs. Palm wine is very sweet when first collected, which is why children usually drink it as soon as it is brought home. Fermentation begins very quickly, and within two days the alcohol content can be up to 10 percent. Older people drink palm wine that has fermented for two or more days so they can get drunk quickly.

It is consumed at home and at matango bars, and no traditional ceremony can be performed in my village without palm wine. In our compound, at a small rock under a particular tree, we would join my father in worship during family gatherings. This little rock was the family god, deemed by my father to be the creator of all his children. During our yearly family meetings around the tree, my father poured splashes of palm wine on the rock to please it and to ask for blessings for the entire family. He usually asked for the god to protect all his children and to change the mind of any enemy with evil intentions against a family member. I had no idea if the family god was listening, but I attended every worship event for the food.

During traditional weddings in the village, palm wine is usually blessed and given to the bride by her father. It is put in a drinking horn, which the bride carries around a crowded room to find her husband. She then serves him the palm wine to show her approval of him as her husband. During the search, people in the room would tease the bride, telling her to serve it to them. Though palm wine is much less expensive than beer, even rich people cannot replace it with commercial wine or beer during traditional ceremonies. At those times and during social events, palm wine is often served with kola nut—a customary pairing of sweet and bitter flavors.

The best thing about helping tap palm wine during the holiday was the opportunity I had to learn how to ride a bicycle. During the third-term holiday, my father started tapping palm wine at one of our farms located far from our compound. He didn't always have enough time to collect all the palm wine himself, so one day he asked me to ride the bicycle to the distant farm to tap for him. Even though I didn't know how to ride a bicycle, I seized the opportunity to learn. On the way back, I couldn't risk spilling my father's palm wine, so I walked the bicycle home. In the course of teaching myself to ride, I had many falls and was often bruised, but I didn't let my father know because he would have taken the bicycle away. Determined, I finally was able to ride a bicycle well.

Third term, or summer holiday, is one of the busiest times on village farms, so my mother was very happy to have me harvest corn, peanuts, and beans, and to pull weeds from our cassava plantings. Corn is the biggest agricultural product grown on our land, and we had to transport most of it in bags on top of our heads for the long walk from farm to home. I was very happy when my mother decided to pay a motorcycle driver to transport some of it.

* * * * *

After three months of manual labor, I was ready to return for my second year of secondary school. It would have been nice to relax for a while, but during the final week of the holiday break, I produced garri from our two-year-old plantings of cassava and sold it at the village market for my back-to-school expenses.

Once again, my father was responsible for paying my school fees and rent. On the day I left, he gave me only part of the school fees. For rent, he wrote a short note to my landlady, promising to pay as soon as possible. Typical of my father, he never chose a specific date when he made a promise. I knew it was a false pledge, and yet I had no choice but to take his note.

Rain had made the road out of our village muddy and difficult, and few drivers would risk driving students to Santa. Travel fare was increased because the road was so bad, but I had to pay because school was starting the next day. The taxi that I took slipped into the roadside ditch far from any houses. All of us passengers tried to push the car back onto the road, but without success. Finally, the driver gave up and advised us to walk back to the village before nightfall.

Some of the passengers began walking back, but I stayed with the car. After a while, a truck loaded with passengers and bags of food pulled up. Behind the wheel was Njunkte Augustin, one of the most experienced drivers from my village. He asked if he could help us, but our driver had given up.

Although Mr. Augustin's truck was full of passengers and luggage, he offered to make space for an older woman unable to walk back to the village. As he was talking to our driver, I climbed on top of the bags of food on the truck. When Mr. Augustin brought the woman's luggage to the truck, he saw me sitting on top.

"Comot from ma motor," he said in pidgin English, yelling at me to come down from his truck.

"Even caterpillar no fit comot me from dis motor," I replied, telling him that even a caterpillar tractor couldn't get me down.

He realized there was no way he was going to leave without me. I sat at the back of the truck for the whole ride to Santa, holding onto the rubber straps used to tie up the luggage. When Mr. Augustin stopped to drop me off, he looked at me and shook his head. "You bi strong head pikin," he said in pidgin English, telling me I was a stalwart kid.

When I paid Mr. Augustin the transportation fare, he gave some of the money back to me. This was the beginning of a special relationship between us. If he saw me walking to the village with other students, he would give us a free ride the rest of the way. And whenever he saw me walking toward his truck in the village, he told people to watch how I was going to bulldoze my way aboard without asking if there was a free seat for me. I also became Mr. Augustin's right-hand man, helping him whenever drivers were hustling for passengers. Whether it was in Santa or the village, I gathered my friends and we would travel with Mr. Augustin.

9

Form Two: New Rival, New Challenges

My second year in secondary school, 2001–02, wasn't going to be easy. My father was going through a tough time financially because the price for the Arabica coffee he grew had gone down drastically. He also bought Arabica coffee from other small growers in the village and resold it at the Baligham Cooperative Union, but that was no longer very profitable. Another negative was that most of the grown-up kids, like me, were no longer in the village to help him buy and transport the coffee. He was still patching clothes and sewing and selling school uniforms, but it didn't generate enough money to take care of his children and buy beer for himself.

When I arrived in Santa for the beginning of the first term, I gave my landlady, Tabitha (aka Mami Tabi), the note from my father, which bought me a few weeks to live in our single room without paying rent. But then Mami Tabi began hassling me to pay my half of the rent—my roommate had already paid his share. She had every right to pursue me for the rent—she was elderly, and the rent money was her main source of income. After running out of excuses, I tried to stay out of her sight. She eventually caught up with me and gave me two options: either pay her the money or pack up and leave. I thought about traveling to the village during the weekend, but there was no guarantee my parents would have the money.

One day, on the way back to my room from school, I saw our

landlady working very hard on her farm plot all by herself. She lived with two grandsons, but they were very stubborn and offered her little help, so I stepped in, knowing it would make it harder for her to kick me out of the room. As I helped her out, she became impressed with my farming skills, and as we chatted, I told her I'd been working on the family farm since I was a little kid. During our conversation, I asked Mami Tabi if she might assign me a portion of her farm to cultivate in exchange for house rent. To my great surprise, she welcomed the idea. I worked on the farm every day after school, and within a week I had completed the cultivation of my assigned section. Mami Tabi was pleased with how efficiently I worked. She struck a deal with me: I could do farm work in exchange for the rent whenever my parents were unable to pay my share.

For the school fees my father had not provided, I started using the tricks he used back when I was in primary school. I lied to school administrators, either telling them that my father was coming in a few days to pay, or that I planned to go to the village on the weekend to get the money. While I was getting better at tricking school officials into letting me stay on campus, my father was busy in the village looking for ways to trick *me*, one time saying he expected some money shortly and would bring it to Santa. He never showed up.

I ran out of excuses and was kicked out of school. When I showed up in the village in midweek, my dad knew it was serious. I didn't even have to convince him. He began walking through the village, trying to borrow money. By evening he had come up with enough so I could go back to school. Think about this: all that trouble for the equivalent of ten dollars.

*　*　*　*　*

During this academic year, I was often angry at my older siblings for paying attention to how well I did in my classes, but not enough attention to how their little brother would pay for school. This was the year when I stopped bothering my parents for help and tried to survive on my own.

Santa is a farming town. Farmers produce Irish potatoes, cabbages, tomatoes, carrots, onions, garlic, celery, parsley, green peppers, and other foods. Most of these products are sold in cities across Cameroon and in neighboring countries like Congo-Brazzaville. I learned that farmers needed help and paid students on weekends. This was great news for me because farming was my area of work expertise. Instead of going to the village on weekends to bother my parents for money, I stood along the road where farmers hired laborers. Some growers might hire ten or more student workers for a day. Generous farmers gave us money in the morning to buy food for lunch, and the remaining balance at the end of the workday. Less-generous farmers subtracted the food cost from our daily wages.

We often had to walk six or more miles to reach the farms. In order to get the most out of their workers, farmers hired us as early as seven in the morning. We went to work as soon as we arrived, and kept at it until five in the afternoon except for a brief lunch break. We nicknamed one farmer "six-to-six" because he made us work from six in the morning to six at night. In the beginning, I had a tough time convincing farmers to hire me because I was small, and they had no idea how hard I could work. But soon they were fighting over me whenever I showed up looking for employment.

Some farmers were strict supervisors who didn't even allow us to stretch. One day, I was hired to pull out weeds at a carrot farm owned by a man nicknamed Joe-Bafut. After several hours of pulling weeds, I stood up to stretch for a few seconds.

"Bend down," Joe-Bafut said loudly.

"You no see sey ah dey ahead all people," I replied in pidgin English, asking if he hadn't noticed that I was ahead of everybody else. He walked away without saying anything. The other student workers made fun of me for the rest of the day, telling me Joe-Bafut wasn't going to pay me. I was worried and wished I could take back my words.

"Lawyer, here is your money," Joe-Bafut said, as he handed me my pay at the end of the day.

After that, he always called me Lawyer and hired me whenever he saw I was looking for work. He also asked me to select a number of hard-working guys to accompany me to his farm. This was how

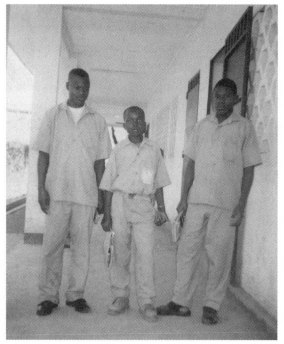

Tekeu Felix (L) and Gabgha Elvis (R) with
their pint-sized classmate, Pierre Nzuah

I gradually became the head of student laborers. Toward the end of each school week, fellow pupils would start begging me to reserve a work spot for them over the weekend.

Doing farm work on weekends was a lifesaver for me and many other students. In addition to what we were paid for a day's work, most farmers allowed us to take free stuff from their farms, such as Irish potatoes, cabbages, tomatoes, and carrots. I didn't have to travel to the village as frequently as in the past because of this food, and I didn't have to figure out ways to bug my parents for money. Becoming self-sufficient improved my relationship with them, especially my dad. Before I earned money as a farmworker, he always knew that my arrival in the village on a Friday meant trouble for him. Now several months would go by without my having to return to the village for food or money.

Back when I first left home to go to school, I was happy to leave farm work behind forever. I had no idea that the skills learned on my mother's farm would help me survive in secondary school. Like many students, I never told my parents that I was doing anything besides schoolwork. Those of us who worked on farms had a code name for it (*mbrah*) so our parents wouldn't know what we were talking about.

It wasn't easy for me to concentrate on studying after a long day of hard work on the farm. Some weekends I was in the fields on both Saturday and Sunday, leaving little time for study. Some of my fellow farmworkers paid a heavy price for doing too much mbrah during the academic year. Many students were dismissed from school for poor academic performances or had to repeat a class.

The benefits of mbrah for me cannot be overstated. Growing up, it never crossed my mind that my parents were struggling to meet my financial needs. Was I the only kid who never bothered to think that my parents might be poor? It wasn't until I reached secondary school that I began to understand the financial challenges they faced, and I was happy to shoulder some of them.

During the third term in Form Two, heavy rain and wind caused damage to the roof of the house where Patrick and I lived. Whenever it rained, we actually collected water right in our room. During the last week of the semester, we decided to find a different studio apartment. The single room we found was in better condition than our previous one, but it cost more. We didn't tell our parents about the move to more expensive quarters because we knew we could pay the extra cost through weekend farm work. Our new room had a ceiling and a cement floor. We were finally going to start our third year of secondary school in a room where we would mop the floor instead of sweeping it. In a sealed and dry room, I thought I might actually be able to get up early in the morning to study before going to school.

10

Form Three, and An Unexpected Loss

When I returned to Santa in September 2002 (at age seventeen) to begin my third year in secondary school, I got the bad news that our school fees had been increased from 15,000 to 25,000 FCFA per year. This was a huge burden on my parents. And Form Three was very challenging: in addition to sports and manual labor—yes, manual labor was a graded subject—every student was automatically enrolled in a total of thirteen subjects.

Studies were intense for Form Three students, and hunger didn't help me concentrate on those studies. I will never forget the time I cleaned the last pieces of white yam we had left in our room before discovering that we were out of palm oil. I went to Mile-12 market, where farmers were loading their produce onto trucks. I got some free tomatoes, celery, beetroot, parsley, and leeks to give my yam meal some flavor. To my surprise, the beetroot I prepared with a grinding stone gave a yellowish color to the white yams, similar to the color of palm oil. I shared this with my close friends and, from that day forward, beetroot became the number one substitute for palm oil for most of us.

As I write this paragraph, I am sitting in my nice apartment in the United States, looking at my first official biweekly paycheck and thinking about how it could have easily gotten me through both secondary and high school, paying for my school fees, house rent, and probably ensuring I had plenty to eat. If one of my siblings had lived abroad when I was in secondary school, he or she could have sacrificed a biweekly paycheck to spare me from all the hardship.

For me and other students who were going to school away from the village, the most painful time came about three weeks before the end of each academic term. That was when we had to resist traveling to the village for food, and instead focus on preparing for final exams. Starvation was typical at this crucial period of the academic year. While preparing for final exams during the first semester in Form Three, I decided to cut back on my farm work. There wasn't enough time to travel to the village, so we usually rationed our remaining food to get us through.

About two weeks before the end of the first term, I got home from school and there was nothing to eat. In front of my building, I noticed someone was moving things around in another part of the building. It was our landlord, who was very rich. I thought it would be awkward to beg him for money to buy food, so I went back to our room, got the machete I used for manual labor at school, and began cutting the grass around the house. On his way out of the building, our landlord stopped and commended me for what I was doing and rewarded me with a 500 FCFA bill. I bought four cups of rice and fresh fish and prepared a *riz sauté*—fried rice—meal for me and my student neighbors. You have no idea how happy I was. In order to survive away from home, I had to make sure my brain never fell asleep.

One skill that helped me thrive was my ability to make friends, and one of those friends was Tekeu Felix, who had grown up helping with his father's construction business. Instead of working on farms as many students did, Felix did a variety of work on construction sites, which paid a lot more than farm labor. He hired me on several occasions to work with him on plastering houses and making cement blocks. I enjoyed working with Felix, and the pay for a half day's work was the same as what farmers paid for a full day.

Felix was very business-minded, dedicating most of his time to making money rather than studying. I was his go-to person for help with schoolwork, and he was my go-to person during my toughest financial times. In addition to his studies and working as a small building contractor, Felix was a popular photographer on campus. He also owned a small store in his studio apartment bedroom, selling rice, salt, sugar, eggs, and other staples. While most of us were blaming our parents for our financial problems, he was able to attend school full-time and support himself through his business ventures. Felix had a knack for making everything work for himself.

I studied hard in Form Three but still came in second behind Kebei Charles—again. This was the fourth successive time I ranked behind Charles since Form Two—an unhappy record in my academic career. It was hard to return home at Christmas with this bad result. Family members taunted me for not being first in my class, and this made it difficult for me to get holiday money from them.

Shortly before Christmas, my brother Vincent came to the village from Douala to deliver presents. I had heard he was paying two boys in Douala to help with his bread-delivery business, and asked if I could help him with his business during the three-month holiday at the end of the academic year. In return, he would pay my school fees. He promised to take me on—but only if I finished the academic year ranked first in my class. I accepted the challenge.

Returning to school for the second term, I was determined to work harder at my studies. I cut down on the time spent working on people's farms during the week. Besides studying every evening before going to bed, I woke up at five in the morning to study before going to school. Whenever a test paper was returned, I went through it to make sure the teacher hadn't miscalculated my score.

* * * * *

On one Wednesday, my roommate, Patrick, stayed home from school because he didn't feel well. I got back home very late because we had some after-school sporting events, and was surprised that he wasn't in the room. Another student told me he had become much sicker and his father had taken him to the hospital.

I started to walk to the hospital to visit him, but about a mile into my walk, a taxi stopped and our friend John Nkuekue got out.

71

"Can you believe Patrick is dead?" he said.

"What?!" I asked in disbelief.

"He died in the taxi before we got to the hospital."

When John started to cry, I knew he was serious. I was dumbfounded and wished I were dreaming. We returned to Mile-12 and spread the bad news among other students. Nobody could believe Patrick was dead. That night, several students from Baligham village joined me in our room, and we stayed up all night weeping and talking about Patrick. Since we didn't have money to hire a car, we gathered in the morning and each of us took some of Patrick's clothing and books to carry on the trek back to the village for the burial.

When we arrived there shortly before noon, Patrick's family compound was jam-packed. No one had gone to work on their farms that day. The sound of people crying and singing traditional mourning songs could be heard from far away. I could barely contain myself when I saw Patrick's mother—so heartbroken. What is life? I saw my longtime classmate, roommate, and friend Patrick lying in bed as if he were taking a nap.

After spending a few days in the village, I returned to Santa, never to see Patrick again. The first night alone in the room was a nightmare. I had shared the same bed, table, cooking utensils, and every other thing in the room with Patrick. Everything I touched triggered a memory of him. When I tried to sleep, I had one dream after another, with him in all of them. I woke up scared in the middle of the night—it felt like Patrick was lying next to me. I turned on the lights. Of course, he wasn't there.

After school on Monday, I was afraid to open the door of our room. I couldn't imagine myself spending another day there alone. A student neighbor, Basil Mbepeb, asked if I would like to stay with him and his half brother until I found my own place, and I agreed without hesitation. The three of us slept in the same tiny bed—so small that one could barely turn over in sleep at night. But none of us complained, and I never went back to my former room. About a month before the end of the semester, I found a room of my own and moved out.

At the end of the second term, I shocked Kebei Charles—my rival in class—by finishing as the top student in our department. Charles was stunned because this was the first time he was ranked second to anyone. I gave all credit to my brother Vincent for challenging me to be the best student I could be. From this experience, I learned that giving an extra push to someone can really make a difference.

When I got back to school for the third and last term, I was inspired to do even better. The final term saw a fierce battle between Charles and me. Our test results were neck and neck, but I finished the academic year as the overall best student in my class—earning a chance to work for my brother in Douala during the three-month holiday!

11

Douala and the Disaster

Impatient to begin work with my brother, I made my own way to Vincent's apartment in Douala, where I would be staying for the rest of the holiday. Vincent, his wife, and kids lived in a one-bedroom apartment constructed from cement blocks and nicely painted. His rent, however, was exorbitant. At night, my brother, his wife, and the youngest child shared the only bed in the bedroom. Mattresses were unrolled on the floor for the older kids. I got the couch.

I thought Vincent was going to give me some time to enjoy city life, but he put me to work immediately. His bread-delivery business was booming, handling over a thousand loaves each day of various types of bread known as *gâteau*. Part of my job was to learn the different kinds of *gâteau* he sold, such as *Kumba*, named after a popular town in the Southwest Region of Cameroon, and *Marimar* and *Sergio*, breads named after the stars of a TV series once popular in Cameroon.

Every day except Sunday, we hauled bread in hand trucks that had built-in boxes for holding the loaves. The whole rig was known as *La Case*. Vincent was in charge of the bigger one, which could carry over 800 loaves. His full-time employee, Bruno, handled the smaller truck, which could carry between 400 and 600 loaves. I helped my brother by pushing the bigger hand truck from behind while he pulled from the front.

On a typical business day, we left home at about three thirty in the morning and paid *benskineurs* (motorcycle-taximen) to transport us to the *boulangerie* (bakery). Leaving there by four thirty with the two fully loaded hand trucks, we pushed them for more than ten kilometers to the Douala seaport, where we distributed the bread to stores, cafeterias, and travelers.

By two in the afternoon, we had finished distributing bread, eaten lunch, and collected money from customers. Back at the boulangerie, we spent a few hours loading the two hand trucks for the next day. I had thought farm work was difficult, but the bread-delivery business took it up a notch. During the first week, my feet were sore and I was exhausted every evening. However, I refused to complain because I didn't want my brother to think I was weak or lazy.

Early in August, Vincent had to travel to the village for the annual cultural week, and he left me in charge. I had mastered the business, particularly the financial side. In past years, I had complained that my brother was not helping with the cost of my education; I thought he was making a lot of money. But I had a change of heart when I was fully in charge of his business and saw how little he made.

While he was away, I faced problems from others in the boulangerie who looked down on me because I was small for an eighteen-year-old. Too bad for them—I was a tough cookie. I had grown up in a very big family where I learned to stand up for myself. When we got back to the boulangerie late one evening, other deliverymen had already selected the best bread products. The man in charge that day tried to convince me to take the poorly baked bread. I refused vehemently and we got into a heated argument. I was given a hard slap across the face. The next day, I told the manager that I wouldn't pay for the bread we sold until I got an apology. He laughed and walked away—maybe he thought I was kidding.

For four consecutive days I took the boulangerie's money home with me—money that they depended on to buy baking supplies. On the fifth day, the manager made the fellow who had slapped me apologize and promise to never lay a hand on me again. Then the manager gave me a ride home on his motorcycle and I handed over the money. After this incident, I earned the respect of everyone at the boulangerie.

*   *   *   *   *

On August 16, 2003—a day I will never forget—at about four thirty in the morning, I was pushing a hand truck loaded with over 400 loaves of bread. I was on the correct side of the road, minding my own business. Out of nowhere, I was hit from behind by a drunk driver. This was the closest I had ever come to dying. It happened so fast that all I could recall was being on my belly and watching loaves of bread rolling down the road.

I didn't feel any pain immediately, but I couldn't get up and didn't understand what was keeping me down. I remember being surrounded by a large crowd of people. Then two men lifted me up and put in the back seat of the drunk driver's car. Bruno and two other men accompanied me to the hospital, yelling at the driver the whole way. I don't know if it was a good idea to make the drunk driver take me to the hospital, but I am forever indebted to these men who accompanied me because they feared the driver would abandon me along the road and run away.

By the time I reached the hospital, I was in a lot of pain. The Nigerian soccer jersey I was wearing was shredded, and bruises covered my body. Both of my legs were painfully swollen. The driver was scared because he knew he was in deep trouble. After a few minutes in the hospital, he told us he wanted to get something from his house but would return. Bruno wrote down his license plate number, took his phone number, and followed him to his house to be sure of where he lived.

For several hours at l'hôpital de District de Deido, my brother's wife Bernadette tried to contact my siblings in the village, but cell phone service was terrible. When the family finally learned of my accident, they were very worried. My mother insisted on talking to me—she was afraid that I had died and that people were trying to protect her from the bad news. She was calmer after we talked. I do believe it was a miracle I survived the accident. I believe God created me out of strong material and won't allow me to depart this world without fulfilling the purpose for which I was born.

Before noon, an x-ray confirmed a fracture to my right leg above the ankle. My left leg was swollen but unbroken. By three in the afternoon, the hospital issued my first bill in the amount of 100,000 FCFA, more than the profit Bruno and I had made in the previous week. My family would have had to sell everything they owned if I stayed at the hospital for more than two weeks.

Bruno called the man who had hit me to find out if he could help with the hospital bill, but he told Bruno that he was in Bafoussam, over seven hours away. He claimed his grandmother had died. Who knows if he was telling the truth!

When my family in the village heard about the hospital bill, they unanimously decided to immediately take me out of the hospital. There was in our village an herbalist—Pa Nkwana—who specialized in treating broken bones. He seemed like the only option for treatment that wouldn't put my family into everlasting debt. My holiday ended prematurely as we left Douala that night with my fractured leg wrapped in a cloth. The trip was hard, traveling with a broken leg on an old bus over potholed and bumpy roads through the night.

When we arrived in the village, a huge crowd of people greeted me. I was humbled. The people made me feel as if I were a jewel. I watched my mom sobbing, so grateful was she to see her son alive.

I sat on a bamboo chair in front of the Pa Nkwana's house, my injured leg elevated on another chair. Pa Nkwana looked at the x-ray we brought from the hospital and noticed that the broken bone in my right leg was dislocated. He gripped my leg and pulled the bone

Resting my fractured leg
on a bamboo chair

into place. I screamed so loud that people around the neighborhood thought someone was being robbed. My parents gave a rooster and 3,000 FCFA before he began treatment of my leg.

As my father supported the leg, the doctor cut it all over with a brand-new razor blade. He then rubbed and covered all the cut spots with his (secret) black-powdered herbal medicine taken from an old black can. He wrapped the fractured part of my leg with a bamboo mat, known in my dialect as a *quala-quala*. Finally, he bandaged over the *quala-quala*.

When Pa Nkwana was done, two of my brothers carried me carefully to the doctor's house, where I was put on one of the two patient beds in his parlor. I was to stay there until my leg was completely healed. Because the native doctor only treated broken bones and related injuries, he sent my brother Vincent to get me painkiller medications from the pharmacy or hospital. Unlike some of the quack doctors in Cameroon who claim they can treat all kinds of ill-

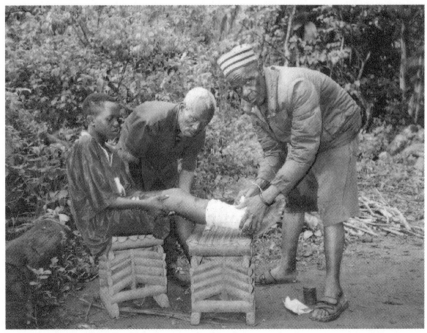

(L-R) Pierre Nzuah, Pa Jean Mofor (my father), Pa Nkwana (native doctor)

nesses, Pa Nkwana was much respected because he never attempted to handle any problem outside of his specialty.

While most of my family was worried that I might never walk again, my greatest fear was that I might be unable to go back to school. Vincent wanted to stay in the village for a while, but I urged him to return to Douala. If he stayed, he might lose customers to other bread deliverers.

My mother stopped going to her farm in order to take care of me. Every day she brought food in the morning and spent the whole day at the native doctor's compound. I got tired of her asking me over and over again how I was feeling. After a week, I finally convinced her to drop off the food in the morning and then go to the farm. It was important for her to take care of the land because family in both the village and the city depended on the crops she grew.

My younger brother, Ntinwa Job, was assigned to take care of me. Job made it clear he was doing this in return for the care I had provided him when he was a child. He warned me never to complain again about having my primary schooling delayed because of him. I couldn't argue with him—I was lying in bed unable to do anything for myself.

This taught me the importance of helping other people in times of difficulty. Growing up, I didn't understand why my mother always cooked food for friends and relatives who had sick family members in the hospital. Well, my injuries gave several people the opportunity to return the favor—and they didn't fail. For the first few weeks, no less than twenty visitors brought me food every day. I can't think of anyone from my neighborhood who didn't visit me with food.

Some lazy people who just wanted free food visited my bedside every day, and we spent the day chitchatting, eating, and playing cards. It was handy that my accident had happened during harvest time—my favorite time of the year because it meant I could eat freshly boiled groundnuts and roasted corn. For a while, I enjoyed being a patient.

12

Form Four: The Challenge of the 2003–04 Academic Year

My life as a patient turned sour when the 2003–04 academic year started and all my close friends left the village for school. Staying behind drove me bananas. I couldn't believe I was going to miss an academic year and would have to return later, a year behind my classmates. I was lying in bed thinking these thoughts, unable to stand on my own two feet.

When school began, my friend Felix made an effort to ride his bicycle down to the village every couple of weeks to keep me updated on what was happening in class. Even though I had endured some hard times being away from the village and trying to support myself as a student, I now realized how important school was to me. I still had a regular group of people visiting me every day, but I felt like a castaway not being in the midst of my secondary-school friends. The effort Felix made to visit me on a routine basis was priceless. This was when our friendship deepened—true friends show themselves in difficult times.

After about a month, I was able to hold on to tables and walk around the room without putting too much pressure on my injured leg. The native doctor recommended crutches, but my parents didn't have the money to buy them. One weekend when Felix visited, he asked if I had thought about the possibility of coming back to school at any point during the academic year. He said a lot of students missed me, and reminded me that I was supposed to prepare for and take the end-of-year national examinations known as Certificat d'Aptitude Professionnelle (CAP). I had given a lot of thought to school, but it seemed like a crazy idea to return because I could barely place my injured leg on the ground. Still, hearing the idea from Felix made it seem less crazy.

After a long discussion with him, I wrote a letter to the principal of my secondary school, G.T.C. Santa. I told the principal that my leg was healing well and expressed my desire to come back to school before the end of the academic year. When Felix was back in the village a week later, he told me the principal expressed sadness about my situation and said I was welcome to start school whenever I wanted. Since this was going to be my final year in secondary school, all class tests and exams were going to be geared towards preparing students for the national exam. This was good news for me: a student could perform very well in class tests but still have to repeat the grade if the national exam wasn't passed.

With all this new motivation to return to school, I asked my brother Festus to go to the bushes and find me a good walking stick as an alternative to crutches. With this stick I was able to limp around on one foot, occasionally testing the amount of weight I could apply to my injured leg. When my father saw me limping around, he expressed his satisfaction at seeing me standing up again. I seized the opportunity to tell him I was thinking about going back to school. He disagreed with me vehemently. He told me to be patient and to let my leg heal completely, and then return to school the following year. I knew he was looking out for me, but I already had the idea of going back to school stuck in my mind.

After about two months at the traditional doctor's compound, I was feeling a lot better and was able to take little walks around the compound with my walking stick. He had cut around my injured leg four times to apply the black powder herbal treatment—there were barely any uncut spots on that leg.

One evening, I asked the doctor about how long he thought I

Taking baby steps
with a walking stick

needed to stay under his care. He estimated I had about five more months to be completely healed. I explained how important it was to return to school and told him I could come back to the village on weekends for treatment. To my great surprise, he accepted my suggestion. My father was furious and tried to convince the doctor that it would be impossible for me to walk the long distance to and from school.

I understood my father's concern, but it was too late. The constant disagreement with him created tension in our relationship, and he stopped visiting me. It must have been hard for my father to have me as his son.

A small party was thrown to celebrate my last day at the native doctor's compound. The total charge for my care was 39,000 FCFA and two roosters.

Family members expressed their joy with toasts of palm wine. When I went to thank the native doctor and say goodbye, he gave me some of the black medicine in a small cup. He told me to find a friend at school to cut my leg with a razor blade every three weeks and apply the black medicine. This was very kind of him, making it unnecessary for me to return to the village for continued treatment. I left his compound believing that herbal medicine can work wonders.

One benefit of being disabled was that I basically watched while my mother and brother Festus put together my food items for school. Festus was at home because my parents couldn't afford to send him to school beyond a primary education—though he eventually became a very skilled wrought-iron worker. Before Vincent returned to Douala, he gave me money to cover my full school fees, and additional cash for taxis to and from school every day because I couldn't walk long distances yet. My father gave me rent money and told me to let him know when I needed funds to register for the national exam. In one way, the accident was turning out to be a blessing in disguise—my parents and brothers were providing assistance without me having to persuade them. My father hired my favorite driver in the village to drop me off right at my doorstep when we reached at Santa.

* * * * *

When I arrived at school for my first day, the Discipline Master told me I was chosen to be the Sanitation Prefect for the entire school. At the time, the best students were chosen to serve in several leadership positions. The Sanitation Prefect position came with a lot of responsibilities, including making sure the classrooms and the grounds around the school were well taken care of.

When I returned to classes, I was dumbfounded that the teachers were already so deep into the syllabus. I tried to catch up by copying other students' notes. Since I couldn't walk for long distances, Sama Ramson, a fellow student from the village, went around collecting notes from my classmates for me to copy, and even helped me copy some of them. What a sweet guy. I don't know what I would have done without him.

2003–04 academic year, school prefects at G.T.C. Santa

I was advised to ask some teachers to excuse me from tests that had already been given, but I refused. This was the year when the national exam would be taken—the gateway into high school—and the school-year tests helped prepare students for the national exam. I had nothing to lose by taking tests I wasn't prepared for. I bombed at most of them.

I finished my first term in Form Four with a failed result. Still, I was pleased with the progress I had made in catching up with my classmates. Even with a failed score, I ranked eighth out of a total of twenty-something students in my department. I had my friends Felix and Sama to thank for helping me get through the term. They were the ones who fetched water for me, helped me with notes, and brought food from my village. I don't know how I would have managed without them.

When I returned for the second term of the academic year, I couldn't afford to buy textbooks to help me prepare for the national exam. The school library's old textbooks were useless. Like other students, I tried to familiarize myself with the national examination format by gathering questions from recent versions. I was lucky to know students in my class who were preparing to take it for the second or third time; they had a lot of examination questions to share with me.

Though I was busy with school, I was still responsible as Sanitation Prefect. When the Discipline Master noticed that the campus wasn't being kept clean, I worked with the class prefects to create classroom-cleaning rosters. For students who failed to clean the classrooms, I assigned them to do much harder work in the school garden. These students were making my job difficult, and the Discipline Master yelled at me each time he thought the campus wasn't tidy. Finally, I had to catch students who were coming late to morning assembly and assign them cleanup duty.

During the second term, I was able to use my walking stick to make the two-mile journey to and from school each day. I could no longer use my injured leg as an excuse for anything. With hard work, I finished the second term with a passing grade and ranked second out of the twenty-one students in my department. This made me optimistic about my ability to pass the national exam.

Students preparing for the national exam weren't allowed to go home for the two-week break after second term. School administrators thought continuous studying leading up to the test was good for them, so all students preparing for the final exam were asked to pay some teachers to tutor us during the short holiday break. I hated not being able to go home at the end of an academic term.

Studying became really intense as the national exam date approached. When we took the mock exam during the third term, I was one of the two students in my department who passed. It seemed as if starting school late scared me into working harder than a lot of my classmates. Most exciting of all, there was a myth that students who passed the mock exam were likely to be successful on the final exam, but I wasn't going to be carried away by the mock results. I kept on studying as hard as I could.

The first part of the national exam was sports. I had to do it because during registration, I refused to complete the handicapped form which would have exempted me from taking this section of the test. I was made to understand that if I completed the handicapped form and passed the national, it would be noted on my certificate that I had a disability. Considering how difficult it was to get a job in Cameroon, I didn't want to have this against me. I figured if I did poorly in sports, I could make up for it by doing well in other subjects. On the day of the sports segment of the exam, I only participated in easier activities that weren't detrimental to my leg, which was still healing. I used the fact that I performed poorly in sports as an incentive to study more during the final days before the written portion of the CAP exam.

Of over forty students who sat for the CAP national exam in Electrical Technology, I was one of the ten successful candidates. I proved to everyone who had doubted my return to school that with hard work, anything is possible; and, most importantly, I won the trust of several people in my family regarding my commitment to education.

13

Seeking Admission into High School

After passing the 2004 CAP national exam, my next step was to seek admission into high school, which is a bit more challenging in Cameroon thanks to widespread corruption practices. Unfortunately, I failed the Common Entrance exam for Government Technical High School (G.T.H.S.) Bamenda, the closest high school around. Other high schools were so far away, it would be difficult to travel to and from the village on very bad roads and still have access to food and family. I spent a week going from office to office trying to bribe my way into G.T.H.S. Bamenda. Bribing is so common and pervasive across Cameroon that it is considered a secondary layer of fee-paying for almost everything. It is the way much of the country's business is accomplished.

In Bamenda, I presented my report cards at every office I visited, but no one was interested in looking at them. I hoped someone would see my high standing and tell me what to do to get into the school. I learned that school administrators didn't take bribes from students directly. An influential figure could have been in a better position to make a case on my behalf. But I had grown up in a small village and my family had no connections to important public figures.

Just when I was about to give up, I learned that Mr. Mantink-ang—the delegate of technical education for the Northwest Region of Cameroon—was from my village and had gone there for the weekend. I quickly packed my bags and headed for home.

It turned out my father knew him well, so I begged him to visit the delegate with me and talk on my behalf. On a rainy Saturday evening, my father and I took a long walk to the delegate's compound, located at a far end of the village known as Gahdiwala. We arrived to find him outside, dressed in a raincoat, pruning his cypress trees. He took a break and welcomed us into his house. Mr. Mantinkang and my father spent some time chatting. Then my father brought up my situation. Without any questions, he told me to meet him at his Bamenda office on Monday morning.

I was at the delegate's office before seven thirty in the morning. He came to work shortly after I arrived, and kept me waiting for a couple of hours before coming out of his office to talk with me.

"Why didn't you come to me before writing the entrance exam?" he asked.

"I didn't know I was going to fail the exam."

"School has already started and I'm not going to bother the principal."

I was speechless. After our short conversation, he got into his car and left for a meeting. I sat in front of his office until five in the afternoon, but he never came back. A night watchman asked me to leave the premises. The next day, I was at the delegate's office again before he showed up for work.

"What are you doing here at this time in the morning?" he asked, and walked into his office without giving me an opportunity to say anything.

I was a little confused, but I persisted. When Mr. Mantinkang came out of his office a few minutes later to talk with me, I told him that education was very important to me and explained what I had gone through just to get into and complete secondary school.

"You are my last hope," I told him. "I don't have anybody else to go to."

The delegate just laughed and went back to his office. Just before noon, he called his secretary into his office and I heard him ask if I was still waiting. Of course I was still there—with no plan to leave until I had a possible solution to my problem. The secretary came out and told me the delegate wanted to see me. I went into his office and he offered me a seat in front of his desk.

"You're very stubborn," Mr. Mantinkang said. "Do you know that?"

"No," I replied, with a short laugh.

"I can't help get you into G.T.H.S. Bamenda, but I can help you get into G.T.H.S. Mbengwi."

"But Mbengwi is too far away."

"That's the best I can do."

I reluctantly accepted the offer even though I had never been to the school and I had no idea where it was located. He wrote a letter for me to take to the principal of G.T.H.S. Mbengwi.

I thought about going to the village to discuss this new option with my parents, but decided to visit the school without their input. I was afraid that my parents would argue against the Mbengwi option because it was so far from my family and village. My father had already suggested that if I didn't get into G.T.H.S. Bamenda, I should stay in the village and retake the Common Entrance exam the following year. After my accident, I realized that education was the only good thing I had going for me, and I wasn't going to let anyone or anything hold me back.

I arrived at G.T.H.S. Mbengwi with the sealed letter from the delegate of technical education and was admitted into the principal's office by his secretary. I discovered that the principal was Mr. Foncham Ephraim, who was principal of G.T.C. Santa when I was in Form One and had been transferred to be in his hometown of Mbengwi. I thought he was going to ask me a series of questions, but he read the delegate's letter and simply told me to prepare to start school as soon as possible because classes had already begun. Then he personally escorted me out to show me where my classroom was located.

When I arrived home in my village, I told my parents that the delegate had not succeeded in getting me admitted to G.T.H.S. Bamenda, and then I paused for their reactions. As I sat down by the cook fire to eat rice and groundnut soup my mother had prepared, my father expressed his disappointment about what had happened because he had been optimistic after our visit to the delegate's compound. On the other hand, my mother told me not to worry because she didn't see any difference in the lives of those who were educated and those who were illiterate in our country.

Then I broke the news to my parents that I had been admitted into G.T.H.S. Mbengwi and had already reserved living quarters. There was silence. I had to prove that I was serious. My mother affirmed her position that I was nuts about education. My father didn't have much to say because he knew any attempt to stop me would be useless.

I didn't have any time to waste because the academic year had already started. With much-needed help from my mother and brother Festus, I sold some garri on village market day to raise money for some of my school needs. The cost of attending G.T.H.S. Mbengwi was 25,000 FCFA per year. Before I left the village, my father gave me 15,000 FCFA, claiming he couldn't come up with the full school fee. He promised to provide the rest as soon as possible.

14

Form Five: A New Town, A New School

Beginning a new chapter of my academic career in a new town presented some logistical challenges. I had to transport my bed, mattress, table, chair, stove, cooking utensils, and several large bags of raw food. I did not expect to return to my village until the end of the first term. No family members were accompanying me, so I had to move everything by myself.

My journey to Mbengwi involved several successive taxi rides. It had rained on the day I made the trip, which made travel difficult on dirt roads. Drivers were only taking male passengers who could help push if the cars got stuck in the wet potholes. The drivers claimed that women didn't like to get their clothes stained and were likely to step out of the car and watch the men push. Once again, women were at a disadvantage. It made me think again about the luck of being born a boy—I thought about the number of intelligent girls in my family who weren't given the opportunity to pursue an advanced education.

The drivers were correct about the condition of the roads to Mbengwi. On two occasions we had to get out and push the car out of potholes. Luckily, we were stacked like sardines in an old Toyota Corona—eight strong, male passengers plus the driver. In other places along the way, the driver asked us to get out of the car so he could drive through dangerous sections without passengers on board. When we arrived downtown at Mbengwi Park, I was covered in red mud stains.

I spent my first two weeks at school copying extensive notes from my classmates to make up for the three weeks of classes I had missed. Class size was considerably smaller than in the previous schools I had attended. More students seemed to pay attention to their studies, setting a very high bar for what they hoped to accomplish. I was no stranger to competition but was a little worried by my studious classmates. Given the remote location of the school, most of the students were area natives who knew each other. Initially, I only knew three students who were from my previous school. Being in a new area and having fewer friends, I spent more time studying.

Each time graded test papers were handed back to us, I saw several students bragging and comparing test scores. Nobody bothered to ask about my score. Even though I kept my test scores secret, I kept track of the top-performing students—I didn't want them studying too hard to catch up with me.

When we received our midterm results, I had the highest average in my class, far ahead of the second person behind me. Many of my classmates were surprised. Up to this point, I was just a short, quiet student who always sat at the first desk in the classroom. After the midterm I gained many friends, and several students started coming to me for help.

Everything was going well until I was kicked out of class for not paying the remainder of my school fees. I went directly to the principal and pleaded for some time. He gave me two weeks, the amount of time I told him it would take for my father to come with the rest of the money.

When my two-week extension was over, I traveled to the village to talk with my father. He said he was struggling to pay the primary-school fees for my younger siblings. I was self-centered and didn't care about fees for my younger siblings; my only concern was for my own situation. I left my father's workshop hoping he would find a solution by Sunday, when I had to return to school.

On Sunday, there was no sign of him until noon. He told me

he had been going around the village trying to borrow money from friends, but to no avail. I burst into tears and told him I was going to sell the only remaining goat in our compound if he didn't come up with the money.

"What? What? What did you say?" he asked.

I didn't reply. I just kept crying, knowing I had pushed the right button to get my father irritated.

"None of your brothers has ever disrespected me like you do. One day, you're going to kill me in this compound because of school."

Luckily, both my mother and stepmom came out of their houses and yelled at my dad to leave me alone. As he walked away from the compound, he warned that if I touched his goat, I should never set foot in his compound again.

An hour later, he came back and handed me 10,000 FCFA, exactly what I needed to complete my school fees. I didn't bother to ask where it came from. Our relationship was complicated, but we really only fought when it came to money, and when he gave me the rest of the cash, he let me know everything was okay. I derived no pleasure from fighting with my dad, so I was always happy when things worked out in the end.

When I got back to school, I was determined to try for outstanding results so that I could easily transfer to G.T.H.S. Bamenda, located much closer to my village. By the last week of the first term I had run out of food, and had only the sum of 1,000 FCFA that I had saved for transportation out of Mbengwi. After thinking it over, I used 300 FCFA to buy the most popular and easiest food staple for students—garri, which I survived on during that final week.

Garri can rise to about twice its volume when soaked in cold water. Every morning and evening, I soaked a small quantity and waited for it to rise. A common African quote says: "Eating garri doesn't mean you're poor, but allowing it to swell before eating epitomizes poverty." Giving it too much time to rise makes it too soft and it doesn't taste as good, but I was only concerned about how to fill my stomach. I experienced severe hunger and it made me wonder if God was busy elsewhere doing good work, while I was left in the anguish of poverty. Some days, I blacked out on the walk home from school under the hot sun. Hunger isn't only felt in the stomach.

I collected my report card on the last day of the academic term and ranked first in the class, which put a little smile on my face. Because I was short on transportation fare, I had to walk the initial four kilometers of the trip home. With a backpack on my back and a duffle bag on top of my head, I joined some of my classmates on the road. As we chatted along, I felt better after learning that I wasn't alone—they had endured a rough first term as well.

At my half sister Marie's apartment in Bamenda, it felt so good to finally have a full meal of white yam and *njama njama*. I don't think I could have waited any longer for food. Before going to work the next day, Marie gave me money to complete my journey back to the village.

When I arrived home, I couldn't imagine how I could return to Mbengwi after the holiday break. Where would the money come from?

"You look like a sick man," my mother said when she saw me.

I had lost my chubbiness without working out. Even though I told her I was okay, she forced me to eat a lot of food that evening.

* * * * *

Leaving the school trauma behind me, it was time to join my siblings to celebrate Christmas, the day when food is most abundant in the village. On this particular Christmas Day, I started visiting relatives at nine in the morning, beginning with my married sister Philomin, who lived at a far end of the village. As I walked from one relative's home to another, I made sure to eat only small quantities in order to have room for sampling the variety of each of their dishes. And because I wasn't in the village except at Christmas, I wasn't shy about begging for money from close family members.

By the time I got back to our family compound at about five in the afternoon, I was too full to eat what my mother had prepared. I had also gathered enough money to buy two beers during the Christmas night party. There is no legal drinking age in Cameroon, and kids could drink whatever kind of beverage they could afford.

One of the ways we had fun on Christmas night was moving from one bar to another. In order to make money, bar owners required that customers purchase beer if they wanted to come in and hang out. I didn't have enough money to buy drinks at every bar, so I kept the empty bottle from my first beer of the evening, filled it partway with water, and as I walked into other bars, I pretended to be drinking so they would let me in. My friends followed my example, so we spent the whole night wandering from one bar to another without necessarily buying drinks.

I was scared about returning to Mbengwi, but stayed positive and went back. The second term was better than the first. I had more friends, and some of the rich students in my class bought food for my lunches in exchange for me helping with their schoolwork.

In class, I had the advantage of having spent time in the French-dominant zones of Cameroon and was fluent in both written and spoken French. Most of the other students had lived in the English-dominant Northwest Region for much of their lives, and their French was rusty. I capitalized on this weakness, making sure I outscored everyone by a big margin in every French-language test. For the other subjects, I worked to score equal to or not far behind everyone else. My strengths were French, math, and all calculation-based subjects.

When we received midterm results in the second term of Form Five, I had studied my way to the top. Besides the simple joy of being ranked first, there were benefits for being a good student. Dating back to primary school, I was never bullied by the big guys thanks to my academic performance. I was always shown a lot of respect by my classmates.

Most of our teachers lived in Bamenda and commuted to school each day. These were full-time, trained government teachers, but living in the city gave them the opportunity to earn extra money teaching at private institutions. Some who were posted by the government to remote areas like Mbengwi refused to show up. It was hard to blame them. Teachers often went months without being paid by the government. Nonetheless, students suffered the most because of it. At the end of the school day, teachers were eager to head right back to the city, especially if rain was coming. As a result, students in Mbengwi didn't have much opportunity to interact with or ask questions of teachers outside the classroom.

For students who came from average (low-income) families and were studying in public institutions, there were a lot of obstacles to overcome in order to succeed. Textbooks were expensive and most of us couldn't afford to buy any. Without textbooks, students depended solely on teachers' notes, which is why I paid attention in all my classes and made sure I took notes as accurately as possible. Because I was so busy writing notes in class, there was no time to ask teachers to clarify things I didn't understand. I made sure to go over my notes at the end of the school day, and if something was still not clear to me, I asked a trusted classmate for help. In that regard, my most reliable classmate and friend was Anoh Pascal, a Mbengwi native who lived with his parents not too far from the campus. We were academic rivals but we liked each other. Pascal often invited me to his home when his mother was preparing the signature dish of the Mbengwi people, *Nan tara*.

Both Pascal and I were Presbyterian Christians. We started attending church services together, though there were times when I refused to go because I didn't have money to drop in the offering basket. When I had money, I liked the offering portion of the service. Everyone went to the left to drop their offering in the basket, and then returned to their seats on the right side. Starting from the first row, people danced their way to the offering basket as they sang this song in pidgin English:

> The thing weh you give wi papa,
> na yi dis wi di givam so,
> Papa eeeh
> Eeeh papa eh, make you takam with all ya heart.

It can be roughly translated as: "What you've given us, God, here it is we are returning to you. Accept it with all your heart."

I felt so ashamed when I had to make way for people to go out and come back from the offering because they knew that I couldn't afford the smallest amount to drop in the basket. As much as I hated this, it forced me to think about saving a little bit of money when Sunday was approaching.

At the end of the third term, I got my report card and packed up my belongings, not expecting to return to Mbengwi. As the best student for all three terms, I thought the odds were in my favor for transferring to G.T.H.S. Bamenda, much closer to my village.

I arrived in Bamenda prepared to submit my transfer application before continuing on to the village for a three-month holiday. My plan was to contact the delegate of technical education who had helped me get into G.T.H.S. Mbengwi, but to my great dismay, he was no longer in the Northwest Region. I couldn't believe it.

I decided there was still a good chance of transferring without a helping hand, considering that my first year's high school results were so strong. I went to G.T.H.S. Bamenda, completed the transfer form, and submitted the original of my report card. By applying early, maybe there was less chance of getting turned down a second time. I then left for the village, hoping for a good decision, which would be made in August.

15

Third Term Holiday, 2005

After the third term in Form Five, I arrived in the village during one of my favorite times of the year: the mango season. My parents and younger siblings weren't back from the farm yet, so I took a sharp knife from the kitchen, looked for the biggest mango tree, climbed it, and sat there among the branches, eating the fruit directly from the source. There was no place I'd rather be.

The first two months of my holiday were spent helping my mother on the farm and engaging in arguments with my siblings, something I had missed while being away at school. Living in the village, I could always find food or the solution to any other problem. When we were working on a far distant farm and my mother cooked something I didn't like, I'd simply make a burn fire in the field and roast yams, sweet potatoes, and cassava. There were avocado trees around the farm, too. Village life was awesome!

In August, I traveled to Bamenda to check on the status of my transfer application. I thought I was in a nightmare when the secretary at the school told me I hadn't been accepted.

"Take a look at my report card," I said. "I was first in my class for all three terms."

"I don't make the decisions," she said.

"I don't understand. I passed all my subjects with flying colors."

The secretary was moving papers around on her desk and was

not paying attention to me. When I asked her to give my report card back, she retrieved it from the very spot she had put it on the day I applied for a transfer. I was certain no one had ever looked at my application. Arriving back at the village that evening, I stood at the door and threw my backpack on the bed in my mother's kitchen.

"What happened?" my father asked.

"They did not accept me."

"What are you going to do now? Go back to Mbengwi?"

"Yes."

Even though I had trouble with my father, he was one of the few people in the family who understood me. He advised me to try to get into Bamenda again after another year at Mbengwi. He knew this obstacle was not going to stop me from pursuing my educational dreams. I told my parents I had made up mind to face the challenges in Mbengwi and complete my high school education there.

While I was still in the village, I met Nchindah Chrysantus, a student from my neighborhood who had passed the national CAP examination but who, like me, hadn't gotten into G.T.H.S. Bamenda for high school. I suggested to him that he stop wasting his time on Bamenda and think about joining me in Mbengwi. He took the idea to his mother, who thought he wasn't tough enough to survive in a place like Mbengwi, but I convinced her to let him try his luck by offering to share my room with him if he was accepted. When he gained admittance, it was a win-win because sharing the room and splitting expenses fifty-fifty was a relief for me.

Preparing to go back to Mbengwi for the 2005–06 academic year, I wanted to make sure life was a little easier this time. I knew which food items were cheaper to buy there rather than transporting them from my village, so I coordinated with Chrysantus about what to bring and what to purchase after we arrived. Leaving the village in September, I was mentally prepared to handle any challenges, and was determined to make sure he didn't have to go through all the hardships I had encountered during my first year in Mbengwi. Chrysantus was going to be in the first year of high school, or Form Five, and I was going to be in the second year, or Lower Sixth.

16

Lower Sixth: 2005-06 Academic Year

This was the year I had to prepare for the national Probatoire examination, which students had to pass in order to move on to the last year of high school. More than half my classmates had taken the Probatoire exam at least once and failed, which was a little frightening for me. But we had nine months to prepare, and my plan was to become friends with some of the students who had taken the exam before so I could get access to the study materials they had gathered over the years.

During the first week, my classmates unanimously voted me as Head Boy, putting me in charge of enforcing rules and making them do all the dirty work, like mopping the classroom floors. Having this kind of responsibility helped me acquire leadership and public-speaking skills.

Once class lectures got going, I didn't find the material as hard to understand as some students had said it would be. As the term progressed and I was doing well in homework and tests, I felt calmer and my confidence grew. To work class problems in my room after school, I used a small blackboard—the secret weapon that helped me ace most of my subjects.

One of my responsibilities was to make sure that Chrysantus was doing well in his classes. Whenever he had a test coming up, I got him ready by giving him a preliminary exam at home. Living with me probably wasn't easy for Chrysantus because I set the bar very high for him. I looked after him like a big brother would, and any of my little brothers will tell you how tough it is to be my younger sibling. After a while, Chrysantus asked if his friends could join him when I was helping him with homework or prepping him for a test. Of course, I agreed. It became the norm for me to help a group of students on a regular basis. Some of them who were natives of Mbengwi brought us food in exchange for the help.

Studying examination questions from the past was one way to prepare for the Probatoire exam. The easiest way to get them was from students who had taken the exam in previous years. By midway through the first semester, I had some of those students as friends. They helped me compile a collection of questions from more than a decade back. Unfortunately, the questions weren't cheap—I had to make photocopies for about 25 FCFA per page, and ended up having more question pages than some of the students who had taken the exam on multiple occasions. I shared these question papers with my classmates who were having a hard time obtaining study materials.

Having the questions was one thing; answering them was quite another. Towards the end of the first term, I wasn't able to answer even half the ones I had collected. My solution was to form a study group with one of the hardest working students in the class, Moma Kelly, who never gave up on a problem until it was solved. The group grew to about eight members, and we met regularly after school hours to brainstorm on problems.

In the beginning, I was frustrated by how little we were accomplishing because several hours were usually spent struggling over a single problem. A few times I wanted to quit and go home, but Kelly kept me there. We would have made more progress with access to textbooks or a tutoring center, but all those resources were too expensive or unavailable. Each textbook cost almost the same as my yearly school fee, which my parents were having a hard time paying.

It was soon time to pay the registration fee for the Probatoire exam. This was one of those blessed moments when my dad sent the money without any hitches. I now realize he didn't always give me the money right away because he was broke. Watching other students struggling to register for the Probatoire exam, I couldn't have been prouder of my dad.

One of the students who almost missed out on the registration deadline for the exam was my friend Lonchi Simon. Back in Form Five, Simon had arrived several weeks after the academic year started. He was having a hard time trying to catch up because other students wouldn't let him borrow their notes to copy. I understood what he was going through because I had been in the same situation. He was grateful that I agreed to help him out and we became very good friends.

When Simon went to register for the Probatoire exam on the deadline day, a counterfeit banknote was discovered in his registration fee. After scrambling around for money, he still fell short. Like me, Simon was many miles away from home and there was no way he could get money from his mother. My roommate Chrysantus and I had 2,000 FCFA in our room, money we had saved to cover transportation home at the end of the academic term. But the look on Simon's face was unbearable. He promised that if I gave him the money, he would repay me as soon as he got back from the weekend trip home, so I rushed to our room and got the cash for him. He was so relieved, and told me repeatedly he was going to get the money to me after the weekend.

Week after week, he never mentioned when he was going to pay me back, and I felt embarrassed to ask him about the money because he was my best friend. Two weeks before the end of the semester, I manned up and told Simon to think about paying me back so my roommate and I would have the money we needed to travel home. He gave me a stare and walked away without saying a word. The next day, he passed me and said nothing. This was the end of our friendship. Even though we stopped talking to each other, I still hoped he would pay his debt, but two days before the end of the term, it looked like we were going to be stuck in Mbengwi.

I went to talk with the woman who owned a small grocery store next to our apartment complex and pleaded with her to lend us the

2,000 FCFA for transportation. It's a shame I don't know her name. In some parts of Africa, married women are simply addressed by the name of their firstborn—a symbol of respect. We simply called her Mami Max because her first child was named Maxwell. I was one of her regular customers, so she knew me well. She told me to come back the next day for the money. I thanked her and promised to pay her back when I returned from the short holiday.

When I got my report card on the last day of school, I was excited to find out my ranking was first in the class and couldn't wait to tell my father. With our bags all packed, I went to Mami Max's store to get our transportation money, but she told me her husband had used all their capital to buy merchandise. I couldn't believe what I was hearing. I was sure her husband was angry that she had agreed to lend money without asking for his permission. I stood at the store, scratching my head and hoping I was having a bad dream. How would we get home?

While crossing the road, I saw a folded 500 FCFA bill lying in the middle of the street. Picking it up quickly, I ran to our room and started telling Chrysantus what had happened. To my great surprise, when I removed it from my pocket and unfolded the money, it turned out to be three 500 FCFA bills, making a total of 1,500 FCFA. The look on Chrysantus' face was priceless. We hadn't eaten since morning, so we used 100 FCFA to buy some doughnuts as we began our journey on foot. The saddest thing about this story is that I didn't think about who might have lost the money—or how to get it back to them. At the time, it felt as though the bills had dropped down from heaven.

* * * * *

Our school courses intensified when the second term began. Within our study group, we realized that the lessons weren't sufficient to prepare us for the Probatoire exam, so we decided to seek a tutor for the subjects that needed reinforcing. Luckily, a few miles away was Ecole Normale d'Instituteurs de l'Enseignement Technique (ENIET) de Mbengwi, which trained technical and vocational schoolteachers. We found a senior student there who was willing to teach us both applied mechanics and math. He was kind of expensive but turned out to be a great teacher. For math we gave him our class syllabus, which he used to prepare lessons. During our sessions, he taught for an hour and then spent another hour solving sample questions, which was exactly what we needed.

I recall that we had a great English teacher who had actually completed his higher education in the United States. We also had a great history and geography teacher who taught these subjects in all the seven classes at G.T.H.S Mbengwi. Other than in English-language class, instructors teaching theoretical subjects only did the lecture part of their courses. As the class Head Boy, I was responsible for dictating notes to my classmates while writing the difficult words on the blackboard. As usual, most of our teachers were anxious to leave for the city right after their lecture periods, especially in the rainy season when they risked getting stuck in the remote area where the school was located.

Among students preparing for the national exam, life is simply all about the exam. If you spent a week on a Cameroonian campus during the second term of an academic year, when studies are in high gear, you could easily identify most of the serious students preparing for national exams. Unlike in secondary school, where some teachers were happy to give us lessons during the short breaks, G.T.H.S. Mbengwi teachers were different—none wanted to be seen in that area during school breaks.

At the end of the second term in March 2006, at age 21, I was ranked first in my class again. This helped to attract more students to my study group. Knowing that we needed to keep up with preparations, we decided to forgo the two-week, second-term break in order to continue studying. I had to make a short weekend trip to the village for some pocket and food money from my parents—it was getting hard to concentrate on my studies with an empty stomach.

At our farm, where I was gathering some raw food, I heard the sound of a village crier from a far distance away. He was announcing that a war had broken out again between the two neighboring villages of Baligham and Awing. The crier ordered all men to carry their weapons to the palace. Other than small children, who were allowed to move to nearby settlements, everyone else was advised to stay in the village during war. Anyone who panicked and left during a time of armed conflict ran the risk of being banished. I was no longer a kid, so I had to stay. I had never used a gun, but I got one of my father's big machetes and joined the heavy crowd of men armed with guns, spears, bows and arrows, and other weapons. Most people believed magic played a big role in successful fighting, so I was scared of being crushed like a housefly on the battleground since I was sure I had zero magical powers.

The experienced fighters were sent to the main battleground, which was a piece of contested land between the two villages. Although no adults were allowed to go into hiding during the war, I was surprised that no one was forced to go to the main battleground. I didn't have to use my machete after all. However, there were jobs for non-gun-savvy boys like me. When women dropped off food at the palace, a group of us youths transported it to the people on the battlefield. Actually, we delivered it far beyond the main battleground, from which we could hear repeated gunfire.

I was most mesmerized by the gun-repair operation. Under a mango tree, several village blacksmiths gathered to provide instant gun maintenance. Other than shooting sounds from the battlefield, the gun-repair area was the busiest and most entertaining to watch during the first day of the fighting. This was an opportunity for me to observe how things were done during intervillage wars. For me, it was an amazing experience to see how my people came together during a difficult time to fight a common enemy. The women played a vital role in supplying food for everyone, though most of it was consumed by people like me who never set foot on the battleground.

After several hours of fighting, both villages ceased hostilities just before dark. I was worried when I saw almost all the fighters leaving the battleground, but was reassured that men would be deployed across the border at night to ensure the enemy didn't sneak in and kill people. At the end of the first day, I was really glad no one from my village had died. I prayed for intervention from the governor of the Northwest Region so that no one would be killed, but no troops had arrived by the end of the day.

The second day of the war was a Sunday and I had to head back to school, but I wasn't sure I'd be allowed to leave during hostilities. My father asked some notables from our neighborhood, and they made it clear that students were not obliged to remain in the village—but could if they wanted to do so. My parents gave me some pocket money and I gathered food from my mother's house. No cars or motorcycles were coming to or leaving our village, so I walked for several miles to the neighboring village of Bagham, where I was able to continue my journey by car.

When I arrived back in Mbengwi to resume preparing for the Probatoire exam, I worried about my family. Throughout years of studying away from home, I had a four-battery AM/FM radio to stay informed about national and international news. At this time, I was paying close attention to local and national news, hoping to get some updates about the war. All I heard was that the governor was planning to send troops to intercede. It was really unbelievable that the government authorities allowed the two villages to battle each other for several days without intervening. When my roommate, Chrysantus, came back from the short holiday, I learned that a father-in-law of my family had been shot and killed. This was sad, and he happened to be one of the few in-laws I really liked.

After the Probatoire exam in June, my brain was fried from seemingly endless studying. All I wanted to do was go home to the village and eat some quality food, which I did. A month later, the results of the exam were published, and I was one of eight successful candidates from the Electrical Technology Department. Most importantly, six of the eight successful students were members of my study group. As for my former friend Simon, he failed the exam. I did not rejoice at this, but I believe his result might have been different if he had been part of our study group.

Studying far away from home, I began to realize that blaming my parents for my problems wouldn't do me any good. It was up to me to find solutions to adversities and obstacles along the way.

17

Upper Sixth: Final Year in High School

After taking the Probatoire in Lower Sixth, it would seem that Upper Sixth would be a little easier. However, there was another national examination standing between me and graduating from high school: I still had to pass the Baccalauréat (BACC) Technique. For aspiring teachers, earning a BACC Technique Certificate was required to register for the national entrance examination into L'Ecole Normale Supérieure de l'Enseignement Technique (ENSET) de l'Université de Douala, the main teacher technical training institution in Cameroon. ENSET was my first choice because I wanted to be a teacher.

My second career preference was electrical engineering. Again, I needed to pass the BACC exam before I could even think about trying to get into École Nationale Supérieure Polytechnique (ENSP) de Yaoundé. Hard as it was to get into a reputable high school, gaining admission to a professional training institution was going to be a whole different kind of challenge.

When I started my final year of high school in September 2006, our class size didn't surprise me. Because national exams held back many students, there were only thirteen in the Electrical Technology Department, and five were repeaters. I was ready to complete the high school chapter of my life and go out into the real world to prosper.

Upper sixth class—Standing (L-R): Roland, Pierre, Walters, Joel, Valentine, Denis, Charles, Kelly, and Emmanuel Kneeling (L-R): Lambert, Jonadab, Elvis, and Festus

Everything was going well until our principal, Mr. Foncham Ephraim, was transferred to another school and his replacement was, well, quite a character. Unlike Mr. Foncham, who was very down-to-earth, the new principal was very bossy and demanded an extreme level of respect from the teaching and administrative staff. He made instructors sign in and out when they arrived and left the campus. He would call teachers to his office and yell at them for showing up late. Students often sympathized with teachers who arrived late—we knew they had to travel on very bad roads to get to school and they used unreliable public transportation. Teachers were also required to make appointments to see the principal, making it hard to talk with him.

Most of the teachers were angered by his behavior and requested that the Ministry of Higher Education grant them transfers to different institutions. In Cameroon, government-trained teachers can be posted anywhere in the country. Although education officials could decide to move them around, teachers could also initiate the process of transfer to better locations. Well, there's an African proverb that describes the outcome of this situation: "When two elephants fight, it is the grass that suffers."

Students were the biggest victims of the bad relations between the principal and the teaching staff. When the transfer decisions were made in early November, most of our instructors were approved for moving on to other institutions—without providing replacements for them at our school. As soon as the announcement was made, some of our teachers stopped coming to school, even though they still had a few remaining weeks before their transfer dates.

Without teachers in the classrooms, the campus looked like a playground rather than a place where students worked toward a brighter future. Many of them wandered around campus because it was boring to just sit in the classrooms. The principal told the Discipline Master to make sure students stayed in their classrooms— whether or not they had a teacher. This didn't work out so well. Most students affected by the teachers' transfer saga were those like me, who needed the guidance of instructors to prepare for national exams scheduled at the end of the academic year. While we were in a bad situation, students in other schools who now had our former teachers were very lucky.

The mass transfer of teachers became a big topic of discussion in and outside of the classrooms. We complained to the few teachers still with us, some of whom were irked because their transfer requests had been rejected. During one of our lectures, a teacher suggested we stop complaining and channel our grievances to the top regional education authorities rather than at the principal.

We weren't optimistic about anyone listening to us, but we agreed it was worth a try. After the lecture, we shared the idea with the accounting students in a nearby classroom. At the end of the school day, all the high school students gathered in one classroom to write a letter that would be sent to top government officials in the Northwest Region, including the governor.

To compose it, students took turns writing ideas on the chalkboard. We then edited and converted those ideas into a single-page letter. We had an English-language teacher proofread our draft because we didn't want government officials to find errors that would make them think we were a bunch of foolish students. Finally, we needed to have the letter typed. Like many students in my class, I had no idea how to type on a computer, even though Computer Science

---

THE STUDENT BODY
G.T.H.S MBENGWI
P.O. BOX 1909 MBENGWI
MOMO DIVISION
DECEMBER 05, 2006

HIS EXCELLENCY,
THE GOVERNOR
NORTH WEST PROVINCE

APPEAL FOR REVIEW OF TRANSFER OF TEACHERS FROM GTHS MBENGWI

We, the students of GTHS Mbengwi, are writing to express our frustration following the recent publication of the list of Provincial transfers in the North – West Province and at the same time appeal to your high office to review the staffing situation of GTHS Mbengwi.

Sir, our appeal has been necessitated by the following justifications:

1) The Department of Mathematics had only one teacher taking the whole school but surprisingly he has been transferred to GTHS Bamenda, which has many Maths teachers and to worsen matters, he was not replaced by anybody.

2) The Accounting Department had only four teachers and two have been transferred without being replaced to GTHS Bamenda and ENIET Mbengwi.

3) Out of the three teachers of Electrical Technology in the whole school, two have been transferred without replacement.

4) Of the five teachers in the Civil Engineering Department, only three are left with only one handling the Second Cycle.

5) Out of three teachers in the Secretarial Studies Department, one has been transferred without replacement.

Sir, from the foregoing analysis of our desperate situation, it would appear that the Provincial transfer rather than redeploying teachers to rural areas like GTHS Mbengwi which that experience an acute shortage have instead chosen to favor schools in the Urban areas, thereby, abandoning us to ourselves and placing our future in jeopardy.

We, therefore, appeal that you should intervene as the boss of the Province to ensure that those teachers transferred by omission or by design be either replaced or sent back to GTHS Mbengwi for necessity of service.

We look forward to hearing from you as soon as possible.

Yours faithfully,

Students of G.T.H.S. Mbengwi

CC
- The Provincial Delegate MINESEC North West Province
- S.D.O. Momo
- Divisional Delegate MINESEC Momo
- Principal G.T.H.S. Mbengwi

was part of our curriculum. We had a student from the Accounting and Secretarial Studies Department type the letter.

We decided to send our grievance letter directly to the governor and top educational officials in the Northwest Region. It was expensive and took a long time to send materials through the post office, so we found some teachers to drop off the envelopes at the regional educational offices in Bamenda, but we didn't tell them what was in the letters. We waited for a few days to be sure the governor and education officials had received them. Our plan was to give a copy to the principal and then go as a group to the office of the divisional delegate of education in Mbengwi to deliver his copy. We thought this would communicate to him the seriousness of our situation.

On the morning we delivered the letter to the principal, students gathered in front of the school gate to prepare for the walk to the downtown offices of the divisional delegate. However, the principal came out of his office, ordered the gateman to lock the gate, and told the Discipline Master to get every student back into classrooms. At this moment, I happened to be going around campus with Tiwara Valentine, selling magazines to raise money for our Journalism Club. We decided to walk to the principal's office to see what was going on. I saw the Discipline Master running after students, trying to force them to get into their classrooms. At first I thought it looked funny, seeing him wielding a long cane while chasing students. Then I heard the principal had told the gateman to keep everyone on campus. He had just read our letter and didn't want us to deliver a copy to the divisional delegate. I was angry because our department was the most affected by the mass transfer of teachers.

I tried to convince my classmates that we should go to the delegate's office against our principal's order. Most were afraid to go because the vice principal had warned that anyone who left the campus would be dismissed from school. I was sad to see that more middle school students were willing to go than the high school students who had written the letter. To be clear, we were not planning any violence, and had no idea the principal was going to stand in our way. We were simply trying to exercise our freedom of speech.

Out of the entire high school class, only three of us—Tiwara Valentine, Moma Kelly, and I—were willing to do everything possible to deliver the letter to the divisional delegate. Unable to get any of our high school classmates to join us, we turned to the secondary-school students and rallied more than fifty to follow us. Then we discovered the gateman had locked the gate and departed. Standing in front of it, Kelly, Valentine, and I concluded that if we left, it would be easy for the principal to dismiss us if we were the only three students to make the trip downtown. Instead, a new plan was hatched: we would get the principal to address the entire school about how he was going to solve the staffing problem. We went to every classroom and soon several students joined us in chanting, "We want the principal to address us!"

When Kelly and I stood in front of our classroom and asked our classmates to come out and join us, Professor Sama Ernest instructed us to return to the classroom or face being personally reported to the principal. I had once respected Prof. Sama, but this was his last lecture because he was transferring to G.T.C. Bamenda.

"What difference is it going to make?" I asked him. "You're teaching your last class and we're never going to see you again," I added in anger.

I don't know where I got the courage to boldly exchange words with a teacher. As Prof. Sama tried to ignore us and continue teaching, several students started banging on the other side of the plywood wall that separated us from the adjacent class. Because of the loud noise, Prof. Sama packed up and left the room.

Some of us walked to the assembly ground, where we continued asking for the principal to come out and address us. We were just a few meters from his office, so I'm sure he heard us loud and clear. Instead of coming outside, he sent out a group of staff members to force us back into our various classrooms. This escalated the situation, and students chased the staff people back into the administrative building. As things worsened, the principal sent the vice principal outside to address the students on his behalf. We liked the vice principal, but he wasn't the person we wanted to hear from at that moment. In the middle of his speech, he asked, "Who are you to demand that the principal come out of his office? It's not going to happen."

This made all the students even angrier, and they began to break up into different factions. A Form One headstrong student deflated the tires on the principal's car. As much as I wanted the principal to come out of his office, I didn't want angry students doing any damage to campus property. Kelly, Tiwara, and I started advising students to refrain from destroying any school property. In order to stop any destructive behavior and stone throwing, we brought all the students together again in front of the administrative building. Hundreds of them gathered and once more began chanting in unison: "We want the principal to address us!"

A group of students directed their voices at his office window. It got so loud that he couldn't stand it anymore.

"Go to the assembly ground," the vice principal said angrily as he came out of the administrative building. "The principal will address you in a moment."

When he stood in front of more than five hundred students, the principal was furious. He told us to form straight lines, as he always did. I never understood why this was so important, but on this day, nobody was interested in lining up. The crowd shouted "No!" to his request.

"We're all affected by the transfer of teachers, but your reaction is unacceptable," the principal said. "You can't just decide to send out letters without my approval."

We all listened quietly as the principal delivered an angry speech. I don't remember everything he said, but the main message was that it was unacceptable to send letters to officials without consulting him. At the end of the speech, he did promise to do his best to solve the teacher problem, and to call for an urgent PTA meeting to discuss the possibility of hiring substitute teachers. The part of his speech that scared me a bit was when he said, "The orchestrators of this protest won't go unpunished."

I hadn't meant to play a major role in what happened on campus.

It happened by default because I was so worried about how I was going to prepare for the national exam without the help of teachers, and their mass transfer put my future at risk.

Before leaving the assembly ground, the principal gave students an opportunity to ask questions, and a number were raised.

"Why did teachers request transfers when you became principal?"

"Why did you stop us from going to the delegate's office?"

"How are we going to prepare for BACC without teachers?"

"What are you going to do in order to improve your relationships with teachers?"

One of the positive takeaways from the principal's speech was the opportunity to ask questions. However, as the session continued, I noticed that the staff member standing behind the principal was taking notes on which students were speaking up or making inquiries. It was too late for me—I had already asked my question.

* * * * *

When we got back for the second term in January 2007, the principal had actually worked with the PTA representatives and hired some substitute teachers. Most of them were recently graduated high school students who were still idling around, looking for work. These substitute instructors weren't nearly as competent as government-trained teachers, but we didn't complain too much because half a loaf of bread is better than no bread at all. For students in the Electrical Technology Department, we were very grateful to Pa Kum, the only professional teacher left in our department. He devoted some of his personal time to give us lessons in subjects he wasn't even assigned to teach. We called him Pa Kum instead of Prof. Kum for good reason: with such genuine interest in our success, he was as much a father figure to us as he was a teacher.

During one of Pa Kum's classes, a gendarmerie officer pulled Kelly and I out of the classroom and issued us warrants to report immediately to the Gendarmerie Brigade of Mbengwi. Our friend Tiwara Valentine, in Lower Sixth, and Little Chi, who had deflated the tires on the principal's car, were also issued warrants.

No reason was given for why we were being summoned, but it was pretty obvious to us. We had to walk to the brigade because the officer had arrived on a motorcycle. This gave us an opportunity to brainstorm on how to defend ourselves. We agreed to tell the truth about what had happened. However, we vowed not to mention the name of the teacher who gave us the original idea to write letters to government officials, or the name of the teacher who had edited our letter. The rumor on campus was that the principal had heard we were guided by an unnamed teacher, and we worried that the teacher would get into trouble.

At the gendarmerie, we were all put in a small room and called up for interrogation, one after the other. I was the first to be called.

OFFICER: "Do you know why you are here?"

ME: "No, Sir!"

OFFICER: "Do you know about the strike that took place on your campus?"

ME: "Oh, it wasn't a strike. It was a protest against the mass transfer of teachers."

OFFICER: "The principal told us you were the leader of the strike that took place on your campus."

ME: "No, that's not true!"

OFFICER: "Tell me exactly what happened."

The officer warned that I was going to be sent to jail if I didn't tell the truth. I can't remember half the things I said because it was a very long interrogation. He pressed me to name the teacher who had given us the idea to write letters, but I didn't crack. He asked me to give him a list of students who led the protest on campus. I knew if I gave him a short list that included me, we could easily face severe punishment. I told him there were no leaders and more than half the student population had been involved in the protest. This was the answer we had agreed upon during our walk to the gendarmerie—keeping answers vague and generalized.

Being interrogated by a uniformed officer for the first time in my life, I was nervous at first, but my confidence grew as I took questions for about an hour. At the end of the questioning, I was locked up in another small room while the other students were being questioned. I wondered how my parents would react if I ended up being jailed.

The interrogation of the other students was brief, none lasting more than twenty minutes. Finally, we were put in a room together, where four gendarmerie officers took turns warning us to never again participate in any kind of campus protest. From our interrogation by these officers, it appeared the principal had exaggerated what had happened. As we left the gendarmerie, we were all relieved because in order to register for the common entrance examinations to the top two institutions for post-high school studies, applicants had to present a Certificate of Non-Conviction. If we had been convicted of any offense, our futures would have been ruined and all our studying would have been in vain.

The day after our interrogation, I was asked to report to the principal's office. "If you fail the BACC exam, don't think about coming back to this school," he said as soon as I entered.

"If only one student passes the BACC exam from this school," I boldly said, "it's going to be me."

"Get out of my office, get out of my office," the principal said, pointing to the door.

When I got back to my classroom, I felt myself getting very angry. I had learned that one of the students from my class had given our names to the principal as the leaders of the protest. I told my classmates about my visit to the principal's office, and I told them I knew who had given my name to the principal. I warned this student to never think about coming to me for help with anything.

Even though several classmates tried to cheer me up, I decided to go home before the end of the school day to avoid saying things I would regret later. The student who gave our names to the principal came to my room and apologized. He said he'd been tricked and had no idea we were going to be punished. I accepted his apology, but I was still mad at him.

It was important at this point to refocus my attention on devising an examination preparation strategy, which involved trying several approaches. For example, I might pick a single problem, such as one on exponential function. I'd use my extensive notes to find and follow how similar problems were addressed, and used that technique to solve the one I had chosen. Whenever I picked one to pursue, I did everything possible to solve it before moving on. Since more than half my courses were calculation subjects, the plywood chalkboard in my room was kept very busy. Sometimes I'd get stuck on a problem and would go to bed, but I couldn't stop thinking about it. When an idea came to me, I'd get up in the middle of the night to write it down out of fear I'd lose the idea by dawn.

After a long period of studying on my own, something happened that I can't explain. It felt as if God had granted me the power to figure things out for myself. When my classmates brought questions to me, I was able to think for a few minutes and then give them the answers. They were surprised when I corrected substitute teachers on topics we had not yet had in class. I had a lot of respect for these teachers who were helping us even without formal training, but when I disagreed with one of them, I would ask permission to prove my point on the blackboard.

I realized that one of the best ways for me to study was to help others. We had a lot of free time during the day because of the teacher shortage, so I agreed with my classmates to meet during some of the free periods to tackle problems together. We usually picked things we'd be studying in class the next day. I assumed the leadership role at the blackboard. We were very organized. Every student was obliged to raise his hand to ask a question or make a suggestion.

Because of my beef with the principal, I decided to expand my involvement across the campus. I wanted him to see my face everywhere he went. As a member and treasurer of the Journalism Club, I worked with the club president to make sure we delivered local, national, and international news to the student population every Wednesday. English was the main language of instruction, so I chose to focus on delivering the news in French. It was unfamiliar to most of the students, so fluently providing news in French in front of hundreds of them elevated my stature on campus.

As a win for me, the principal had to stand in front of the administration building and listen to me reading the news to almost a thousand students. The price I paid for my fame was the amount of time I spent helping students with their French-language assignments. Because of all the assistance I was providing across the campus, I was nicknamed "Prof." I had been debating whether to become an engineer or teacher. Now, with the pleasure derived from other students' respect for me, I was leaning towards the teaching profession.

During the 2007 Bilingualism Week celebration, the two French teachers at G.T.H.S. Mbengwi enlisted me to help them organize and create activities such as sketches, songs, and teaching students how to sing the national anthem in French. On the final day, we presented our sketches and songs in front of other students, and under the watchful eyes of the principal, staff, and representatives from the Ministry of Secondary Education (MINESEC).

I was presented with many prizes for my effort, small things like eighty-sheet notebooks. The best moment was when the principal had to congratulate me and hand all the prizes to me. I wondered what was going through his mind. Although I seemed like a delinquent student to him, I hoped he was starting to realize that I wasn't that bad.

I became a completely different kind of student from the day our principal told me I wouldn't be allowed back if I failed the BACC exam. I was known for being punctual, but began coming to and leaving school whenever I wanted. I developed a new kind of stubbornness that I didn't understand. There were times when I asked myself, "Who am I?" and couldn't really answer. On many occasions, if I arrived at the school gate in the morning and saw other students being punished for tardiness, I

Skit: "Je Veux me Suicider"

would simply U-turn and go back home, where I would study on my own for the morning and return to school during lunch break, when the gate was opened. I didn't miss much in the classroom because of the lack of teachers.

* * * * *

This was surely my best academic year yet. I was making money from teaching prep classes and feeling very positive about my preparation for the BACC exam. Finally, I wasn't starving anymore. However, I felt as if my siblings had forgotten me and didn't care about my education. Just as I began feeling that way, a surprise letter arrived from my brother Innocent, who was living in Douala.

> Dear brother,
>
> Here comes once more the voice of your beloving brother who comes from the Douala town. Thieves visited me on the 17/02/2007 and did away with my phone and money mounting up to about 40,000 FCFA. The only good thing is that they did not take any of my properties. But all equal I have struggle to get another phone.
>
> Dear brother, you should know that all our hope now is on you in so far as school is concerned. So, you should take your studies extremely serious. Also try to succeed at your examination and also with flying colours. You should always call if conditions are not withstanding.
>
> Here is the sum of 5,000 FCFA. You should use it to be managing for this while. I would have given more but my conditions have not permitted me to do so.
>
> Extend my warm greetings to everybody.
>
> Your brother,
>
> Kenne Avent Innocent.

His letter came at a time when I was seriously preparing for the mock examination. The 5,000 FCFA he sent was enough money to feed me for a month. But most importantly, it was so encouraging to read a letter of support from a family member. It meant the world to me. It had taken weeks to reach me, but it arrived at the right moment to lift me up. There's no feeling like knowing a family member thinks the fight you're fighting is a good cause.

When the mock BACC results were published in May, I was ranked at the top of my class, ahead of the second student by a wide margin. I don't tell these results to brag, but to underscore the importance of ranking as a motivating factor for my academic success. As short as I was, this is how I attained respect from my peers. Ranking is also a big part of the Cameroonian education system, and when I was so far from home, it induced me to study hard without pressure from my parents.

In June, when I had finished the eleventh and final subject of the BACC Technique exam, I was very relieved to be done with studying, at least for a while. Standing outside the campus gate, I picked up a stone and threw it towards the schoolyard. This was my way of saying, "Farewell! Hopefully I won't be seeing you anytime soon." I learned this gesture in the village—whenever we were done cultivating a large piece of land, we'd throw stones back onto it.

After the BACC testing was over with, I traveled to Douala to help my brother Vincent with his bread-delivery business while awaiting the exam outcome.

In late August 2007, the BACC results were published. I was one of ten students of the thirteen in the Electrical Technology Department to pass. This was a great percentage, considering that we did it with an unprecedented lack of teaching staff.

On the Saturday I heard the BACC results, my siblings took me out to the bar to celebrate. At times when I needed money from them and we went out drinking, I would order inexpensive sweet drinks rather than beer. But if I asked for a beer, they would know there was nothing on my mind because, as a gesture of respect, I refrained from drinking when I needed help. My brothers had noticed this practice, so on this occasion, when I ordered beer, they all laughed. I was so filled with joy.

18

Decisions!

With high school behind me, I had decisions to make. Brother Vincent was providing all my basic needs and wanted me to remain in Douala to continue helping him with his bread-delivery business. I, however, didn't want to feel dependent on anyone else. All my siblings in Douala were taking good care of me, which made it difficult to think clearly about my long-term future. I knew that adversity had always helped me make decisions throughout my academic journey; being away from family and having to cope on my own had motivated me to carve out a personal path.

After working with my brother for some months, I told him I wanted to travel back to Bamenda, where I could concentrate on preparing for the Common Entrance examination into ENSET de Douala and Polytechnique de Yaoundé. Working at his business—pushing hundreds of loaves of bread in a hand truck for more than ten kilometers a day, six days a week—left little energy for opening books to study at night. I was so exhausted from the work that all I could do at night was eat and sleep. But my brother wanted me to stay and help. I wanted to tell him I wasn't an endless-energy robot, but I couldn't find the courage. I was counting heavily on his financial support, and was reluctant to argue with or anger him.

All my life I have had a weakness—and, maybe, a strength—if I set my mind on doing something, I'd persist until I achieved it or fell over trying. In early August 2007, my brother told me he was going to be traveling to the village for the annual cultural week and, again, he was going to leave me in charge of the business.

As my brothers were preparing to leave Douala for the soccer tournament in the village, I thought about one of my greatest allies in the family—Aunt Manyi, who believed in me like no one else. Most importantly, she was an independent woman and thinker who would speak her mind. So I wrote a letter to Aunt Manyi, telling her that I couldn't succeed in electrical engineering without being computer literate, and the only place I could study computer science was in Bamenda, but that Vincent wanted me to take a course in Douala, where the schools were not as good. Finally, I told her that the computer training year in Bamenda would begin very soon, and I needed her help to get me out of Douala as soon as possible. I stretched the truth, but I was desperate to leave the city.

Vincent tried to convince Aunt Manyi that I could stay in Douala and accomplish all the things I wanted to do, but she took my side. From then on, my relationship with Vincent was strained. We no longer had interesting and deep conversations during the workday, and news from the village came to me from my other brothers. It was painful working with Vincent under those conditions. Deep inside, I knew I had hurt his feelings.

I felt a little guilty about leaving, but there was no turning back. The day of my departure, I stopped at the boulangerie after work to load up on bread to bring home. My family in the village would go nuts if I didn't bring bread from the city. Vincent walked with me to the bus station for the overnight trip. I knew our relationship was at a low point when he gave me the exact fare and not a penny more.

As soon as I arrived in the village, I went to see Aunt Manyi and thanked her for getting me out of Douala. Late in September, I left for Bamenda to investigate computer training schools. Unfortunately, the cost of attending was far beyond the amount I had expected. The year-long course at FLEXCOM Institute was too expensive, so I signed up for their six-month version for 60,000 FCFA. This was a huge amount of money for my parents, so I arranged with the school secretary to pay in two installments. With classes scheduled to begin on October 2, I returned to the village to discuss with my parents how to come up with the first installment. When I told my mom about the school cost, she was shocked.

"Hoôkolokolo," she exclaimed, a reaction in dialect to something out of the ordinary. "Where are you going to find that kind of money?"

"From you and papa," I replied.

My mother laughed. I told her it would be very easy for me to find work after I completed the computer training program. I had no idea if this was true because getting any kind of decent job in Cameroon was very hard, regardless of one's level of education.

I must now take a pause to thank whomever introduced the cassava plant to my village. My dreams would have been dashed as a young child if my mother wasn't growing cassava as one of her main agricultural products. This is true for most children in my village. In the case of computer-school fees, I was going to process some garri from my mother's cassava to raise money for the first installment of 30,000 FCFA. However, with the fluctuation in the price of garri from market day to market day, based on weather conditions and the number of wholesale buyers, she planned to borrow money to supplement whatever money we raised from selling the garri. This time I didn't bother my father to contribute to my school fees. My intention was to stay with one of my siblings in Bamenda during my computer studies so I wouldn't have to pay rent.

A day before I planned to leave the village for school, I visited my grandmother, Ma Mbohlang Suzanne, for inspiration and wise insight. She was one of the sweetest people on earth, and her spirit still shines through my mother. I can't count the number of times she received me with open arms when I was at odds with my parents. During this visit, she roasted a yellow yam for me, which I ate with an avocado picked from her backyard. My grandma was very special to me, and I enjoyed talking with her more than with my parents. She was always nice to me, and I don't remember her ever criticizing me as my parents did.

When I told Grandma that I was going to be leaving the village for school, she asked me to kneel in front of her three-mud-brick fireplace so she could say a prayer for me. This was something Grandma did every time I was going back to school. She said her prayers in dialect, the only language she knew. As I knelt in front of the fireplace on her dirt floor, she grabbed a chunk of soil and rubbed it on my forehead, a symbol for her blessing. As she rubbed my forehead repeatedly, she started saying a prayer: "God will protect you as you go back to school. If you hit your leg on a rock, it's the rock that will crack. Any man who has evil thoughts against you will not succeed because I have never wished for bad things to happen to another man's child...."

She said this prayer in a way that had depth beyond the words. Before I left, Grandma told me to stop by her house the next day to collect some cocoyam she was going to get from her nearby farm.

The next day, I was walking back from dropping my father's tailoring equipment in the market when someone told me that my grandmother had just passed away. I couldn't believe it. "No way! My grandma can't be dead. I was with her last evening and she wasn't sick."

This world is really strange to me. You are with someone today who is good in spirit, and the next day she is gone. On that morning, it seemed as if my grandma knew what was happening. She sent my cousin Pinata Cleris, who was living with her, to get my mother, who arrived and spent a few minutes with Grandma before she passed away. There was no record of my grandmother's age, but judging from my mother's age, we guessed she was about eighty years old. Oh, she was a sweet grandma and it was sad to bid her farewell.

Because she was a respected older woman from the Bamiléké tribe, Grandma's funeral was a major event and involved a great deal of preparation that included all her children, grandchildren, in-laws, and other close family members being present for the ceremony and burial of her casket. Since I was still a student, I wasn't expected to contribute financially, but I was the main man when it came to preparing for the funeral.

While waiting for relatives to arrive in the village for the burial, I gathered some of the younger children in the family to help me build sheds. By using sticks and fronds, we built a large shed that almost filled the compound yard. With the basic electrical knowledge I had from my schooling, I got cables, switches, and bulbs from my uncle who owned a bar and had a generator. I wired all four of the houses at my grandmother's compound where family members would be staying. I also wired the outdoor shed where traditional dances would take place. *Kana* was one of those traditional dances performed all night.

A Bamiléké family such as mine pays more respect to the dead than the living, spending large amounts of money on rituals and ceremonial events. On the night of my grandma's death, close family members spent the night in her house in the presence of her body, which had been nicely dressed and lay on her bed. Before 8 a.m., relatives from Douala, Yaoundé, and other parts of Cameroon began to arrive. After a series of traditional rites were performed, the beautiful white coffin was brought outside and placed on a table. Several family members came forward to give short speeches, mostly telling grandma to watch, bless, and protect us from her place in heaven above. Everyone, regardless of age, was given a chance to walk close to the coffin to pay last respects, after which the casket was buried.

Following the burial, it was time to choose my grandmother's successor. A common custom of many tribes in Cameroon is for an elderly person to choose his or her successor and confide this choice to one person who is able to keep it secret. According to Uncle Barnabas, my grandmother had chosen her successor more than two decades earlier when she was very sick in the hospital and unsure if she'd survive.

Now, when the moment arrived to reveal her selection, Uncle Barnabas tricked my brother Vincent into joining him inside the house. Vincent had no idea he had been chosen by grandmother to succeed her—until our uncle grabbed his hand and started running across the compound yard as the crowd erupted, "*Wu tililililili ...*," shouting in dialect. This is a sound Bamiléké people make while tapping their mouths with their hands, which amplifies the volume. A series of gunshots followed, mostly from blacksmith-made firearms loaded with gunpowder. For a week, traditional dances and rituals were performed to mourn and celebrate the life of an amazing woman.

After a week of helping out during my grandmother's funeral ceremony, it was time to turn my attention to school. Time and again, grandma had told me not to play around with my education, and I felt the best way to put a smile on her face in heaven was to return to school. I talked with my mother, who said she had spent all the money I was supposed to use for my first installment. From the look on her face, I knew she expected me to be very angry, as I had always been when barriers were put between me and my education. However, Grandma had been one of my favorite people, and I couldn't be angry that my school fees were used for her funeral.

My mother was surprised when I said I understood that she had to use the money. With the help of some of my younger siblings, I processed another batch of garri and sold it during the village market day. I made 20,000 FCFA, which wasn't enough for the first installment of my school fee. I couldn't ask my brother Vincent for financial assistance because he was still mad at me for leaving Douala against his will. We had hardly talked during the funeral week. I was angry with my siblings for not coming together to help with the 10,000 FCFA I still needed.

So, just two weeks after losing her mother, my mother borrowed money to help me complete the first installment. My brother Innocent gave me 5,000 FCFA for spending money. Once again, I felt the truth of how hard poverty can be.

19

Computer Training School

On October 21, 2007, at age 22, I left Baligham for the next chapter of my academic career at FLEXCOM Institute in Bamenda. I had one goal in mind from computer training: to type as fast as some of the people I had seen in Western movies, who did it without looking at the keyboard. Before starting at computer training school, I didn't know anything about computer software—all I knew was that people typed on computers. After one week of attending classes, I realized there was a lot more to computer studies than just typing.

Initially, I was simply fascinated by being able to create the Cameroonian flag (green, red, and yellow with a yellow star centered in the red band) in Microsoft Word. Compared to my previous academic studies, computer training just seemed like fun. Although computer school was expensive, for the first time in my life I was attending a school that did not have a teacher shortage. I now understood why wealthy people send their children to private institutions. As with all Cameroonian schools, FLEXCOM Institute used a ranking system, which wasn't a surprise. At the conclusion of the first trimester, I was ranked fifth out of 117 students. Because I was contented with my ranking position, it seemed as if I had lost my competitive edge.

I was yet to discover the importance of computer training, and computer school was a second priority for me. My main goal remained getting into a professional teachers' training institution,

ENSET de Douala, or into Polytechnique de Yaoundé, the best engineering institution in the country. While in the village for a short break, I realized how much I needed financial help from my brother Vincent in order to register for the entrance examinations for these two professional institutions. It was almost impossible to ask my parents to help me since they were already struggling to come up with the remainder of my school fees.

Now I realized the full consequences of my falling out with Vincent. I couldn't send him a letter asking for money because we had not been communicating for months. I decided to write him an apology letter. If he forgave me, then I would ask him for financial help. I told him I hadn't meant to disrespect him by forcing my way out of Douala against his will, and that I was very sorry. By the end of the short school break, I still hadn't heard anything from Vincent. Either he didn't have time to reply or he was still mad at me.

Leaving the village for the second trimester, I was so lucky it was my mother's turn to benefit from her njangi contribution group. She easily gave me 30,000 FCFA to complete my school fees. On the first day of classes, I went to the treasurer, Loveline Fonyuy, to pay my fee. She tried to convince me to switch from the six-month program to the full-year version, which cost a lot more money. The founder and director of FLEXCOM Institute, Mr. Khan Felix, heard us talking and joined us from his office.

"You're a good student," Mr. Kahn said. "You should really consider going for the one-year program."

"I don't think my parents can afford to pay for the one-year program."

"In the six-month program you get a certificate. But with the one-year program you'll be awarded a diploma."

"That sounds interesting."

"The best student in the one-year program receives a desktop computer during the graduation ceremony," Loveline said.

I didn't believe I had a chance against all the smart students in my class, but this got me thinking about the benefits of switching to the one-year program. Nonetheless, I was more concerned about the upcoming professional exams. I had never really considered pursuing a career in the computer science field. When it was time to register for the common entrance exams, I decided to phone my brother Vincent. After school, I stopped at a callbox along the roadside. Right at the beginning of our conversation, he acknowledged having received my letter. I took that as a way of saying he accepted my apology, which I had made, honestly, because I needed his help. I still believed I had been right to force my way out of Douala.

We had a good conversation. Later that evening, he sat down with my other brothers, Daniel, Innocent, and Festus. Together they came up with the money for processing documents and registering me for the two professional exams. The money was transferred to me via Express Union. I took both exams and failed them. More than twenty classmates and friends who took the exams with me also failed. With all the preparation I had put in, it seemed I should have passed at least one of them. But with the level of corruption in the academic system, it is unclear if I actually failed, or if I simply hadn't done something extra beyond taking the exams. In Cameroon, it isn't unusual for students to use their connections with people in power to gain admission into higher institutions.

From my years in school, I had developed a passion to be a professor, but that dream was dashed by my failure to pass the ENSET de Douala Common Entrance exam. My backup career was to be an electrical engineer, but that dream was dashed when I failed to get into Polytechnique de Yaoundé. I was discouraged.

Corruption is a very bad thing. It has an adverse impact on the aspirations of so many young people. Growing up in a country where no one in power was under the age of sixty is also a problem. The old leaders have lost touch with what it's like to be young. I found myself thinking I was born in the wrong country. Given my academic achievements in secondary and high school, I believed I had earned the right to a scholarship and entry into an advanced educational institution.

As soon as I found out I had failed both of the entrance exams, I went back to the FLEXCOM Institute office and had the treasurer switch me from the six-month to the one-year program. This cost a total of 107,500 FCFA, not a small amount of money. I made the change without consulting my parents. This longer program was known as Data Processing, geared to training students on a variety of computer software.

Changing my program meant I was going to have to extend my stay with my half sister Marie. Her husband, a taxi driver, had a second wife. Eight of us lived in a three-bedroom house in a section of Bamenda known as Nitop-one. I shared a small bed with Maximinus, a boy Marie's husband, Ni Sama, had with a girlfriend.

Living in a house with seven other people, it was a struggle to have enough food for everyone. Even with Marie's job as a private nurse and her husband's job as a taxi driver, it wasn't easy to put food on the table every day. Luckily for me, I was very close with a brother-in-law, Nana Robert, who was an apprentice at a car mechanic workshop. He rescued me each time I came home from school and found that there was nothing to eat. When Robert's boss gave him 150 FCFA to take a taxi home, he would walk instead and save the money. We'd take it to a nearby restaurant, where we each ordered rice for 50 FCFA and topped it with black beans for 25 FCFA. Because we were regular customers, the waitress usually threw in a few pieces of fried plantains.

It would have been considered disrespectful to my half sister and her husband if they discovered we were eating out, so I kept it secret. Robert and I referred to our restaurant meals as "black beans." Each time one of us complained of hunger, the other would whisper "black beans," and we would head out without letting anyone know we were going to eat at a restaurant.

* * * * *

Now that computer study was the only good thing going for me, I began to take it much more seriously. I got up each day at 5 a.m. to fetch water from the closest public tap, and made sure that all the twenty-liter water containers in the house were filled before I left for school. Even at that early hour there were long lines for water.

Knowing that the best student in the class would receive a

desktop computer at the end of the year, I started spending more time after classes studying and familiarizing myself with all the software programs we were working on. One goal was to attain increased typing speed—my original reason for enrolling in the school! While some of my friends were busy learning how to play computer games, I dedicated my time to a program called "Mavis Beacon Teaches Typing." Midway through the second semester, my typing speed was up to seventy words per minute without looking at the keyboard. This was a big accomplishment for me.

An amazing thing about FLEXCOM Institute was that it had internet service, though only intermittently. Each time a student realized there was a live connection to it, he or she would yell, "There is internet!" and everyone would try to do something on it before the connection disappeared. The slowness of the connection allowed us to multitask. One could type an address, use the restroom and return, and a page would still be loading.

My studying paid off. I did very well in all my courses during the second trimester, in both the theoretical and practical aspects of each subject. My Microsoft Word teacher, Mr. Temeyen Godlove, nicknamed me "Pa Microsoft," which he called me when he handed out test papers. Although I was fascinated by the magic of performing complex calculations in Microsoft Excel, my favorite subject was Microsoft Word. To my surprise, I finished first in my class of eighty-seven at the end of the second trimester.

Mr. Kahn, the director of our school, came to read our results and tell us what to expect during the final trimester. At that time, FLEXCOM Institute was divided into two different departments: hardware, for students learning how to repair computers; and data processing, for lazy students like me who only wanted to learn how to use a variety of software programs. Standing in front of the class, Mr. Khan read the names of the top three students from each department and asked them to come to the front of the classroom. I was the shortest and smallest of the six students.

"Look at him," Mr. Khan said, pointing to me. "If ranking was according to size, he'd be the last in this class."

Everyone laughed. Mr. Khan reminded all students to come back at the beginning of the third trimester with the remaining part of their school fees. I was still thinking about how I was going to inform my parents that I had switched to the longer program, which cost an additional 47,500 FCFA.

"The best students from my school are not going to be walking home," Mr. Khan said at the end of his speech.

He announced that the first student from each department would receive 2,000 FCFA, the second would receive 1,500 FCFA and the third 1,000 FCFA. I was delighted because I had no money for transportation back to the village, and I had been worrying about again asking my half sister Marie for transportation fare. The 2,000 FCFA covered it, plus I used the extra to buy bread, biscuits, and some bonbons for my siblings in the village. When I arrived home, my mom thought I was done with my six-month course.

"What are you going to do now?" she asked.

"Mama, I switched to the one-year program and it's going to cost an additional 47,500 FCFA."

"You must think money grows on trees," she said.

"Mama, you are starting to sound like my father."

My mom was shocked—not about the extended program, but about the money it would cost. Really, there is no one I can talk to in my family like my mom—she is one of a kind. When I decided to stop going to my father with my financial needs, my mother assumed total responsibility and did everything in her power to make sure I could continue to pursue my dream.

When I returned for the final trimester, I was required to do a one-month internship. I was accepted as an intern at Maryland Internet Complex, a cyber café on Commercial Avenue in Bamenda that offered internet access, typing of documents, and computer repair services. The internship was exciting because I was exposed to so many new possibilities and learned so much. I often worked more than my ten hours a day in order to spend time with the senior staff. Late in the evening, with less traffic at the cyber café, I was able to watch and learn from them about repairing computers and installing software. My regular work at the cyber café included typing and formatting documents, designing postcards, and helping customers access the internet. This work prepared me to become one of the most skilled cyber café attendants in Bamenda.

Asang Elvis, a computer technician at the cyber café, taught me how to download drivers for a variety of computer operating systems. This type of work paid very well. Elvis also taught me how to download free software programs and how to perform minor computer repairs. Because the manager, Mr. Etienne, was brilliant at computer maintenance, his services were sought by people throughout Bamenda. When the café brought in a lot of money, Mr. Etienne would reward us by buying everyone lunches of roasted plantains and avocados.

At the end of the internship, I returned to school for the last part of the final trimester. The year ended with a final exam on fourteen of the sixteen courses we had studied. Luckily, many of the students had not completely paid their school fees, so the director allowed us to take the exam with the stipulation that the fee had to be paid to attend graduation and receive a diploma. I still owed 10,000 FCFA, and having totally tapped out my parents, I had no idea where the money would come from.

Two days before graduation, my half sister Marie surprised me with the 10,000 FCFA to complete my school fee. This was unexpected, considering Marie's monthly wage of less than 50,000 FCFA and the number of people who depended on her for food and housing. In my family, we all refer to her as "Mama Marie," and she lives up to that name totally. It is an understatement to say I owe her for rescuing me during an important moment of my life.

On the eve of graduation, all the students gathered at the proprietor's house, where we slaughtered and fried chicken, popped popcorn, made a variety of snack foods, and filled hundreds of goody bags for graduation guests. With so much competition from other computer institutions in Bamenda, the director wanted our graduation to be a successful occasion; he saw it as a marketing tool for his school. He rented graduation robes for all of us, and we were required to wear suits under them. Yes, more money. I did not own a suit. My brother Innocent paid 25,000 FCFA so that I could have a tailor make one. When I dressed up in my black suit with well-polished black shoes, I was proud of the man I was becoming.

As people were seated and the graduation ceremony began shortly before noon, we lined up outside and danced our way into the graduation hall, singing a song we had all been practicing for about a week. The hall was packed and looked more dazzling than I had anticipated. There were representatives from the Ministry of Employment & Vocational Training, and several influential public figures from the Northwest Region. The director hired a famous

(L-R): Elie Leussa (classmate) and Pierre Nzuah

musical group to perform during the ceremony. I even had an opportunity to see a famous comedian perform—an entertainer whose pidgin-English comedy program I followed on local radio.

After the entertainment, it was time to hand out student prizes. Prior to graduation, the director had contacted small businesses across the city to contribute small items as rewards for graduating students. Some of the donors were present at graduation to personally hand out their gifts. Out of a total of fourteen software programs we had studied, I received the prize for best student in more than half of them. I also received runner-up prizes in other subjects. My name was called out repeatedly, to the extent that the emcee said in jest that I shouldn't return to my seat.

The individual subject prizes were something of a surprise. The only one I had my eye on was the desktop computer, but I didn't think my overall class average was high enough to win the grand prize. A very smart girl in my class, Wirba Laura, had definitely given me a run for my money. When the big moment came, the director stepped on stage and gave a brief speech.

"The first prize in data processing goes to ____?" Mr. Khan asked, turning the microphone toward the audience.

"Pierre Nzuah," the audience responded.

Oh, man! I would have collapsed if I hadn't won first prize. As Mr. Khan confirmed that I was the winner, I could hear my half sister Marie screaming from the top of the hall. This was the high point in my academic journey to that day. It was an opportunity for me to shed some tears of joy, but the best I could do was have a big smile on my face.

I received an enormous Pentium III desktop computer and monitor. The emcee, Mr. Muluhngwi Simon, who was our accounting teacher, asked Marie and her husband to come forward to take the computer so that I could return to my seat. At the end of the ceremony, Marie hired a taxi to transport my prizes back home so I could stay and mingle with classmates and have pictures taken.

This was such a gratifying day for me. I had worked really hard through my educational career but had never received such tangible

Receiving the grand prize, a desktop computer

rewards. I was not only the first person in my family to be computer literate, but also the first to own a computer. And the value of the prizes exceeded what I had paid to attend computer school for a year.

* * * * *

During the period when I had been studying in Bamenda, I also spent some time back in the village attending to family matters. On one occasion, I returned home for a short break from school and learned that my half brother, Mofor Amos, had become extremely stubborn. Amos had completed primary school three years earlier and, like me, had tried to force his way into secondary school. He was not successful. Realizing that he would almost certainly be spending the rest of his life in the village helping my parents on the farm, he decided to make everyone miserable. Unfortunately for Amos—and my other younger siblings—whenever I was around, they had to put away their stubbornness and shove their willfulness in their pockets. On this particular trip to the village, I saw my stepmother, Mami Suzanne, frying garri alone.

"Mami Suzanne, I see you're frying garri all by yourself," I said, before asking, "Where is Amos?"

"Amos doesn't listen to me anymore," she said. "He must be somewhere on the street with his stubborn friends."

Well, there was a time when my parents thought I was unbearable, but I never failed to help on the farm, and I always helped my mom fry garri because I knew it was the main source of income for the family. Above all, I never hung out with kids in the neighborhood who were known for belittling their parents.

I cut a long branch off a eucalyptus tree and started wandering around the neighborhood, looking for Amos. Being whipped with a eucalyptus branch is no fun. I had my butt whupped this way in primary school. I found Amos standing by the roadside chatting with his friends, just as Mami Suzanne had told me. I hid the cane behind my back. When I was close enough, I gave Amos a series of lashes on his back and asked him why he wasn't at home helping his mother fry garri. I would have beaten him more but he outran me.

Amos' friends stood there laughing, thinking I wasn't going to do anything to them because they weren't my brothers. I went back and delivered their share of the whipping. They ran away, yelling back at me, "You are crazy!" By the time I got home, Amos was with his mother frying garri, and he hadn't mentioned what had happened. When I showed up with the remaining eucalyptus branch in my hand, my stepmother began laughing and said she had wondered why Amos rushed into the house and shoved her away from the frying pan. Mami Suzanne was glad to have me home.

A few months later, my half sister Marie had an operation and my stepmother came to spend some time with her in Bamenda. She told me that Amos had returned to being defiant as soon as I left the village. I told Mami Suzanne that the best way to change his behavior was to send him to secondary school away from the village. I encouraged her to forget about the tradition of the father shouldering the cost of school, and to find a way to send him even if she had to borrow money. She wondered if school would help Amos.

Speaking from personal experience, I told her that if Amos was in a situation where he had to become independent in a place away from home—including cooking for himself and facing all kinds of challenging situations that students go through—he would not have to be forced to mellow down and take responsibility. He would instead *have* to be respectful in order to obtain the money and food needed to live on from family members in the village.

"I will do anything to get him out of my house," my stepmom said.

Well, Amos was eventually sent to my former school, Government Technical College in Santa, where he chose to study electronics technology. After the first term, my stepmother admitted to me that school had transformed Amos into a much better person.

There were other issues in my family at this time. I could never understand why the first and last children in our family got the most attention from our parents. For children like me, somewhere in the middle of the seventeen children my father had brought into this world, it was a struggle to get any attention. In spite of this, things did not go well for Mami Suzanne's youngest, Mamekem Cynthia. She had completed her primary-school education, but then had to stay home because my father couldn't afford for her to continue. Because she was a girl, it was less likely he would pull out all the stops to find money for her education.

While I was studying in Bamenda, my niece Kebunjion Gillian had a baby boy, and Cynthia was brought from the village to babysit. I had a chat with her and asked how she felt about staying at home while her classmates continued their education.

"I'm tired of the *jogmassi* work," Cynthia said. "I don't want to return to the village."

By *jogmassi* she was referring to the kind of work people do without being paid. Listening and looking at the sad expression on my little half sister's face, I felt sorrow that her hopes for a promising future were being dashed at such a young age.

"What if I convince Mama Marie to send you to school here in Bamenda?" I asked, trying to get a response from her because I had been thinking about this for a while.

"I would really like that," she said, with a tiny smile on her face.

Now I had to find the right words and the perfect moment to have a serious talk with my half sister Marie. Again, she was Mama Marie because she played such an important role in our family.

One day after school, I decided to stop at the private health clinic where she worked, which was right across the street from my computer school. In order for me to go home and start cooking before she returned from work, I often stopped there to get money for grocery shopping at the Bamenda food market. But I was on a different mission this day.

When I arrived at the clinic, my half sister asked in pidgin English: "You donc come for cause trouble again, eh?" She asked this question because I tended to distract people every time I showed up at her workplace.

"Massa, na hungry go kill ya pigin oh," I replied, holding my stomach as I told her that hunger was about to kill her son. I wasn't kidding because I hadn't eaten anything since morning.

My half sister sent me to Sonac Street to buy four roasted, ripe plantains for 200 FCFA and two avocados for 100 FCFA. As we sat eating our plantains on a bench in front of the clinic, I asked her a question.

"Mama, what do you think about these girls in the village who are getting married at early ages and giving birth to children they cannot support?" I was trying to get her opinion before bringing up the topic of my little half sister.

"Nzuah, why are you asking me this question?" Marie asked in typical Cameroonian fashion—answering a question with another question.

"I think if we allow Cynthia to return to the village, she might end up like one of those girls," I said, referring to the ones who are forced to work on the farm because their parents cannot afford to sponsor them beyond primary school.

"What are we going to do, then, for Cynthia? I can't think of anything she can do in the village."

"We can send Cynthia to a secondary school here in Bamenda?" I suggested.

Of course, by "we" I meant her because I wasn't in a position to contribute a penny towards Cynthia's education.

"That's a good idea," Marie said. "Let me talk to Ni Sama."

141

Considering the number of people living in Marie's house, I didn't think it was a good idea for Marie to ask her husband if he wanted Cynthia to extend her stay. "I think you should talk to Ni Sama only after we have found a school for Cynthia. That way, Ni Sama can be upset for a while, but he won't allow Cynthia to return to the village if she has a school to go to in Bamenda."

Marie laughed at how I was talking about her husband right in her face. "Dis pigin, you know ma man like book," she said in pidgin English, amazed at how much I had come to know her husband. To be clear, Ni Sama was a very nice man, and I believe he would have embraced the idea of sending Cynthia to secondary school in Bamenda. Nonetheless, I didn't want to complicate the situation by having to go through too many people.

At the end of our discussion, Marie agreed to help Cynthia further her education. To fulfill my part of the deal, I took Cynthia to City College of Commerce (CCC) Mankon in Bamenda, where she was admitted to the accounting studies department. She was overjoyed at the chance to attend secondary school.

Although jobs are very scarce in the Northwest Region, this part of the country is home to some of the best academic institutions in Cameroon. As a result, people from other parts of the country often send their children to secondary and high school there, particularly in Bamenda. Formukong Meldrick, the firstborn son of my eldest brother Vincent, had completed his primary-school education in 2008 in Douala, a French-speaking area. My brother wanted Meldrick to attend secondary school in an English-speaking region so he would be fluent in both languages. Vincent decided to send him to my former school, G.T.C. Santa, which had been upgraded to a Government Technical High School.

Meldrick had passed the Common Entrance exam, but missed the face-to-face interview because he lived seven hours away in Douala, and the school had no way to communicate with him about the appointment. Vincent called me and was very nervous. Meldrick was his eldest child and he was worried that he wouldn't be admitted into secondary school.

At the time, I had a blue NOKIA 3310 cellphone that allowed me to communicate with siblings in other cities. As a former student and prefect of G.T.H.S. Santa, I had a good connection with some of the administrative staff still working at the school. I told Vincent to send Meldrick to meet me in Bamenda. At the age of eleven, Meldrick was put on a night bus in Douala, and I picked him up at the Vatican Express bus station very early in the morning in Bamenda. After breakfast we traveled to Santa, which was about ten miles away.

It had been four years since I graduated from G.T.H.S. Santa, but most of the staff still recognized me. This made it easy to start a conversation and for me to make a case for my nephew. Everything went smoothly. Meldrick was interviewed and admitted on the spot. In addition to the normal school fees, Vincent had given Meldrick an additional 20,000 FCFA in case we were asked for a bribe. Fortunately, and surprisingly, we were only asked to pay 3,000 FCFA as a late admission fee. Helping my nephew get into secondary school worked out well for me, too—it helped to heal the tenseness that still existed between Vincent and me ever since I had chosen to leave Douala against his will.

With a diploma in data processing from FLEXCOM Institute, I registered for the August 2008 national diploma exam in Secrétariat Bureautique. This test was given once a year by the Ministry of Employment and Vocational Training. I scored third best from the Northwest Region, and dedicated the diploma to my younger brother, Mbohlang Festus, who paid for the exam registration cost.

20

Job Hunting and
Moving to a Different City

With my strong academic background, I thought I was ready for the job market. I made photocopies of my Probatoire certificate, high school certificate, FLEXCOM Institute diploma, and proof of my success on the national diploma exam. In addition, I created a fairly decent resume and included this in my job application package. Then I went to several places across Bamenda, applying for jobs. At multiple locations I was told they weren't hiring. Some people took my job application package and promised to get back to me. I followed up with those people, but to no avail.

After a month of job hunting in the city, it was clear to me that no one was interested in my services. I was learning firsthand why youths with high school and university credentials were constantly complaining about the alarming unemployment rate. I vividly recall something that President Paul Biya used to say to young people on the eve of Youth Day, celebrated on February 11: "I am fully aware of the difficulties you are facing. I know your doubts and worries. I know especially that you have difficulty getting a job."

I started asking questions: if the president knew what young people were going through, why hadn't he done something to avert the skyrocketing rate of youth unemployment during the decades of his leadership? Despite my education, I now saw myself in the same

145

situation as some people who never had the opportunity to attend school. How was I different from some classmates who dropped out early on, or never got beyond primary school? I was having negative thoughts like I used to have in secondary and high school when faced with tough situations. I started feeling as though I was trapped in the wrong environment and became resentful toward society. During this difficult time, I tried to keep in mind the common saying, "L'impossible n'est pas Camerounais," meaning that "The impossible is not Cameroonian."

Because I had worked hard and so many people had helped me get to this point, there was no turning back. Growing up in an environment where I had to self-start and self-inspire, I held my head up and made another major decision: it was time to move to another city. I didn't want to return to Douala because I had so many siblings there—it would be too easy to rely on them rather than being independent. I decided to move to Yaoundé, the capital of the Centre Region and the administrative capital of the country. I was a bit more hopeful about finding work there, and to reduce the cost of living, I called my cousin Yimely Samuel to see if I could live with him.

"No problem *petit frère*," Samuel said. "Just let me know when you're coming."

In early September 2008, I packed and left Bamenda, leaving some of my graduation prizes with Marie and taking the rest to the village. These were mostly dishes, which I distributed to close family members who had supported me in some way throughout my education. After a week there, I traveled to Yaoundé for job hunting.

Upon arriving, I assembled my credentials and was ready to begin searching, with Samuel's help. We visited several internet cyber cafés and computer training institutions, leaving a copy of my credentials at each stop. No one was hiring at more than twenty of the places we visited. Most said they would contact me as soon as a job opportunity opened up. In the meantime, I was at my cousin's welding workshop, helping him by sharpening knives and machetes, painting doors and windows, and doing whatever I could to be useful. For over a month, I waited in vain for a job-offer call.

21

A Job, But ...

On Friday, January 16, 2009, two months before my twenty-fourth birthday, I received a job offer. I was at my cousin's workshop, painting a gate with anti-rust treatment, when Nchinda Pius stopped by on his motorcycle. He was the manager of eCentre Cyber Café, located at Carrefour Carrière in Yaoundé. This was one of the many cyber cafés owned by his brother who lived in London.

"We want to start a computer training program," Pius said, "and I'm looking for someone who can teach in both French and English."

I accepted this job offer without even asking the terms of employment. I just wanted to work.

I started on January 19 without signing any contract or negotiating what my monthly salary would be. I was just delighted to be in a place with the opportunity to use some of the knowledge and skills I had acquired in school. In addition to being the only staff person teaching the use of a variety of software programs, I was responsible for helping clients who wanted to learn how to use the internet to communicate with family in Cameroon and abroad. I was also in charge of selling internet-access time tickets and typing and formatting documents.

At the end of my first month, I went to the manager to collect my salary. Based on my qualifications and responsibilities, the owner of the cyber café had set my monthly salary at 40,000 FCFA, which was more than the 23,514 FCFA minimum wage decreed by the government. Sadly, I didn't get my much-anticipated first month's salary.

"Look at the cashier forms," Pius, the manager, said to me. "Where do you want me to get money to pay you?"

I was speechless. My colleagues at the cyber café tried to make me feel better by telling me they couldn't remember the last time they got paid at the end of the month. But my situation was different than my seven colleagues at the café—I was one of the two employees who was not a family member of the owner. Based in London, the owner had his relatives run his businesses in Cameroon, and this may not have been a good decision. They used the company money to solve personal problems, so at the end of each month there wasn't enough left to pay bills and wages. They didn't appear to care much about the success of the business or about the negative balance in the accounting records.

Even without getting paid, I continued to work at the cyber café. I made sure I woke up very early each morning to fetch water for my cousin's wife. Even in the nation's capital we had to walk a long distance for water. After doing morning chores, I walked two miles to work with Samuel, whose shop was about a half mile from the cyber café. I was working six or seven days a week. If I walked to work with Samuel, I knew he'd buy me breakfast. I only had lunch on special days when a satisfied customer might tip me. Luckily, I didn't have to worry about dinner. Samuel always left money for his wife to buy food, and 99 percent of the time, even when I got home very late, there would be food for me on the table.

After seeing me work several months without pay, my cousin got really angry about the way I was being treated.

"You cannot be working for these people and I'm still responsible for buying your food. If things don't change, I'd rather have you come back to my workshop."

I loved my cousin very much, but I didn't want to go back to welding and the pain it caused me. I decided to contact the director of the café in London instead of relying on his family members, who didn't seem to care about me or the business. After a long negotiation with him and the manager, it was agreed that I would take home a maximum daily amount of 500 FCFA for my transportation costs. This might seem like a small amount of money, but it made a big difference in my daily life. I was able to buy lunch and take a taxi home at night. I didn't bother asking for the rest of my salary at the end of the month; it would have been a waste of time. I couldn't quit because there was no other place to go. Just having an unpaid job in Cameroon was an honor.

With the knowledge I acquired from my training at FLEXCOM Institute, combined with my internship at the busy Maryland Internet Complex cyber café in Bamenda, I excelled at eCentre 1, both as a bilingual instructor and a cyber-café attendant. The director revised my schedule and I was assigned to spend three days a week at eCentre 3, located in an area known as Kondengui, not far from the famous Yaoundé prison of the same name. Because this branch was beyond walking distance from where I was staying with my cousin, I managed to persuade the director to increase my daily allowance to 700 FCFA.

I was generating a lot of revenue for the eCentre businesses, but half my monthly pay was being spent on transportation. There was no sign that the remainder of my monthly wages was ever going to be paid, so I followed my cousin's advice and quit my job on October 6, 2009. I wrote a resignation letter and waited until students were seated in the classroom. Then I told them about my decision before emailing my resignation letter to the director in London. I copied all his siblings who were in charge of running the business. As students left the classroom, they demanded their training fees be returned to them. I left the cyber café, but I knew the owner would try to persuade me to return because it wouldn't be easy to find another bilingual computer teacher. Here is the resignation letter I wrote:

> Dear Director,
>   Please accept this as my resignation to eCentre, effective immediately. I regret the inconvenience it will cause, but circumstances have left me no choice.

Working for eCentre has been a wonderful experience. I have grown in many ways here and will always treasure the opportunities provided for me in my close to eight months stay at eCentre.

I started working with eCentre on the 19th of January 2009 with two weeks of test. That is, I was official affirmed to be a staff of eCentre on the 4th of February 2009. From that period till now, I have collected the sum of 20,000 FCFA at eCentre 3 and 82,900 FCFA at eCentre 1 making a total of 102,900 FCFA under my account. Subtracting that sum from my seven months' salary, 40,000 x 7 = 280,000 FCFA, I will be owed 177,100 FCFA. I will be very grateful if you use your high position to pay what is due me by your well-known company eCentre.

If you have any questions, please feel free to ask. I wish you and the company all the best. I do hope our paths cross again in the future.

Sincerely,
Pierre Nzuah

The day after my resignation, I joined my cousin at his welding workshop. I wasn't happy with this work, particularly since it was done without proper eye protection, but I was guaranteed breakfast and lunch each day. At lunch time, I went to a cyber café near my cousin's workshop to check my email. The director of eCentre had sent a lengthy response to my resignation letter.

Pierre,

It is unfortunate that you have had to take this course of action. You must understand that it is an act of absolute disregard for protocol and disrespect of management authority for you to be writing to me about a sudden resignation, leaving students who are depending on you for training and without first expressing any grievance to any of your direct supervisors/controllers.

As for any issues of staff wages, everyone must note that for the survival of the business, it is necessary for staff to be fully aware of the link between their productivity and their income—what they put in and what they take out. Accordingly, all wages have been reviewed so that they become linked to your individual and your site performances. Further, each site supervisor has been given the responsibility to make their site succeed, in whatever way possible. So it is entirely up to the site supervisor to pay whatever money is available to staff even when there is no money to pay for electricity, or to choose to pay the electricity to ensure that the site can continue to work and pay the staff wages tomorrow. One thing you must assure yourself of is that I will not pay money for people to sit around doing nothing!

One issue to be addressed is training and the plan was to get all trainers to eventually be working on a shared income basis, where for each student that they take on, they would get up to 50% of the training fee. That is all part of a bigger arrangement where the site will be promoted as a training centre and classrooms equipped to offer those services. This offers great opportunities for serious people who want to succeed.

I must remind you however, that under your contract of service, your action to abandon a class of students without prior notice constitutes an adverse action to actively undermine the interest and reputation of the business. I will therefore ask that you contact Pius immediately to discuss any grievances you may have and resume duties until at such time that there is mutual agreement to terminate the contract. If you fail to follow this advice then be aware that not only will there be no further payments to you, but eCentre may seek other means of redress to the financial and consequential loss arising from your actions. I hope however that you will choose to do the right thing and continue to work for the greater opportunities ahead at eCentre.

Kind regards

███████████

This was the second time I had irritated the director. On another occasion, he had promoted me to site supervisor, and I told him I'd only accept the offer if it came with an increase in monthly wages. He got angry and rescinded the offer. Perhaps I hadn't followed normal procedures when I resigned my position, but there was no "contract of service" as far as I knew. I can't remember signing a single piece of paper at the time I was hired. The director's siblings lied about my resignation, claiming they had no idea I was dissatisfied enough to leave. I hadn't bothered telling Pius, the manager, because I knew it was a waste of time. After reflecting on the director's reply to me— which I think was meant to scare me—I sent a response. I don't think he understood what a hardheaded kid I was.

> Director,
>
> I am sorry for the inconveniences I might have cause with my sudden decision of resigning, but I refute the statement that it was an act of absolute disregard for protocol and disrespect of management authority. I have always told most of my colleagues that issues are best resolved through dialogue than in writing directly to the Boss who knows less of what is happening at the site. So, if I wrote to you this time, though every staff is claiming he was not informed, I have done so before writing to you.
>
> First and foremost, I talked with Pius on Friday concerning training and his response was that I should carry the training publicity papers I have produced and put at the site and move along the street to inform people that training is going on at eCentre. Furthermore, he said he had discussed with the Director that if

training is not moving the classroom will be given out for rent. Concerning salary, he said I should not complain too much about that because even him the General Manager has not been paid and he still went ahead to repeat those words yesterday when I told him I was resigning in front of Erick and Obi. In what way again was I expected to discuss with him?

As for Erick, I came in the morning and he was not there, else I would have told him since he is the person I always tender matters to for resolution. He came to work at about 10 am when I have already sent my resignation letter, and I still called and told him about my decision. So, if he has replied and said that I never contacted anybody, that means he has not contacted Obi or Pius.

As for Obi, I discussed with him on Friday and told him that if things have to continue this way, I will not cope and will have no other option than to quit. On Monday he was ill and never came to work, and yesterday I still told him that I was resigning.

From the above judgements, you will understand that I never disregarded or disrespected the management authority nor abandoned training without prior notice. Not only Pius, but I have also contacted other staff like Erick, Ignatius, and Mirabeau that for the business to succeed, we have to hold meetings at least once a month to redress matters affecting the business, to no avail.

I have discussed with Pius and my condition is that if I am to resume duty:

1. I should be paid a certain amount of money to be using now.

2. My salary should be fixed because I don't want to work on contract, commission, or any other method.

3. The setup of the training room should be looked

into because there are three students now with only one computer.

If the above conditions are alright, I will be able to resume duty tomorrow. If the management of eCentre deems that it is not possible for me to work under those conditions and that they will not refund any money to me, there will be no problem but I believe that I deserved what I'm owed by eCentre.

Pierre Nzuah

For about a week we all went back and forth via email. They soon realized nothing was going to force me to return without money in my pocket. Finally, I was enticed with 20,000 FCFA and returned to work, but money wasn't the only reason I went back. I was thinking about my future, and knew returning to the cyber café was in my interest. At this point, I had to figure out other ways to make money if I wasn't getting paid at the end of each month.

* * * * *

As a side job in Yaoundé, I started installing software programs on private computers, charging customers from 1,000 to 2,000 FCFA for this service. Although my employer was still not paying me a real wage each month, I didn't care as much because I was beginning to make as much money from my side jobs as I should have made from a monthly café salary.

Occasionally, the director shipped secondhand computers from London to Cameroon. Some of these were used for the cyber-café business, and some were sold to other people. On my own, I learned how to use parts from broken computers to repair other machines at the cyber café. Initially, I was repairing computers by simply using the trial-and-error method, but gradually I became good at identifying and fixing computer hardware problems. I had also learned more about how to search, download, and install drivers for printers and computer operating systems. With this do-it-yourself computer repair and troubleshooting knowledge, I was able to start earning extra money.

One of my secrets was to never fix computers in front of my customers. Many people would be reluctant to pay a fair fee if they discovered that I solved their problems in a few minutes. In Cameroon, you have to side-hustle like crazy and be able to think outside the box in order to survive.

From the start of my work at eCentre, I spent a good portion of my time helping students from the University of Yaoundé I and the University of Yaoundé II with online research. Most of them started at the university right out of high school and had very little computer knowledge. I also assisted students searching for information about foreign universities for study-abroad programs and helped them fill out application forms. For those who were accepted, I assisted with the next three steps: completing online visa applications, scheduling visa appointments at various embassies, and prepping them for visa interviews. When students were scheduled to interview at the US embassy in Yaoundé, for example, I used reputable online sources such as travel.gov to create a three-page paper of questions and answers frequently included in visa interviews. I charged 500 FCFA per copy, with 300 FCFA of this fee going to my employer's account for printing and 200 FCFA for my own pocket. This was a win-win-win arrangement for all involved.

After a while, I started asking myself why I was helping others travel abroad while I languished in poverty in Cameroon without any hope for a prosperous future. With that in mind, I started searching for schools abroad that offered electrical engineering programs. I centered my searches on schools in Britain, the US, and France because I was confident in both French and English languages. I had always dreamed of sleeping and waking up in one of these western countries.

Thanks to my experience as a cyber-café attendant, I was aware of online scammers who extorted money from students desperate to get out of Cameroon. When I started exploring colleges and universities abroad, I checked out their institutional websites and read any Wikipedia background on them, all to verify the legitimacy of the school. The two things I was looking for were affordability and the availability of an electrical engineering program. Initially, I was fascinated by the fact that whenever I sent emails to admission counselors abroad, their responses came back to me faster than when I sent emails to people within Cameroon.

I also began aggressively searching for study-abroad scholarships. I found descriptions of many, but few had application links. Gradually, however, I became obsessed with the idea of leaving the country to study. One day, on the way to work, I proposed the idea to my cousin, Samuel. We got along very well, and I was comfortable talking to him about any dumb idea that crossed my mind. I told him that I had been in touch with some schools abroad.

"Petit frère, I have a friend called Monsieur Theo who helped my friend Donald travel to Belgium," Samuel said.

Before we separated at Carrefour Mbankolo to head to our respective work sites, Samuel promised to have a talk with Monsieur Theo, a moringa oleifera farmer who spent much of his time at the cyber café researching plant information and communicating with his international business partners. (Moringa oleifera is a drought-resistant plant with many uses, some of them medicinal.)

I had to wait until the next day on our way to work to find out from Samuel how his talk with Monsieur Theo had gone.

"What did Monsieur Theo say?"

"He said he can help us, but we have to talk with our brothers in Douala."

Samuel knew a lot of people who had traveled abroad and knew about the financial burden involved in sending someone out of the country. During a family reunion in the village, he brought up the topic of sending me to study in the United States and how important it could be for the whole family. Most of my close family members were skeptical about investing their money in a project that seemed very farfetched. My aunt Manyi got annoyed and yelled at everyone.

"What kind of children are you? Why is it impossible for you to ever get together and agree on anything that involves money?"

She went on and on, asking questions and blasting everyone in the room. I knew my aunt trusted me, and that I was perhaps one of her favorite family members. She could see the pain on my face. I was in disbelief that my relatives weren't excited about the possibility of sending one of their own abroad. Eventual, Aunt Manyi convinced everyone that it was a good idea.

About a week later on a Saturday, four of my brothers from Douala arrived in Yaoundé. We stayed up late at Samuel's house, talking about how significant it would be to have a family member abroad. The next morning in Carrefour Mbankolo, seven of us met at a bar: my four brothers from Douala (Yemeli Vincent, Tafortio Daniel, Kenne Avent Innocent, and Mbohlang Festus); Monsieur Theo and my cousin Yimely Samuel, both from Yaoundé; and me. Monsieur Theo was going to talk to us about the process of seeking admission to an American college.

During our meeting, Monsieur Theo told us that the school he had chosen for me was SUNY Potsdam in New York. He presented a list of admission requirements. We had a very successful meeting, after which my siblings pledged to split the financial burden of my admission process equally. We agreed to keep the process secret so that we didn't run the risk of getting ridiculed—just in case the project failed. In my community, traveling abroad is prestigious, while failure in this endeavor is equally shameful.

One of the admission requirements for international students was to take the Test of English as a Foreign Language (TOEFL), which I thought was going to be an easy multiple-choice examination. The registration fee for the exam was $150, but we paid about twice that because Monsieur Theo had to pay a friend abroad to register me for the test.

Without much preparation, I took the TOEFL and scored 52/120, which was way below the 79/120 minimum score required by SUNY Potsdam. I didn't think the results accurately reflected my English skills.

My brothers were concerned that I was never going to be able to improve my score to the necessary minimum. Nonetheless, they put their money together to have Monsieur Theo register me for a second time. According to him, the friend abroad who was supposed to register me again squandered the money and never signed me up for the test. We suspected Monsieur Theo may have spent the money, but we didn't confront him because we needed him to help us with online payments—something that could not be done easily in Cameroon at that time.

The 2009 admission deadline for SUNY Potsdam (July 1) was fast approaching and we had no time to spare. Once again, my brothers came up with the necessary registration fee, and this time Monsieur Theo succeeded in registering me for the TOEFL. I was scheduled to take the test at the American Language Center in Douala because the test dates in Yaoundé were all booked.

In order to prepare, I downloaded some free study materials and made use of them late at night after my work at the cyber café was done. Besides the fact that TOEFL prep materials on Amazon and eBay were very expensive, I didn't have a debit card to purchase them. I relied on my ability to download some of these materials online for free. Studying at night after working long days was not easy. Finally, I took the TOEFL for the second time and scored 76/120, falling three points short of the admission requirement. That was the last straw. My brothers gave up, which was understandable considering how each of them struggled to meet their basic, day-to-day financial needs. To make matters worse, Monsieur Theo moved away from Yaoundé to live and work on his farm permanently.

I was ashamed of disappointing my brothers, but being desperate and determined to leave the country, I wasn't ready to concede defeat just yet. Still, after working more than ten hours a day for six months, I hadn't even saved a hundred dollars. In hopes of getting ideas about how to get out of Cameroon, I began talking to friends who had successfully made their way to Europe and the United States. Some of these people were having a hard time making a living abroad and suggested I might be better off staying in my homeland. I read articles about people from Western countries warning others not to put their lives at risk by seeking greener pastures abroad. But listening to them would have stripped me of any hope for my own future. There was nothing left for me in Cameroon.

Although I complained about the lack of opportunity in my native country, there were times when I told myself to shut up. Although we weren't rich, I was still fortunate to be part of a family that always helped me have something to eat and a place to live. I knew many who didn't have that much. During the time I was in Yaoundé, the common phrase on the streets was, "La galère va nous tuer," which means, "Poverty is going to kill us."

It's true that I spent a lot of time thinking about my own future, but I also imagined what it must have been like for people starving or trying to flee oppressive governments just to have a chance at life somewhere else.

When I rescinded my resignation from eCentre, I did so because of their internet access. Without it, I couldn't continue pursuing admission to a foreign university. Despite the setbacks, I hadn't given up that dream.

22

Hanging in Limbo

In January 2010, the eCentre cyber-café branch at Carrefour Carrière was shut down because the landlord wanted to use the space for a personal business venture. I refused to join other employees in moving to other branches. I'd spent almost all my wages on transportation, and they were a fraction of what I was supposed to be paid.

I rejoined my cousin Samuel in his welding workshop, but also did a number of side jobs for pocket money. During my time at eCentre, I had established a special connection with some of the customers. In addition to computer repairs, I was known for my skill, speed, and accuracy in typing and formatting documents. I was able to toggle between the French and English keyboards, including using the necessary accent marks such as *accent aigu, accent grave,* and *accent circonflexe* when typing French documents. With the connections I had, teachers and university students gave me their documents to type. I used my home desktop machine—the computer I received as a prize after completing classes at FLEXCOM Institute—but had no printer, so I charged only 150 FCFA per page. My clients then had the documents printed elsewhere.

Adjacent to my cousin's welding workshop was GIC-SIIM Cyber Café, where my friend Koebou Marcel was the only employee. He worked from eight in the morning until midnight, seven days a week, for a monthly salary of 40,000 FCFA. As an unemployed

161

customer, I was more interested in spending time helping my friend Marcel than assisting my cousin Samuel in his welding workshop. One day, Marcel asked if I would like to work with him. I said yes gladly. Since Marcel's boss didn't want to hire another employee, Marcel paid me 15,000 FCFA a month out of his own salary.

On the days I was in charge of the cyber café, I generated a lot of revenue, to the surprise of the owner, Tamafo Leopold (aka Tonton Leo). Despite the fact that I was simply an employee of his employee, Tonton Leo did recognize my contributions to his business. On many occasions, he rewarded me with 500 or 1,000 FCFA for a job well done.

Although I had a part-time job at this cyber café, I didn't see it as employment that would pave the way to the future I wanted. For much of my life I had believed in the saying, "The patient dog eats the fattest bone." But my patience and endurance had begun to waver, and I started believing in a statement from a famous Cameroonian musician, Prince Afo Akom: "The patient dog that has been waiting to eat the fattest bone may soon be dying of starvation."

I decided to contact Kelly Crosbie, the international student admissions counselor at SUNY Potsdam. The TOEFL had tormented me and I was hoping there was an alternate way for achieving admission into SUNY Potsdam. In my email to Kelly, I attempted to get the English proficiency test waived, considering that English was one of the official languages of Cameroon. Unfortunately, Kelly confirmed that I had to take the TOEFL and achieve the minimum score required. Although I was scared of the test, I told her I was going to give it another try.

Since my brothers had given up on my study-abroad dream, my challenge was to bring them back on board. I knew if I could persuade my brother Vincent to give me one more chance, the others would follow his lead. As the eldest, he was like a father figure to the younger siblings. I made a surprise trip to Douala to have a serious talk with him.

I spent about a week there simply helping Vincent with his bread-delivery business. On several occasions, I tried to bring up the topic of the "study-abroad project," but I was too ashamed because I couldn't explain why I had been unable to pass the TOEFL. I hoped Vincent would mention it, but he never did, so I decided to use my backup plan: initiate the subject in front of Vincent's wife, Bernadette, who was my second go-to person, right after aunt Manyi. One day after work, when we had finished eating dinner and were watching a Nigerian movie on TV, I gathered the courage to bring up what was on my mind.

"Pa Meldrick, I have been in touch with SUNY Potsdam. The admission counselor said that I can take the TOEFL and reapply for admission."

"I think we should forget about this America thing," Vincent said.

"With more preparation I can improve my TOEFL score."

"I think you should try the Common Entrance exam into ENSET and Polytechnique again," Vincent said.

As much as I had dreamed of getting into one of these programs after high school, I was no longer interested in staying in Cameroon. America was the word ringing in my head.

After the back and forth between Vincent and me, Bernadette was infuriated and jumped into the conversation, mostly yelling at Vincent. This was what I had hoped for. My brother was as stubborn as me, but one of the few people capable of getting under his skin was his wife.

"I can't understand how you can give up so easily," Bernadette said. "How many strangers have you helped to go to the white-man's country? They are not going to help you like your own brother."

She went on and on as Vincent said nothing in response, lying on the couch and listening. She accused my brother of neglecting his own family and helping strangers who might never be there for the family. She mentioned a few people whom my brother had helped financially to travel abroad and from whom he had never received a word to thank him for his support. I felt indebted to Bernadette for everything she said because her words made my brother reconsider his position.

"I think we should discuss this as a family," Vincent said.

He picked up his cellphone and called my three brothers in Douala—Daniel, Innocent, and Festus. A small family meeting was arranged for the next evening. As we gathered in my brother's apartment, he used his wife's words to convince my other brothers. They came to the conclusion that I should take the TOEFL as soon as possible, and in case I didn't get the required score, they were going to make sure I kept taking the test until I achieved the minimum required score.

I was the happiest person in the house, promising to do my best to succeed on the TOEFL in the fewest number of tries. At that time, the registration fee had gone up from $150 to $175, which was a huge increase, considering that I was only making about $30 a month. Before I left Douala to go back to Yaoundé, my brothers joined together and raised the exam fee. My cousin Samuel was very excited about the possibility of me getting to the US. His dream was to someday visit—if even for just a week—so he could come back home with stories to tell his friends.

In order to prepare properly for the TOEFL, I arranged my work hours at the cyber café to be from midday until closing, about eleven o'clock or later. My co-worker Marcel was okay with this. Again, working at this particular internet café was such a luxury. I had free access to the internet, which allowed me to download free TOEFL reading materials, free TOEFL essays, and other useful materials onto my flash drive.

On August 20, 2010, I traveled to Douala for the TOEFL test, and learned my score on September 2. It was 83/120—not impressive, but I was more than okay with breaking the curse of not obtaining the minimum 79 required for admission into SUNY Potsdam.

The day after I got my test score, I sent an email to the international admissions counselor at SUNY Potsdam, Kelly Crosbie. She recommended that I attend a different campus called SUNY Canton, which offered electrical engineering technology. I read about the four-year electrical engineering technician program available at SUNY Canton and found out that it was indeed a perfect fit for me. Most importantly, the attendance cost was less than at SUNY Potsdam. After doing some research about SUNY Canton and looking at the college's Facebook page, I sent an email to the international admissions counselor there.

I got a reply from Erin Lassial on September 14, 2010, containing a list of all admissions requirements. In order to save the 28,000 FCFA it would take to send SUNY Canton my admission documents, I asked SUNY Potsdam to forward my admission materials over to Canton. However, Potsdam wanted to keep those documents: "Everything you mailed to our campus will remain here. You will need to send all new documents to SUNY Canton because the documents you sent to us are no longer considered official since we have opened them. The bank statement will need to be resubmitted regardless of the campus you are considering as the figures can change from semester to semester and from campus to campus."

Still looking for ways to be economical, I arranged to scan and email my admission documents to SUNY Canton rather than mailing them, saving me about sixty dollars, which was twice my monthly salary. A few days later, I received a message saying, "We will need all your educational documents evaluated by WES. That includes high school and anything you have completed beyond that."

I had to find out about WES (World Educational Services) because I had never heard of it before. Getting my educational credentials evaluated by WES was not easy. First, I had to travel from Yaoundé to Douala so Mr. Martin at the American Language Center could help me pay the $174 evaluation fee. Then, since WES doesn't accept online submissions, I had to mail my educational documents through the postal service, which was a lot of money for me. I tried to get them to receive my materials electronically, but they were adamant about not accepting online submissions, so I mailed copies to them on November 12. Five days later, WES acknowledged they had received my documents—and had sent photocopies of them to the Cameroon General Certificate of Education (GCE) Board for verification. As a result, WES placed my file on hold while waiting for a written response.

I wasn't surprised. Even in Cameroon, before registering for a professional exam, education documents must be certified. I kept checking on mine at wes.org, and by November 28, their status had changed from "Pending Evaluation" to "Waiting for Verification from Institution." Curious about what was going on, I sent an inquiry to WES.

"It looks like the Cameroon General Certificate of Education (GCE) Board is taking a long time to verify my certificate and transcripts. My admission deadline is also fast approaching. Is there anything I can do about the problem or should I continue waiting?"

The following day I got a reply from a representative of WES:

> Hello,
>
> Thank you for your message. The verification request was sent out on 11/17/2010 to them. To ensure that they receive the verification request, you may request for the verification request to be sent via courier for a fee of $60. It will give you a tracking number and ensure that somebody will receive the request there. Please note, this is completely option and offer for your convenience only. If you would like for such request, please request this in writing and inform us how you like to pay (i.e., charge the credit card on file, etc.). Thank you.
>
> Sincerely,
> Shirley

Going through the whole online payment process to get WES to resend my documents to the GCE Board would have been a waste of time, and I didn't have time to spare. I called Vincent and he said I had to go to the GCE Board office in person.

I took a bus from Yaoundé that evening and spent the night in Douala. The next morning, I continued to the GCE Board office in Buea, in the Southwest Region, a two-hour bus trip from Douala. When I arrived just before eight o'clock, there was already a long line of people waiting to enter the office building for a variety of services.

166

Finally, at about three in the afternoon, I was called to come into the office and explained to the young man at the reception desk the purpose of my visit. He scanned through the letters the GCE had received from WES, but mine was not there. I told him that photocopies of my certificates had been sent to the GCE by WES via the US Postal Service about two weeks earlier, and mail usually took about five days to get from the US to Cameroon.

"The person who delivers our mail from the post office has not brought in anything for more than a week," he said.

This statement led me to believe the photocopies of my certificates and the verification request letter sent by WES were already in the Cameroonian Post Office. Someone just needed to pick them up.

"When is he going to bring your mail from the post office?" I asked, hoping that he'd be delivering mail that day.

"I don't know," the receptionist said.

I tried explaining the urgency of my situation, but he didn't seem to care much. I thought that this young man was more likely to be helpful than the older bureaucrats I'd dealt with in the past, but, no, that was not the case. I told him to call the post office but he said that wasn't possible. I asked him to consult his coworkers to find out when a mail delivery might be expected, but he assured me they wouldn't know. I asked for his cellphone number so I could call and come back once the mail had been delivered, but he told me he didn't give out his personal number. Before coming to the Buea office, I had called many times and no one ever answered.

It is discouraging that the office in charge of all English-language exams across the entire country doesn't have someone who oversees their mail on a daily basis. In addition to explaining that I had traveled all the way from Yaoundé, no amount of pressure made any impression on the receptionist. Even though I was getting frustrated, I tried to keep a cool head. I knew from past experience that it's never a good idea to start an argument with a government official.

I was exasperated, but I had only been at the GCE Board for a day. I met some people outside who had been coming back and forth for more than a week. Reluctantly, I left Buea and returned to

Yaoundé because I had to work. My brothers were taking responsibility for the money to process my documents, but I was responsible for all transportation costs.

During the next week, I called the GCE Board office many times but could never get through. I decided to return to Buea, arriving this time before seven in the morning so I'd have a good position in the line. Many people were lined up well before the opening time of eight o'clock. During this visit, I learned that the board had received copies of my educational certificates and the verification that needed to be signed by someone. Unfortunately, I was there on a day when the board registrar had an off-site commitment, and no one knew if he was going to stop by the office. Nobody else there was able to sign documents in the registrar's absence. This meant that nothing requiring an official signature could be completed for the entire day. I sat in the waiting room outside of the main building with a number of other people, but the registrar never showed up.

Board staff started to leave the offices at about four in the afternoon, and none of them were bothered by the many people still sitting in the waiting room. Throughout the hours we sat there, no one came to update us about the likelihood of the registrar arriving, so we waited and hoped he would show up, even as the workers left.

Since time was running out for me to meet the admission deadline, I had to stay overnight in Buea so I could get to the GCE Board office very early and secure a good spot in the waiting line. I couldn't think of any relatives who lived in Buea, and being short on cash, I couldn't afford a motel room. For a few hours I wandered the streets, reflecting on how the government of my country was making life miserable for me. I was angry, annoyed, and going crazy.

Later in the evening I went to a bar, sat at the far end, and bought a beer. My plan was to sit there nursing it until daybreak, when I could head back to the GCE Board office. This was not a great plan, but it was all I could think of at the time.

Sitting at the bar, bored, I started scrolling through my cellphone contacts to distract myself and came across the name Stanley, one of my best friends from computer training school. I vividly recalled him telling me that he was going to continue his education at the University of Buea (aka UB). When I called him, it turned out he was on campus for an evening class—and I happened to be on the Molyko-to-Buea Town Road, the same street where UB is located. I walked from the bar to the school entrance, where Stanley met me after his class. I spent the night at his studio apartment, which was close to campus. Sometimes things work out in this world.

The next morning, I was in front of the GCE Board office by six thirty and had a good position in the line. I was called in at about ten o'clock and was asked to pay the sum of 3,000 FCFA, the signage fee for the WES verification letter.

"What would happen if I wasn't here to pay the 3,000 francs?" I jokingly asked. I thought the verification process was between the GCE Board and WES, designed to confirm the authenticity of my education documents.

"We would have waited for you," said the woman who was taking care of my case, laughing.

Finally, it was nice to chat with someone with a sense of humor. I was sent back to the waiting room, to be called back when the registrar had signed the verification letter. I bought some beignets from a nearby store because it was taking a very long time for the registrar to put his signature on a single-page document that had already been prepared. Finally, I was called into the office and was handed a stamped envelope containing the verification letter WES needed signed and mailed back by the GCE Board.

"I thought the GCE Board was supposed to send this document directly to WES," I said. I didn't think it made sense for me to handle a document that was supposed to confirm the authenticity of my educational credentials.

"So, you want us to use our money to mail your verification document to America, eh?" the woman attendant asked me.

"Yes."

She laughed. I was actually dumb enough to think the GCE Board would charge 3,000 FCFA to sign a verification and then spend 28,000 FCFA to mail it to WES.

I had done some research on the various methods for sending the verification documents back to WES because I was worried about the imminent admission deadline. However, more frustration awaited. I asked a GCE Board staff person to fax the document to WES, but was told that the board did not fax internationally. Then I told the worker to scan the document and email it to WES. Unfortunately, she said they had lacked internet service in their office for a long time. I offered to buy an internet time ticket from the cyber café across the street so that we could scan and email the verification letter using a GCE Board email address.

"We can't send a confidential document from a cyber café," she said.

Although this woman was very nice to me, I didn't believe that the staff at the GCE Board office understood their actions could define the course of my future. I took the stamped envelope with me, traveled back to Douala, and had a talk with my brothers, telling them how I had decided to get the verification letter to WES.

Instead of sending the letter through the Cameroon Post Office (CAMPOST) for 28,000 FCFA, which would have taken up to five business days to reach WES, my brothers contributed a total of 58,000 FCFA to send the letter via UPS, which would take two to three days. I put the stamped verification envelope from the GCE Board into another envelope and mailed it with the Cameroon GCE Board's address. I wanted to avoid the risk of WES suspecting foul play if they noticed that the verification letter had passed through my hands.

On December 22, 2010, three days after I mailed the verification letter, the status of my submission had changed to "evaluation in progress." This was a huge relief. I kept checking it as frequently as I checked my Facebook page. On December 28, I received an email notification from WES that the evaluation of my academic certificates had been completed.

I was stunned that it took the Cameroon GCE Board over a month just to sign a document, and it took WES less than a week to evaluate my entire educational history. This made me even more eager to set foot in the United States, a country where I assumed everything would be perfect.

I immediately forwarded the WES email to the international admission counselor at SUNY Canton. I wanted to confirm with Erin Lassial that my evaluated education credentials and report had been sent to her by WES.

> Hi Madame,
> It has been a long time that I have not heard from you. Below is the message I received from WES concerning my transcripts.
> I will be delighted to hear from you as soon as you read this message.
>> Happy Merry Christmas,
>> Pierre Nzuah

I received a very nice reply from Erin just a few hours later. Comparing the polite, friendly tone of her email with the experiences I had with government officials in my country, I felt as though Cameroon and the United States were in alternate universes.

> Hi Pierre,
> Your enthusiasm to have this process completed is appreciated. I am sorry I concerned you by not writing back right away. I did not write back because it was too early to have received your transcript evaluation and I had several others to process that have come in. I did check today, but since we get two mailings in per day, I wanted to wait until the second one had come in before I got back to you. The evaluation is still not here. Please understand this is normal; however, they should be in this week. I will be sure to notify you as soon as they come in.
>> Thank you,
>> Erin Lassial

Knowing that I had provided everything required to be considered for admission, I had to (impatiently) await the final decision. From my previous communication with Erin, I knew she usually sent emails to me on weekdays at around six in the evening Cameroon time, which would be early afternoon in the US eastern time zone. The waiting was intense.

On Thursday, December 30, at 6:34 p.m., I received the long-awaited email, a message that changed my life forever: an acceptance letter from the international admissions counselor at SUNY Canton. My dream to further my studies in electrical engineering technology was about to become a reality.

> Hi Pierre,
>
> Great news … your WES evaluation came in today and is acceptable. Congratulations! I will have your acceptance packet sent to you on Monday, both via mail and email. I will send your documents to our international office so we can process an I-20 for you right away. Thank you for all your effort.
>
> Cheers,
> Erin

When I opened the acceptance email at the cyber café, I screamed wildly. The people there and at the bar next door thought I was going crazy. I wish I could articulate how joyous and excited I felt from my toes to the top of my head. This was a rare moment in life when I actually shed tears of joy. I immediately called my brothers in Douala and told them the great news. They were all ecstatic. My acceptance into SUNY Canton was one of the best things that had ever happened in my family—and absolutely the most important thing as far as my educational career is concerned.

23

Too Much Paperwork, Too Little Time

I was walking on air so I didn't care at the time, but there was an unbelievable amount of paperwork required after receiving the acceptance letter. First, I had to complete and submit the DS-160 form, the online Nonimmigrant Visa Application. After doing so, I received an email from SUNY Canton advising me to complete an I-901 form and to pay the $200 SEVIS fee to the US Department of Immigration and Customs Enforcement (ICE) as soon as possible. Time was running out; I needed to pay this SEVIS fee and obtain a receipt prior to my visa appointment at the US embassy in Yaoundé. Unfortunately, Cameroon was one of very few nations from which online payment was not accepted by ICE. This restriction was in place because there were so many fraudulent transactions involving the cited countries. After much frustration and many failed attempts, I finally found a way to make the payment.

While waiting the next few days for my receipt to arrive, I made a visa appointment at the US embassy. But the earliest one available was on January 26, two days after the start of the spring 2011 semester at SUNY Canton, and I was required to be on campus by January 19 in order to attend freshman orientation and take some placement tests. After explaining the urgency of the situation, I was able to get an expedited appointment.

When people know how to do their jobs and there are clear

protocols in place, it makes life easier for everyone. The international admissions office at SUNY Canton had sent my I-20 form via UPS and had emailed me all the information I needed for my visa appointment.

For years I had watched people I knew travel abroad while I hustled for survival in Cameroon. Finally, I was beginning to feel that my dreams about America were not so farfetched. Everyone in my family was feeling happy and high.

On the day of my interview, I dressed in a black suit and my polished, pointy dress shoes. As I walked from the house to find a taxi at the junction, neighbors gave me strange looks—they hadn't seen me dressed professionally before. Everything went well during the visa interview, until one question made me stop and think carefully: "What are your plans after graduation?" the consular officer asked.

I was so excited about studying in the United States, I hadn't thought about post-graduation plans. I knew it would not go over well if I told the officer that I planned to stay in the US, so I gave the safe, expected answer: "After graduation, I'd like to come back to Cameroon and teach in remote areas where there is a shortage of teachers. I attended school in these types of areas and I understand what students go through."

Even though I had a strong passion for teaching, saying that I would return to Cameroon after college was a questionable answer. Like many people in developing countries, I perceived America as heaven on earth: who wouldn't dream of remaining in such a place? But I knew it wasn't wise to tell the consular officer this. Then I heard the words everyone hopes to hear at the embassy: "Congratulations, you have been granted a visa to study in the United States."

The smile on my face was endless. Walking out of the US embassy, I felt incredibly blessed and my heart was filled with so much happiness.

I collected my passport with the stamped US visa and took a taxi to a travel agency to pay for the plane ticket I had reserved (purchasing it wasn't possible until I had my visa). Unfortunately, the travel agency had sold my reserved ticket.

We had settled on the travel agency because other flight agencies were much more expensive. The female worker at Moabi Travels did a new search for me, and the cheapest one-way flight she found was the next day, January 20. This was a day earlier than planned, but we had to take this ticket for $1,396.90 on Ethiopian Airlines, departing out of Douala. I reached into my pocket, and the only cash I had left after two years of work in Yaoundé was 2,000 FCFA. I used it to tip the travel agency lady, which made her day.

From the moment I received the SUNY Canton acceptance letter, I had planned to make a trip to the village to say my good-byes, but my schedule was now so tight that there wasn't time for this. Instead, we arranged for some family members to meet us at my brother's house in Douala. By the time we arrived there, it was filled with family members and close friends. There was beer, gospel music, and dancing. This was my sendoff party. Everyone was talking and hugging and making speeches and proposing toasts. It was a unique moment for my family.

When we all arrived at the airport before noon, we sat outside eating fried chicken that my brothers' wives had brought from home. As my departure time approached, we paid a cameraman-for-hire at the airport to take a group picture, and then one of me with each and every immediate family member who was present.

From childhood to this moment, as I was about to leave the country, my relatives perceived me as a stubborn, hotheaded kid. This was true. But from an early age, things had never come easily to me. As a result, I often had to ask for financial help from my family, sometimes tormenting them in the process. Now, looking at my siblings, I had no doubt they were all very proud of me. I felt like I had been chosen by God to write a new story for my family. As I hugged each relative for the last time, it hit me how hard it was to say goodbye to loved ones, particularly as the person who was leaving.

At a Douala International Airport checkpoint, I was asked to present proof of MMR immunization. Unfortunately, things had happened so fast, I hadn't found time to have this test. I bribed the agent with 3,000 FCFA.

175

Before departure: Douala International Airport

Sitting in an airplane for the first time in my life, several questions raced through my head. Where would I be if I had never had the opportunity to attend school? Where would I be if I had allowed adversities to stop me from pursuing my dreams? Would I be sitting in this airplane if I hadn't worked hard and believed in myself? Born in a country where jobs are scarce and nepotism and bribery are common practice, I could have ended up living a miserable life in the streets. To every young person going through tough times and thinking all hope is lost, I urge you to stick to your plan—don't give up. I made some of the most important decisions in my life when I was trying to overcome adversity. I know not everyone can be as lucky as I have been, but it is better to work hard and fail than to never really try.

After growing up in a subsistence family, the opportunity to travel to America completely changed my perspective on the world. Being born without a silver spoon in my mouth made my early years tough, but having experienced hardship, I knew how to welcome an opportunity when it knocked at my door.

PART II

OVERCOMING DAUNTING
ODDS IN AMERICA

24

Coming to America

After a flight that seemed very long, I was relieved to hear the pilot announce our landing at Syracuse Hancock International Airport. His update on the local weather made me look down through the window. I saw that the earth was completely white. I have never seen such a thing. After picking up my luggage, I looked around for the person from SUNY Canton who was to meet me. I waited for about thirty minutes without seeing anyone who was looking for me. Getting nervous, I decided to go outside and look around. As soon as I went through the door, it felt as if someone with huge palms was grabbing and squeezing my face—it was so freaking cold! I rushed back inside. Now I understood what the pilot meant by 20°F below zero. I had left Cameroon during the dry season when the temperature rarely fell below 80°F. I was still dressed in my black suit and pointy dress shoes. I had no winter coat, no hat, and no boots. I'm going to die here, I said to myself.

Then I saw someone waving a sign with PIERRE NZUAH in large letters. It was Rebecca Blackmon, secretary at the SUNY Canton International Programs Office.

As we walked to the car, I pointed at the snow and asked, "When is this going to be over?"

"I'm sorry, not anytime soon."

Despite the research I had done about the United States, it never crossed my mind to search for information about winter. Leaving Cameroon at 80°F and arriving on a sub-zero windy day in Syracuse was one of the most shocking experiences of my life.

"Do you have winter clothing?" Rebecca asked, because I kept bugging her about the weather.

"No, I don't."

"Oh, we have to stop at JC Penney and get you some winter clothes."

I was lucky that before I left Cameroon, my brothers had given me an emergency pocket allowance of $400. At JC Penney, we bought a winter coat, a hat, and gloves. Even with three layers of clothing I didn't feel warm enough. In Cameroon, we have two seasons, rainy (from April through September) and dry (for the rest of the year). I had never felt the need to own a sweater. I can't ever remember checking the weather forecast in Cameroon.

As we drove along, I saw no leaves on the trees and all the branches were covered with snow. Although I had just met Rebecca and didn't want to seem really dumb, I had to ask one question.

"Why are all these trees dead?"

"They are not dead," Rebecca replied, laughing.

I was mostly quiet after asking all my weather questions, though I should have been asking a lot about school since I had missed freshman orientation and placement testing. Rebecca tried to engage me in conversation.

"What's your favorite type of music?" she asked.

"I like *Makossa* and *Coupé-Décalé*."

"Sorry, I don't have any of that."

"It's okay, you can play any kind of music."

Driving from Syracuse to Canton, I didn't see the America I had imagined—no skyscrapers, few cars on the road, and the towns we drove through didn't even look as thriving as Yaoundé. SUNY Canton was located in the village of Canton, which looked about the size of my home village except that the buildings were brick instead of mud. These were the thoughts going through my mind because I had imagined attending college in a place like New York City.

25

Spring Semester 2011 Begins

Rebecca dropped me off at Heritage Hall on the SUNY Canton campus sometime after eight in the evening on January 21. There was more than half a foot of snow on the pathway, and I got a lot of it in my shoes as I walked into the building.

"Don't hesitate to contact our office if you need anything," Rebecca said before leaving.

Inside I met Felicia, the resident assistant on duty that night. As she guided me through the check-in process, another RA, Andrew Squire, came into the office. I noticed his arm was covered in tattoos.

"Andrew, this is Pierre," Felicia said. "He is an international student from Cameroon."

"No kidding," Andrew said. We shook hands and did all the nice-to-meet-you stuff.

"Where the hell is Cameroon?" Andrew asked. "I'm so bad at geography."

"Cameroon is located in West Central Africa—on the Atlantic coast."

"I gotta look it up," Andrew said, pulling out his phone.

After reading about Cameroon, he asked, "You speak French? And English?" He was asking too many questions. All I wanted to do was to go to sleep.

"Yes, I was forced to learn both languages in school."

"Good for you, man," Andrew said. "English is all I know, and I'm not even good at it."

"Your English seems perfectly fine to me," I said.

"I don't know about that," he said, and then changed the topic of discussion. "Have you picked a major yet?"

"Yes, I'm going to be majoring in electrical engineering."

"No shit. I just switched my major to electrical engineering, but I gotta complete my associate in psychology this semester."

"That's cool," I said. "We might be in the same classes next semester."

"True. Do you have a course checklist?"

"No."

"Let me get a copy for you."

Andrew went to his room in Heritage North, Room 102, and got me the course checklist for the Electrical Engineering Technology Program. It was at this point that RA Felicia interrupted our conversation in order to take me to my dorm room. Even though I was exhausted from my long journey, I really enjoyed my conversation with Andrew. He made a good first impression and I would never forget it.

"May I please use your computer to send a quick email to my family back home?" I asked.

"We don't allow residents to use the office computer," Felicia said. "But, I'm gonna make an exception for you just for this time."

I sent an email to my siblings to tell them that I had a very long but successful journey to SUNY Canton. Felicia then took me to my room, Heritage South 109. I had chosen to live in a triple because it was about $500 less expensive than the double rooms. Since I was the latecomer, my two roommates had already chosen the bottom beds and I was stuck with the top bunk bed. I didn't meet either of my roommates until Saturday, when Austin showed up with his girl-friend. She lived off campus, but nearby, and that's where he spent most of his time. My other roommate, Brendan Keating, had spent the whole weekend partying with his friends in other residence halls. He finally showed up on Sunday evening to get ready for the beginning of classes, and we had a chance to introduce ourselves.

"I'm going to be playing hockey for the school team," Brendan said.

"What is hockey?" I asked.

After laughing at me, Brendan showed me a few video clips of hockey on YouTube. They looked interesting, particularly the hockey-fight videos. The commentaries accompanying them were the most entertaining.

"… and now, we've got a hockey fight; gloves are off, here we go; that's his first fight in the NHL and he looks pretty good …" Then the referees stood by and allowed the players to go at each other for a while. I would totally watch a hockey game just for the commentary and the fights.

I asked Brendan if I could use his laptop to check out my schedule for the semester. This was when I discovered I had been signed up for only five classes totaling twelve credits. One of the five courses was Beginning Algebra. I didn't understand how math courses were organized in the United States because in Cameroon, mathematics is simply mathematics in every class, except that the depth of the topics increased as students advanced into higher grades. Nonetheless, the word "beginning" made me feel that the course was probably below my level.

This was the result of showing up too late to take the math placement test, which would have helped the college assign me to an appropriate course. I told myself there was no way I was going to start at the basic level. On the first day of classes, January 24, instead of going to the Beginning Algebra class, I found my way to the International Programs Office. It was here that I was told to talk with my advisor, Dr. Stephen Frempong. I didn't even know that college students were assigned advisors. Again, this was because I had missed orientation and was from a different country.

Before I left the office to see my advisor, Rebecca gave me two pairs of winter boots she had brought for me from home. I had been wearing a pair of sneakers on a frigid, snowy, winter day. This was so kind of her.

I finally met my advisor, Dr. Frempong. He was the first person I had met who also had a heavy accent, though his had been Americanized. I explained to him that with the level of math I had acquired through my education in Cameroon, I should be enrolled in Calculus I, or at the least, Pre-Calculus.

"I can't move you from Beginning Algebra to Calculus I," Dr. Frempong said.

"How about Pre-Calculus?" I had only learned about the different types of math courses required for my program from the checklist that Andrew had given me.

"No. I'm going to move you up to Intermediate Algebra."

"Thank you."

"Where are you from?" Dr. Frempong asked, as he printed out my updated schedule.

"I'm from Cameroon."

"I know Cameroon very well. I'm from Ghana, but I worked in Nigeria for a while before coming to this country."

"That's awesome."

"How did you find SUNY Canton?" he asked.

I gave him a brief overview of the tedious process I had been through to find my way to the United States. It turned out that Dr. Frempong's journey from Ghana to Nigeria and then to America wasn't an easy one either. However, the immigration visa process during his time was less strict than what I had been through. I had a very interesting conversation with him. Like everyone else had been saying to me, Dr. Frempong told me not to hesitate to stop by his office if I needed help with anything.

Before coming to America, I had looked at pictures of the dorm rooms on the campus website and thought the rooms would be exactly like that. So, I only had one bedsheet with me, which I used to make the bed during the day and as a blanket at night. The bare mattress on my bed was hard and uncomfortable.

"Do you need some stuff for your bed?" my roommate Brendan asked when he saw me lying on the bare mattress and having a hard time falling asleep.

"Oh, yes."

"I'm gonna call my aunt to get you some sheets and a blanket, okay?"

"Thank you so much."

His aunt eventually sent me bedsheets, two pillows, a blanket, and a sweatshirt. You have no idea how grateful I felt to find myself in a strange land with people supporting me, even though they knew almost nothing about me. Someday I'd like to find Brendan's aunt and thank her in person for her kindness and generosity.

On day two of classes, I met with Erin to thank her for patiently guiding me through the admission process. She had already heard that I arrived in the US unprepared for the harsh North Country winter, and when she said I could use some of the winter clothes her husband wasn't using, I couldn't possibly refuse the kind offer. She also cautioned me to avoid associating with the delinquent students on campus, or I could risk being sent back to Cameroon, and all the effort I put into coming to America would have been in vain.

Later that evening, Erin knocked at my door and gave me a large box filled with winter coats. By the end of the week, the director of Heritage Hall, Kristen Roberts, had brought me another box filled with personal hygiene items, laundry detergent, and other miscellaneous supplies. This meant a lot to me because I was new in the area and didn't know where stores were located—and the freezing temperatures were simply too intense for me to even consider walking downtown to buy supplies.

During the first week of classes, my lips cracked and my face was numb each time I left the residence hall. For a while, my limited path of movement was from the residence hall to my classes and the dining hall. And, oh, my experience with the dining hall wasn't very good either. Because I hadn't attended high school in the US and I didn't know anyone on campus, I had no friends to sit with while eating, and often found myself all alone at a large, circular table. Sometimes I was reluctant to go to the dining hall because of the shame of being in a room where nobody wanted to sit with me but everyone wanted to stare at me. I felt so lonely and homesick.

One of my more interesting dining experiences was discovering that I didn't know how to order food. Some of the offerings in the dining hall looked similar to the food back home, but I didn't know the American names for them. During one of my early visits to the dining hall, I listened to the student ahead of me place her order.

"Can I have a burger with Swiss cheese and French fries, please?" she asked.

When it was my turn to order, I placed the same order. This was my order every time for a long while until I got sick of it. The first time I tried the dining hall's chicken, it was tasteless to me. It took me a long time to discover that I had to use items from the condiment bar—ketchup, honey mustard—to spice up my food. With all this trouble in ordering food, I turned to the salad bar, which was self-service. This worked well for me because I didn't have to know the names of the items I put on my salad. Never before or since have I eaten so much salad.

Eventually, I came up with a strategy to learn the names of different food items so I could order whatever I wanted to eat. Whenever I approached the food stand and the server asked what I wanted, I simply pointed to a food item and asked, "What is that?" If the server replied, "pork chops," I would politely ask to have some. I still looked a little stupid having to ask the names of everything, but this trick helped me to learn about the different types of American food.

26

First Semester: The Money Problem

Sorting out my class placement, learning about food, dealing with the cold—these turned out to be less stressful than the big problem: money. My total cost for the spring semester was about $10,000, excluding textbooks and miscellaneous expenses. I was offered an international grant of $2,000 per semester, which brought my base cost down to $8,000. Before I left Cameroon, some of my brothers agreed to pay my expenses—in installments. We had no idea that in the United States, students are expected to pay all their attendance costs at the start of the semester. The $8,000 I owed is about four million FCFA. It never occurred to us that we might be expected to pay such a sum all at once.

Not long after the semester had started, my brothers got together and sent me $3,000 for the first installment on my fees. Since my arrival in the US, I had been having trouble communicating with my family back home because I didn't have a laptop. With the six-hour time difference, the library was usually closed when it was convenient for my family to chat with me online. Most importantly, it was difficult to depend on library computers to do my school assignments. A laptop is an essential tool for any twenty-first-century college student.

I used $320 of the $3,000 from my brothers to purchase an Acer laptop at Walmart, and took the remaining money to the Student

Service Center to pay for part of my spring semester cost. After counting the money, the clerk gave me a strange look.

"Where is the rest of the money?" he asked.

"That's all I have for now. My brothers are going to send the rest of it later in the semester."

"Oh, no. You were supposed to pay your full tuition before the first day of classes."

"I did not know that," I said, not that my family would have been able to raise $8,000 all at once.

"If you don't complete your billing soon, you risk being dropped from all of your classes."

"Let me talk to my brothers back home. I'll be back as soon as I hear from them."

Now I was worried. Looking back, it was crazy that when I was in Cameroon, desperate to leave the country to continue my education, I didn't pay attention to the cost of attending SUNY Canton. When I first looked at the numbers online, I assumed the $10,000 was an annual fee, not a semester cost. As I left the Student Service Center, I had bells ringing in my head—how would my family come up with such an amount of money in a short period of time? As soon as I reached my dorm room, I emailed my four brothers and my cousin—these were the people who had been most involved in helping me get to SUNY Canton. I told them that I risked being sent back to Cameroon if the remainder of my fees weren't paid very soon.

Two days later, I still hadn't heard back from any of my siblings. I went to Walmart and bought a prepaid calling card. One of the Walmart clerks allowed me to make the call on the service-desk phone. My brother Vincent was shocked when I told him I could be deported back to Cameroon.

"No, they cannot deport you. Over my dead body!"

"I'm really nervous, bro," I said. "I've been told I was supposed to pay the full amount before the semester started."

"Tell them to give you some time," Vincent said. "I was planning to go to the village next week to pay my wife's bride price, but I'm going to cancel that."

188

I didn't think his father-in-law was going to be happy about this. Many village parents dream of and count on the day when the traditional rites of a marrying child are performed, including the payment of a bride price. It was also going to be a big disappointment for people in the village who wait for occasions like this to eat free food and drink free beer and palm wine. Before I got off the phone with Vincent, he promised to call for an emergency family meeting about my situation and that he would get back to me as soon as possible.

Meanwhile, I was doing badly in most of my classes because I didn't have textbooks. One of the problem classes was Oral & Written Expression (English 102), an English language course taught by Professor Melissa Lee. I explained my situation to her, and she promised to give me some time to make up assignments once I was able to purchase textbooks. She also promised to contact some people on campus to see if there was any financial help for me, but the financial-aid office told her nothing was available. Nonetheless, I very much appreciated her effort.

The longer I waited for my family to act, the more distracted I became. Dr. Daun Martin, my First Year Experience (FYE) instructor, noticed my absentmindedness in class. After one of her classes, she took me aside and asked if I was okay. I explained my predicament, and she said she would talk to some people to see if there was help. As with Professor Lee, Dr. Martin's effort yielded nothing. She talked to most of the same people Professor Lee had already contacted. Again, I was grateful for Dr. Martin's willingness to go the extra mile for me, though nothing came of it.

In Cameroon, my brother Vincent continued to deliver bread, and also played the role of secretary for the business, collecting money from the other deliverymen. He had a stable livelihood. Nonetheless, when he tried to get a bank loan, he was turned down because he did not own enough valuable collateral as security.

Vincent traveled to the village and asked every family member to contribute whatever they could to help me out. He warned relatives that those who failed to contribute should never expect to ask me for help if I pulled through college and became a (relatively) rich

189

man someday. My village family members, who earned so little from subsistence farming, did their best to make contributions of $10 to $50. Altogether, in less than a week, they raised a little over $4,000 and sent it to me via Western Union. This was an amazing accomplishment: in Cameroonian currency, it equaled more than two million FCFA. While the amount was extraordinary, it was still not enough to cover the remainder of my college costs, but I so appreciated my brothers pulling together the family to raise a great deal of money, trying to get me out of a difficult situation.

With the money in hand, I wondered what I was going to say to the clerk in the Student Service Office. I asked myself: what would happen if I used all this money for part of my remaining tuition and then failed some of my courses because I didn't have textbooks? My brain was heated up and I was confused, feeling as though it was always my destiny to be in financial trouble no matter where I was in the world. After thinking it over, I used some of the money to buy all the textbooks I needed. Oh, Mon Dieu! I couldn't believe the cost of textbooks in the United States, especially at the campus bookstore.

The student clerk in the Student Service Center didn't look pleased when I presented him with an incomplete payment for the second time. He must have been sick of listening to me talk about my family's financial situation, and about how they had raised the money I was presenting to him.

"I understand your situation; I just don't know how I can help you here."

"I'm sorry, sir," I apologized.

"This is what I'm gonna do," the student accountant said. "I'm gonna put you on academic deferment, and you will have up until the end of the semester to pay the rest."

"Thank you so much, sir."

I felt a little relieved, and thankful to the student accountant for giving me some extra time to complete the tuition payment. However, I had no clue about where the remaining $2,424 would come from. I told my brothers back home to keep looking for ways to borrow money while I explored financial aid options in the US.

I met with the director of financial aid to find out if there were any scholarship opportunities. Unfortunately, there were no direct ones for undergraduate international students, and my international status disqualified me from almost every other scholarship. Someone on campus suggested I contact the Cameroonian embassy in Washington, DC, or the Cameroon Students Association in the US to see if they had any financial assistance. I wrote to my country's ambassador in Washington but never received a reply. I also emailed the Cameroon Students Association in USA (CAMSA-USA), hoping that someone among them had gone through an experience similar to mine and could help me out. But the chairman could offer no assistance, although he invited me to attend their spring-break bash in Washington so I could have the opportunity to mingle with CAMSA-USA members.

I started asking questions to God again. Often, I laid on my bed in my dorm room and cried, wondering, "Why, me? Why me, Lord?" With the situation as it was, I feared never having the chance to live up to my God-given potential.

I owe much to Rebecca Blackmon and Marela Fiacco, both of whom worked in the International Programs Office at the time. They were good listeners and put up with me. I visited their office time and time again, and they always consoled me and assured me that everything was going to be alright. As I continued to go around the campus looking for help, someone asked me a question I couldn't really answer.

"Just outta curiosity, why did you decide to attend college in this country knowing that your parents couldn't afford to pay for it?"

I struggled to come up with an answer. Then, this same person tried to clarify the question, wondering why I couldn't attend college in my own country. Unbelievably, it was actually more straightforward gaining admission to an American college than an institution of higher education in my own country. Looking at my history to this point, I had always managed to get through school by postponing and paying fees in installments. If I had worried about money first, I probably never would have gotten through high school.

I wasn't getting questions just from people in America. In fact, I was hearing from more and more people back in Cameroon who wanted to know how I had managed to get out of the country and into the US. They asked a lot of questions.

"What scholarship did you win?"

"Did you win the DV lottery?"

"Bro, you have to help me get out of Cameroon."

I didn't bother explaining the financial problems I faced because I didn't think they would understand. However, I did explain that it was a collective family effort that made my travel to America possible, but most people didn't believe me. Many of them knew my family and couldn't believe they could pull together the financial resources required. To make it easier to answer all the people hoping for help from me, I simply referred them to the Tuition & Fees page on the campus website.

Still struggling with how to cover the remaining $2,424 first-semester tuition, I asked the international admissions counselor, Erin Lassial, to help me find an on-campus job to pay off the amount due. She reminded me that as an international student, I was only allowed to work a maximum of twenty hours a week, and even if there were any jobs available, working twenty hours a week would not earn enough to pay off my tuition.

However, she scheduled a meeting for me with the director of admissions, David Norenberg. When I showed up at his office, we exchanged greetings and shook hands.

"Why did you do that?" he asked.

"What did I do?" I was worried that I might have done something wrong in just the few seconds I'd been in his office.

"As we shook hands, you grabbed your right hand with the left hand," David explained, while demonstrating by shaking my hand again.

"In my culture," I told him, "we do that for older persons as a sign of respect."

"I like that," David said. He offered me a seat in front of his desk and asked, "What exactly is going on?"

I described my background, plus the many obstacles I faced before arriving at SUNY Canton, and how highly I valued the chance for a college education. We had an interesting conversation, but he made it clear that work-study jobs were hard to come by, especially mid-semester. He promised to talk with the associate director for advancement, Julie Parkman. I left his office with my fingers crossed.

Things did not work out as quickly as I had hoped, so I became kind of a nuisance in David's office. I went back there many times, and when I was feeling embarrassed by all these visits, I emailed him to find out if there was any news on the work-study situation. I give a lot of credit to the college staff who put up with me.

David succeeded in finding a $500 work-study job for me. I thought this would be directly applied to my account balance, but later realized that taxes would be taken out of my paychecks. This job would not take care of everything I owed, but would reduce it to about $2,000. I was grateful for the employment—international students have a hard time finding these jobs.

The position was in the admissions office, assisting staff, including David, the director of admissions. To round out my work-study hours, I also got a job at the circulation desk in the college library. During my first day of work there, a student came down from upstairs to sign out a calculator.

"Can I have a graphing calculator, please?" the student asked, handing over her student ID.

"Sure."

"That's not a graphing calculator," she said, laughing at the simple scientific calculator I had given her.

"What does it look like?" I asked.

This was the moment when I learned about calculators that will plot graphs based on the math problem entered. I was shocked. I wasn't allowed to use a calculator in primary school. In secondary and high school, I only used one to solve trigonometric problems or simplify complex answers. Most of our math teachers actually encouraged us to leave our final answers in fraction form so we didn't have to worry about using calculators.

I asked a co-worker to help me find the graphing calculator, but it had been checked out by someone, so I tried to explain to the student how to use a simple calculator to solve her math problem.

"Why do all that work when a graphing calculator can do it for me?" she asked. "I'll wait."

When the graphing calculator was returned to the circulation desk, I used it to plot a quadratic function before signing it out to the student who had asked for it. From this point forward, I knew it was unlikely that I would ever fail a graphing problem. Colleges should really consider offering work-study jobs to all their foreign students so they're exposed to the many opportunities available. It might have taken me forever to discover the genius machine that was capable of finding turning points, points of inflection, local min, local max, and asymptotes of functions in a matter of seconds. I planned to tackle function problems from this day forward by plotting them before solving so that I could double-check my numbers as I solved. Unfortunately, when I went to Walmart and discovered the cost of a graphing calculator was ninety-five dollars, I thought, no thanks, and continued using the two-dollar calculator I brought from Cameroon.

27

First Semester: The People Problems

Life was challenging during my first semester. I had arrived in the middle of the academic year from a foreign country. From the first day of classes, I realized it was going to be tough to make friends. About five minutes before the end of every class, students would begin to pack up their bags—something that would be considered disrespectful in classrooms back home. At the end of class, students were out of the room before the teacher had finished wiping the board. This was different than in Cameroon, where students often stayed for a while at the end of a lecture to chat and discuss questions about the material with their peers. Here, I was finding it hard to connect with anyone after class. I was lonely and wanted to make friends, but it wasn't easy. After growing up in a big family in a village where I was surrounded by people, it was extremely painful to live inside an isolated bubble in America. For me, socializing was just as important as getting an education.

Before coming to the US, I didn't realize I would face certain challenges adapting to the campus environment. The diversity of the SUNY Canton population turned out to be a little challenging for me, which was surprising considering that I came from a country that has about 250 distinct ethnic groups and more than 200 dialects. I was having a hard time trying to fit into the campus community, and wasn't familiar with most of the topics of discussion in the hallways or in the residence hall. People were divided into groups—Hispanic, white, dark skin, brown skin, African-American, etc. Initially, I couldn't tell the difference between white and Hispanic people—they all looked white to me. As much as people had a hard time understanding me because of my heavy accent, the pace of speech of most people was too fast for me to understand. On many occasions, I just said "yeah" to things I didn't really understand. It was hard to be an outlier.

It took a while to learn about the different American ethnic groups. For example, during my early days on campus, I wondered why most black students were referred to as African-Americans, while someone like me, born in Cameroon, didn't have the continent hyphenated before my home country, African-Cameroonian. I understand the importance of ancestral roots, but it was difficult for me to understand why someone born and raised in America—most of whom had never set foot on the African continent—would have that continent hyphenated before their country of birth. I was even more confused to find out that only people with roots in black African racial groups were referred to as African-American. Why weren't nonblack people from countries like Egypt, Tunisia, or Algeria called African-American?

The first time someone remarked on my accent and asked if I was from Africa, I was taken aback. I may even have answered no. I had lived in Cameroon my whole life and only learned about other African countries in the classroom. Yes, Cameroon is located on the African continent, but if I agree to the broad generalization that I'm from Africa, I cannot tell you about life in Zambia. But more to the point, I have never heard anyone ask a German if he was from Europe, or a Korean if he was from Asia. I was baffled that people talked about Africa as if it were a country, considering that Africa is the second-largest and second-most-populated continent. It was surprising that people thought of Africa as all-black, and did not include northern countries like Tunisia or Egypt as part of their understanding of the African continent.

In an anthropology class, the instructor referred to Africa as the origin of modern humanity. Some white students argued about this in class. While I had grown up in a developing country where I often complained about the lack of opportunity, I was shocked to hear how students in this class tried to distance themselves from a place they had never visited. My classmates gave me the impression that, because of the higher standard of living in the US, they didn't want to acknowledge the possibility of ancestral ties back to early human life in Africa. Yes, life in many countries there is difficult, but listening to people talk about Africa during my first months in America, I felt they painted a dark picture of the entire continent, recognizing nothing of the positive. Considering how much I learned about the US during my school years in Cameroon, I was surprised at how little American students knew about Africa.

Struggling to overcome homesickness, boredom, and loneliness during my first months at SUNY Canton, I went to the International Programs Office to seek help.

"What is the best way to meet people on this campus?" I asked.

"You can start by joining clubs," Rebecca said, and gave me directions to the Student Activities Office.

I went there and was given a brochure with a list of all the clubs and organizations on campus. I started attending meetings of groups that sounded interesting, and the one I fell in love with was the Brother-to-Brother club. At my first meeting, George Lawrence and other club leaders gave me a very warm reception. Joining turned out to be a great way to integrate into campus life. I started making friends and also knew many others casually. Finally, when I greeted people on campus, I actually got a "hey" back instead of a weird look or a fake smile.

Another one I joined was the Newman Club, which had its meeting house in downtown Canton, where gatherings were open to students from all the area's colleges. I heard about this club from its coordinator, Sr. Bethany Fitzgerald of the SUNY Canton Campus Ministries. Through membership, I made friends with students from St. Lawrence University (SLU). There were no other black students in the club, but members went together to the annual African Night at SLU. We ate free food together, and I met several international students from Kenya.

Gradually, I was adapting to the village community. I visited the Campus Ministries Office and asked about local Presbyterian congregations.

"The Presbyterian church is downtown, on the park," Sister Bethany said. "It's a ten-minute walk from campus."

"Oh, thank you."

"I can give you a ride on Sunday morning. You're going to like Reverend Mike."

That Sunday, Sister Bethany picked me up and drove me to the church.

"Reverend Mike, here is Pierre, the young man from Cameroon," Sister Bethany said as she introduced me.

"How in the world did you end up here?" Rev. Mike asked after we exchanged greetings.

"It's a long story."

"Welcome to the Church on the Park."

At the beginning of the service, Rev. Mike introduced me to the congregation, which was a nice thing to do. I can't really explain his preaching style because my words won't do justice to the unique way he connects his sermons with his own life, the lives of the church members, and scripture. Listening to Rev. Mike, you don't need anyone to tell you how well he knows each and every person in the congregation, and how much he knows about the wider community.

Once again, I couldn't help comparing my life and experience in America with my life back in Cameroon. During church service, I noticed that the congregation was mostly older people, even though the church was located about halfway between two colleges, St. Lawrence University and SUNY Canton, with a combined student population of more than 5,000. At most of the churches I attended back home, congregations were comprised of mostly younger people.

When it was time for the offering, envelopes in holders on the backs of the pews were used to put money in, and the envelopes were collected in baskets carried up the aisles by church elders. This was different than offerings back home, and I liked it. In Cameroonian churches, the attendees had to walk from their seats in a specific order to drop offerings in baskets at the front of the church. If you had nothing to offer, everyone would know.

Church lasted for about an hour, whereas back home it could last for hours. At the end of the service, Rev. Mike stood at the top of the stairs to greet and speak with everyone as they left. I shook hands with him and he invited me to join the others for coffee hour. This was where I met Richard W. Miller, a SUNY Canton distinguished professor emeritus and the man our student center was named after. I had a nice talk with Professor Miller, and he pointed out the importance of the cultural diversity that international students like me were bringing to campuses across the United States.

My welcome at the Presbyterian church was special. From day one I was made to feel that I was part of the church family.

Back on campus, I was still looking for more free-time activities. I wished I had more courses to keep me busy, more than the twelve credits I had been signed up for. And because I was placed in a math class well below my level, I was doing extremely well while some of my classmates were complaining about their grades. I thought it would be good to volunteer time to help the students who were struggling in their math courses. I sent an email to the director of tutoring services, Johanna Lee.

"Thank you for your interest in the math lab," Johanna said. "We are always looking for talented people. I would like to meet with you to discuss your math experience and how that could best be used."

After a few email exchanges, I scheduled an appointment and met Johanna in her office at the entrance to the math lab.

"Why do you want to volunteer your time in tutoring?"

"I just want to help."

"That's very nice of you."

After a few minutes of discussion, Johanna gave me a form to complete. It was surreal to me that I would be asked to do paperwork for a volunteer service—and I hate paperwork. Johanna said she'd get in touch with me. I thanked her and left, feeling confused about why she couldn't just take me up on my offer, considering that I had come in with a note of recommendation from my Intermediate Algebra instructor.

It was soon time for spring break, and I received an email from the Residence Life Office indicating that every student had to vacate the dorms during the break. Well, the residence hall was my only home. I had no other place to go. I contacted the residence life director, Courtney Bish, and she granted me permission to stay on campus.

With my housing problem solved, I had to worry about how I was going to eat during the week-long break. The dining hall would be closed and there was no kitchen in my residence hall. Luckily, each of the three wings in the residence hall had a microwave room. On Friday, the last day of classes before the break, I walked downtown to the Dollar Store and bought two boxes of ramen beef/chicken noodles and a bowl. I was set for spring-break food. About the time I was getting used to having Ramen noodles three times a day, the winter break was over and I was back to eating campus food.

In one math class, when we were given our test papers back, I had a perfect score plus the bonus points. However, I noticed that the black student adjacent to me had scored 47/100. At the end of class, I followed him outside and offered to help him with his math. His name was Monti and he was from Senegal.

Before long, I had arranged to meet Monti and some of his friends at the library on a regular basis to solve homework assignments and prepare for tests. They couldn't believe I was willing to sacrifice my time to help them out for free. Actually, this was a win-win situation because I was looking for ways to make more friends across the campus. We started working as a group of three, but friends started bringing friends and the group grew in size. As time went on, students started knocking on my dorm-room door for help with their homework assignments. I started feeling like I was a valuable campus resource, like my earlier school days in Cameroon. Most importantly, I was no longer sitting alone at a large table in the campus dining hall.

28

Making It to the End of the First Semester

Among the emails I received inviting students to apply for scholarships, an offering of $1,000 towards housing was one of the few that weren't limited to US citizens. I applied for and received the funds, which would be split between my next two semesters. On the alert for any similar opportunities, I kept asking teachers and administrative staff if there were any other scholarships available.

It started to get a little warmer after spring break, so I spent some of my free time exploring the village of Canton. To my great surprise, every house was locked and there were no kids playing outside. This looked strange to me after growing up in an environment where children were always outside playing, without adult supervision, and doors were always open to people who might wander by. How do you know someone is at home if the door is locked? This was the question I asked before learning that it's customary in the US for people to call before visiting.

As the semester continued after spring break, the office of Advising and First Year Programs sent an email to everyone advertising for the Orientation Leader position, which included pay of $150— enough for me to buy one of the less-expensive textbooks. I applied and was selected to be part of the orientation leader crew for the fall 2011 semester.

Then came another email, one that I didn't like. On-campus students were reminded to pay the $105 housing deposit in order to reserve their rooms for the fall semester. I was completely broke because I had used all the $500 from my work-study job to pay down my tuition balance. I spent a week wondering what I was going to do. One day, I was surprised to receive a letter from my fellow Cameroonian and old classmate, Sunday Isaac, who was living in Portland, Oregon. Inside the envelope there was a fancy card and a brand new $100 bill. He wrote, "To God be the glory. It is with great privilege to have such a wonderful brother like u. After going through a tremendous circle of education, the God almighty has gathered us again in a blessed land of opportunities. Let us work hard and bring the best out from it. Let us remember where we are coming from but not where we are leaving. And in education, u will always be a winner. Let your heart not be trouble of the finances."

I rushed to the Campus Center and paid my deposit just a couple of days shy of the deadline. When I called Isaac to thank him, I didn't really know what to say—he had saved me.

At long last, my family had raised and sent a total of $2,000 to complete my tuition balance. I didn't even bother to ask how they had managed to raise this money. I went directly to French Hall and paid the amount due.

* * * * *

The most interesting episode in my first semester was about to happen. An email from the Residence Life Office alerted students to make arrangements for either going home or living off campus during the summer break. The message, issued a few weeks before the semester's end, said all on-campus students were expected to vacate their dorm rooms, including taking their belongings, on May 21. I had been in touch with some Kenyan international students at St. Lawrence University, where on-campus housing was provided for students who couldn't afford to go home during the summer. I had ignorantly assumed that SUNY Canton would do the same for me, not understanding the difference between a relatively low-cost state college and a private institution like St. Lawrence University.

I emailed the director of Residence Life, requesting permission to stay on campus as I had during the winter and spring breaks. She replied that there were no exceptions for the summer break; no students could stay on campus in the residence halls. With my brain starting to heat up again, I talked to my residence-hall director, but she confirmed the message. My next stop was the international program director's office. She felt sorry about my situation but could do nothing to help. I started to think about the imminent possibility of becoming a homeless man in the United States. I went to see my advisor, Dr. Frempong, who had become a father figure to me during my roller-coaster first semester.

Dr. Frempong called the director of international programs, but their talk yielded no solution. Dr. Frempong told me to contact an economics professor from Congo who lived within walking distance of the campus. I emailed him but never received a reply. I don't want to blame anyone except myself for this predicament. I was so desperate to leave Cameroon that I didn't anticipate the obstacles that might arise. But this was the story of my educational history: beginning with primary school, I would always attend classes without necessarily knowing how I would pay my fees or house rent. If I had thought too far into the future during my early years, I probably never would have made it to America.

Two weeks before the end of the semester I was still stranded, not knowing where I would stay for the summer. Meanwhile, other students were busy preparing for their final exams. Each time I picked up a book to read, I found myself looking at the pages but not really seeing anything. My mind was wandering. I asked myself why life had to be so complicated. My family back home was still paying back the money they had borrowed to get me through my first semester. Worst of all, I had no idea where I was going to get the money to pay for the upcoming fall semester.

I went back to the International Programs Office, where the director, Marela Fiacco, came up with a great idea.

"Are you willing to do dirty jobs?"

"I'm willing to do anything."

She urged me to talk with Terri Clemmo at the Career Service Center about on-campus summer cleaning and painting jobs, which were paid positions and came with free summer housing. When I arrived there, Terri was expecting me. Marela had called to let her know I was on my way.

"Why didn't you come to us earlier?"

"I didn't know about summer campus jobs." In fact, I didn't even know there was a Career Service Center to help students get jobs.

"Human Resources is responsible for summer employment," Terri said.

She advised me to go to the HR office and complete a job application form immediately because it was getting late. I got the form, filled it out, and submitted it the next day.

"When should I expect a response?" I asked the HR director.

"We should get back to you by Monday."

"But we're supposed to be out of the dorms by Saturday."

She was referring to the Monday after the semester was over, and I had to be out of the dorm two days before that. There was no guarantee I would get the job, and I had no idea where I could spend Saturday and Sunday nights.

With the option of an on-campus summer job seeming improbable, I continued to talk with my instructors and administrative staff. At some point, I realized I was being referred to people I had already talked to. Finally, someone sent me to talk to one of the campus counselors, which I did without first knowing what the counselors do. He gave me a chance to introduce myself and tell him what I was going through, which I was happy to do. Then he started asking questions.

"How long have you been away from home?"

"Since I got here in January."

"Do you miss your family?"

"Yeah."

"Who do you miss most—your mother or your father?"

"I just need a place to say," I yelled, standing up and getting ready to leave. "I'm not crazy."

The counselor tried to calm me down because I had become so emotional. This wasn't his fault—I just had so much on my mind. Unfortunately, I took my frustrations out on him, which wasn't fair. "I'll email you as soon as I talk to a few people," he said, after taking my contact information and giving me his business card. He never got back to me.

From this encounter, I imagined how I must have been driving everyone crazy. This was the point where I stopped bothering people on campus with my problems. I was wishing I could just fall asleep and forget all my troubles.

On Sunday, May 15, I woke up early enough to walk downtown and attend church service. Whenever I was feeling low, the First Presbyterian Church on the Park was the place to go. Somehow, Rev. Mike never failed to put a smile on my face. As usual, at the end of the service, I lined up with other church members to shake his hand before walking back to campus.

"Good luck on your finals," Rev. Mike said as we shook hands. "Just out of curiosity, where are you staying during the summer?"

"That's my biggest problem right now. I've talked to everyone I know on campus, but nobody has been able to find summer housing for me. I hope to be deported on a free flight."

"Pierre, you've come a long way. If you step foot in the airport, you're never going to have another opportunity to come back here. I have some thoughts we can explore, and, in the worst case, you can stay with us here in the church."

God does work in mysterious ways. I walked out of church on that day feeling like an elephant had been lifted off my shoulders.

After our conversation, Rev. Mike emailed some church members. One of them recalled seeing a message from Ellen Rocco, the manager of North Country Public Radio (NCPR), sent out to the campus. She was looking for students who might be willing to help out on her farm in exchange for room and board. Rev. Mike then contacted Ellen and her husband, Bill. "Pierre Nzuah is fluent in French and English, well-motivated, has experience working in electronics, and grew up on a farm. He is willing to do anything that will allow him, quite literally, a future," he wrote. "I'm writing to ask if you would be interested at all in exploring the possibility of Pierre coming on as one of your interns."

I anxiously awaited Ellen's reply, considering she had no idea who I was. After taking my first final exam, I checked my email and Ellen had replied to Rev. Mike. I was hoping for a positive response, but I was a little less worried since he had offered me a backup place to stay.

After further email exchanges, Rev. Mike picked me up on campus and took me to Ellen's office on the other side of Canton, the studios of NCPR. I thought Ellen would be interviewing me, and I was prepared to tell her about my years of experience on farms while growing up in Cameroon. When we got to her office, however, she only asked me to pronounce my last name.

At the end of our meeting, Ellen arranged to pick me up in front of the residence hall on May 21. Rev. Mike emerged as my hero during this excruciating time. As for Ellen, I wondered if she was crazy for taking in a foreign student from Baligham village without asking any tough questions.

With my summer housing dilemma solved, I was motivated to prepare for the rest of the final exams. I was also helping four of my classmates prepare for the math final, which benefited me as a way of studying for my own tests. My personal principle was to go the full distance to help a friend prepare, but during an exam it was each person for themselves. The good news was that all my study buddies did pretty well on the math finals.

Throughout the semester, I had very little time to talk with my roommate Brendan. He was busy with hockey and with his many friends. On the night of May 19, we had the best conversation we'd ever had. We talked while he packed up his belongings to prepare for departure the following day. I didn't have much to pack. I was sad to hear that the person who had introduced me to the game of hockey would be transferring to a different college closer to his hometown.

When Brendan's father and a friend came to pick him up the next day, we all sat in the dorm room talking. I wished that Brendan's aunt had come to pick him up so I could thank her for all the things she had bought and sent to me at the beginning of the semester, without even knowing me. Brendan's father was funny and fun to talk with. A few minutes after they left, his father sent Brendan back to give me sixty dollars—three twenty-dollar bills—before they left the campus. The importance of this money was huge. I was about to start the summer break without a dollar in my pocket.

29

Summer 2011: Part One

On Saturday, May 21, 2011, I packed up my stuff—which didn't amount to much, actually fitting into a single suitcase—and was outside my dorm before ten in the morning, waiting for Ellen to pick me up. I watched with envy as graduating seniors walked around the grounds in their commencement robes. For me there was still a long way to go—at least three more years—and I had no idea if I was ever going to be able to graduate from college. As always, a lack of money stood in the way.

When Ellen arrived, I put my suitcase in the back seat, and was about to get into the car when I noticed seniors lined up, walking toward Roos House, the new athletic center where the graduation ceremony was about to take place.

"I wish that was me," I thought, not realizing that I had spoken out loud.

"Don't you worry, we'll get you there," Ellen said. A few years later she told me, "I was saying that just to be nice, but I had no idea where the money was going to come from."

If you saw me the day Ellen picked me up from campus, you'd have thought I was a miserable young man. Even though I'd eaten a lot of campus food during the semester, I had lost weight and looked like a scrawny, unhappy kid.

"We don't live in a fancy house," Ellen said when we arrived at her home outside of DeKalb. "I've done my best to arrange a nice room for you upstairs."

I didn't care at all about a fancy house. I was simply happy to have a place to stay. It was good to have a change of scenery after a semester that seemed to have lasted forever and had been quite stressful. Though I had no problem with the schoolwork, adjusting to the new environment and worrying about my financial situation had exhausted me.

My little upstairs bedroom had shelves filled with books on all four walls. I couldn't believe that one person could own so many books. My high school library hadn't had half the number of books in Ellen's collection. After unpacking, I took a short walk with her to a field behind the barn to meet her husband, Bill, who was working on the sheep fence.

"Can you drive a tractor?" he asked right after Ellen introduced us.

"Nope."

"You're gonna have to learn how to drive the tractor."

Bill sounded very serious, so I understood I hadn't been offered a place on the farm just to eat, relax, and get away from school for a while. Nonetheless, I was excited about the opportunity to learn how to drive a tractor.

"You can go to your room and take a nap," said Ellen after our meeting with Bill.

I went upstairs and tried to sleep, but couldn't doze off. Peeping through the window, I saw Ellen working in the garden and decided to go out and help her.

"You should be catching up on sleep," she said.

"I couldn't fall asleep," I said, and grabbed a spading fork to help her turn the soil.

Ellen was surprised at how fast and effective I was without having to show me what to do. She thought she was going to have to teach me like she did the younger students who had interned there in the past.

"I can tell you grew up on a farm," she said.

I smiled and took this as a compliment. We started chatting comfortably, and Ellen asked a lot of questions—I could tell she wanted to know all about me. She sounded like a journalist.

"How many hectares do your parents cultivate?"

"My mom is actually the one who does the farming, but we've never bothered to measure the size of our farm."

Besides explaining to Ellen that my father made a living mainly from his tailoring work, I told her that different plants did well in different sections, which is why my mother cultivated various crops on pieces of land across the village. When Ellen insisted on getting a sense of the size of the land my mother cultivated, I told her it was between ten and fifteen hectares.

"Is that enough to feed your entire family?"

"Yes, but she has to sell some of the excess in order to buy cooking oil, salt, and other supplies."

I forgot to tell her that most of my siblings living in the city relied on the corn, beans, and other crops from my mother's farm.

"You must have really good soil in Cameroon."

"Yeah. People would die in Cameroon if the soil wasn't fertile."

"I like Cameroon already," Ellen said, laughing. "How many siblings do you have?"

"Sixteen," I replied, after pausing for a few seconds to make sure I got the number right.

"Your poor mother!"

"Not from one mother," I clarified. I told Ellen that my father had two wives, and he also had a daughter each with two mistresses.

"Is that a common practice in Cameroon?"

"Yup. I know a lot of people in my village who are married to more than four wives."

"What about the women?"

"I don't think women are allowed to marry more than one husband."

"That's not fair," Ellen said. "How does your father manage to go to the farm with two wives?"

"He doesn't go to the farm with either of them."

As far as I knew, in order to avoid conflict between them, my father never accompanied his wives to their farm plots. But both my mother and stepmother claim that he was simply a lazy man as far as farm work was concerned. Actually, my father did other kinds of farming. Besides tailoring, he was a palm-wine tapper, keeper of chickens and goats, and took care of Arabica coffee and plantains around the family compound. Unfortunately for my dad, none of those fit into the definition of a real farmer in my village. Real farmers trekked several kilometers on a daily basis to cultivate and do physical work on their plots.

I attempted to switch the conversation from me and my family background.

"Is this the only garden you have?" I asked Ellen.

"It might look small to you, but it's bigger than a typical American garden."

Hers wasn't even a quarter the size of a farm plot behind my mother's house.

From chatting and working with Ellen in the garden, I felt she was a very down-to-earth person.

When we returned to the house, Ellen's husband, Bill, was busy packing and getting ready to leave the next day. He had been a full-time potter for over forty years and owned a business, Red Truck Pottery, in Chestertown, about a three-hour drive southeast of the farm. After marrying Ellen a few years earlier, Bill started splitting his time between the farm and his pottery workshop. As I sat at the kitchen table with my laptop, scrolling through Facebook and chatting with Ellen, Bill walked into the kitchen and interrupted our conversation.

"Are you ready for your first tractor lesson?" Bill asked.

"Yes," I said, closing my laptop and following him outside, hoping I wouldn't make a fool of myself because I had never even driven a four-wheeler.

After a driving lesson of about fifteen minutes, I was able to drive the Kubota tractor around the field, in first gear only. Bill told me to keep driving in first gear until I was comfortable enough to upshift. I couldn't wait for him to leave so I could find out how fast the tractor could go. He wanted me to learn to drive it right away because it was used to do most of the regular work around the farm: cleaning the chicken and turkey coops, cleaning the sheep pens in the barn, haying, and transporting heavy loads.

I was very excited to drive the tractor, and while using it to clean out the turkey coop for the first time, I had Ellen take some pictures of me, which I immediately sent to my brothers back in Douala. I told them to print a few and send them to my mother in the village because she was really worried about my well-being and how I was getting along. As for my father, he was telling everybody that I could survive anywhere.

On the same day as my first tractor-driving experience, Bill gave me a quick lesson on using the lawn mower. It was amazing to me that Americans had power equipment to do so much of their work, and I was surprised that I was able to learn how to use it so easily.

Out to clean the turkey coop

The last power tool he taught me how to use was the weed whacker.

"Have you used a weed whacker before?" Bill asked.

"Nope."

"How do you trim your lawn in Africa?"

"You mean in Cameroon?" I asked, with a smile.

"Yes, and don't be a smart-ass."

"We use machetes."

I was going to say "cutlass," but had already learned during my first semester that Americans refer to cutlasses as machetes and groundnuts as peanuts.

Weed whacking

Before leaving for Chestertown, Bill gave me a list of jobs to do around the farm. Hoping to make a good first impression, I planned to complete everything before he returned from four days away.

"Don't work too hard," Ellen said as she left for work. "You just got through a rough semester."

As soon as she left, I attacked the chores. As much as I enjoyed doing the tractor jobs, the weed whacker was my favorite tool. After years of using a machete to cut grass in my father's palm wine and Arabica coffee farms, I imagined how the weed whacker would have made that job so much easier.

Before Ellen returned from work, the lawns in front of the house and barn were mowed, and every edge was neatened with the string trimmer. I switched from the string to the three-point blade trimmer to cut the grass behind the barn and around the front pasture. Although I was doing valuable work, it was also fun operating all the different farm tools for the first time.

If I were to go back in time to my school years in Cameroon and could choose one piece of equipment to own, it would definitely be the trimmer/weed whacker. Having such a tool during my days in primary, secondary, and high school would have made life so much easier, and I could have avoided all the blisters I suffered from swinging the machete when manual labor was required at school. This is a crazy thought, of course—I probably would have used any money back then to buy beignets rather than gas for power equipment!

I completed everything on Bill's list in two days. Then I spent the rest of my time doing basic chores: watching the sheep during the day, feeding the chickens and turkeys, gathering eggs, and updating my Facebook status. When Bill got back from Chestertown, he was impressed—he didn't think I was going to finish all the jobs he'd left for me. Back in Cameroon, my parents would have expected me to do more work in that amount of time, but both Ellen and Bill praised me for what I had accomplished.

With Ellen busy working at the radio station, Bill and I became farm work-buddies. Each time either of them commended me for a job well-done, I replied, "Well, I have been a farmer all my life."

This was a joke between us. It was a phrase I stole from an older neighbor, James (Jim) Vanornum, who lived about a quarter mile down the road. The first time I heard Jimmy using that phrase, I thought it pretty well summed up what I had been all my life, too. I like farming because it is good work that doesn't strain my brain. On the other hand, who would have thought I would be doing it in America? Definitely not me. Despite all the skills I had acquired through my academic years, it was farm work that helped me find a place to stay during the summer. Growing up on a farm turned out to be a real asset.

After less than a week living with Ellen and Bill, I managed to cause trouble with our neighbor, John McLusky. Bill had asked me to trim along the roadside with the three-point blade, which really chews up the grass and weeds. When I reached our neighbor's mailbox, I thought I'd do him a favor by trimming all the grass and plants growing around the mailbox.

Later that day, Ellen received a phone call from John, who was very angry. Apparently I had cut a lot more than grass—I had trimmed a decorative stand of daylilies completely down to the ground. When Bill got home from town, he told me we should go and apologize. I said no. I was scared because John had sounded so angry. On my behalf, Ellen and Bill went to apologize—with a dozen eggs and a loaf of homemade bread. I was eager to know if the visit turned out OK.

"How did it go with John?" I asked.

"Everything is fine," Ellen said.

"We basically told him you're from Cameroon, where there are no lilies," Bill said.

"Are you kidding? We have lilies."

"So, you want to go say that to John?" Bill asked.

I had an opportunity to meet John at a neighborhood potluck some time later. I had been avoiding him, but it was time to finally meet him face to face.

"Hi, John, I'm Pierre, the guy who weed-whacked your lilies."

"Don't worry about it—they're back and look just fine."

As the summer progressed, Bill thought it was time to introduce me to all the closest farm neighbors. One of our stops was at an Amish home. Bill loved the Amish culture and was friends with many of the families who lived nearby. The first time I had heard anything about Amish people was in my Oral and Written Expressions English-language class. Some students had described them as farmers who lived without electricity, power tools, or motorized vehicles. I learned that they used horses and wore the same simple clothing every day. That description of the Amish sounded very much like the way people in my home village lived, but with one important difference: while almost everyone in Baligham led a similar, simple life, they wouldn't choose to live that way if there were other options.

Bill was chatting with one of our Amish neighbors, Abe Stutzman, who referred to furniture he was building for an "English" friend. I was a bit confused because the Amish looked just like every other white person, except for dressing a bit differently. To me, they and all the other white people were just that—white people. I was curious to know what made them different from each other.

"Why did Abe call them English?" I asked Bill

"The Amish refer to all non-Amish people as English."

I learned that the Amish emigrated to the United States from Germany a couple of hundred years ago, and that they chose to preserve their culture and language. Abe seemed pleased when Bill said that Amish families are one of the few groups in America where kids grow up bilingual; they learn German at home. With this brief background on them, I wanted to know more.

"What do you call black people, especially someone like me who is not from America?" I asked Abe.

"I've never thought of that."

"Well, you can call me black Amish because I grew up on a farm like yours."

We all laughed. This was my first encounter with an Amish family and it was definitely a learning moment for me.

Perhaps the most memorable thing about my first encounters with Amish people was the reception I got from the children who had never seen a black person before. Once, when we were going towards Abe's barn, a group of about ten Amish kids came out and stared at me as if I were a mystery creature who had just fallen out of the sky. One kid pushed his way forward to get a better look at me. I picked him up and swung him around. He started screaming, and the other kids backed off. When I put him back on the ground he ran as fast as he could to the barn. I apologized to Abe for scaring him, but Abe assured me he'd get over it. It turned out this child was a neighbor's son, and we later learned that he was terrified because he thought I was going to kidnap him!

Apparently the story had spread through their community, for this incident was often referred to when the Amish people I knew introduced me to other Amish folks. But as time went by and I interacted regularly with their families, the kids overcame their fears and came to think of me as a favorite play buddy and friendly "uncle."

I must take time to talk about my experience with American food during my first months in the United States. From what I'd eaten in the college dining hall, my conclusion was that American food was terrible. Often, when I was asked what I missed most from home, the first answer that came to mind was food. (Then I'd feel ashamed when people asked, "What about your family?") In Cameroon, there are few food regulations and no big restaurant or food chains. This makes it easy for people to open small restaurants and food stands all across the country. Because there are few widely used food preservation practices, the fare prepared at restaurants is usually fresh from the farm, delicious, and very inexpensive.

I must admit that I jumped to some wrong conclusions about American food based on my campus experience. The first time I tasted Ellen's homemade apple pie, I was blown away. Both Ellen and Bill were great cooks and I was a happy eater. While I still missed fufu and *njama njama*, *achu* and yellow soup, water fufu and *eru*, Bill and Ellen's homemade food helped reduce my constant desire for traditional Cameroonian dishes.

As it turned out, I wasn't the only student helping on the farm that summer. Billy McNamara, who had just graduated from St.

Lawrence University, needed a place to stay for a few weeks before leaving to start a summer job in Maine. Really, God has to bless Ellen and Bill for providing much-needed temporary housing for young people who would otherwise have been stranded.

Bill taught me and Billy how to use a chainsaw, a vital tool on the 120-acre farm, about half of which was forested. Wood was important as a source of heat because Ellen preferred burning it in a cookstove and heat stove rather than using fuel oil. We spent the early part of the summer felling and bucking up firewood, loading cut wood onto a flat wagon, and transporting it to the house. From Bill, I learned this saying about cutting your own firewood: "Wood warms you three times; when you cut it, when you split it, and when you burn it."

Whenever Bill left the farm to work at his pottery in Chestertown, one of my main responsibilities was to split and stack wood. Luckily, I didn't have to split all those huge chunks of wood with an axe. Bill had a hydraulic splitter that made the job considerably easier. The first time he returned from Chestertown and saw how much work I'd done on the wood pile, he was impressed. I had split all the wood we had moved down to the front yard and stacked it along the fence between the house and barn. In the process of stacking, I had created some decorative random designs to make the stack look fancy.

"What is that?" Bill asked, pointing to the designs.

"That's my signature stack," I replied.

"You're so full of shit," Bill said, laughing.

During the summer, Ellen came back from the barn one day and told Bill that we were losing chickens. She had seen a lot of feathers in the coop area in the barn, and we were getting fewer and fewer eggs. Ellen said it looked to her like a raccoon was attacking the chickens, so Bill decided to camp out in the barn. He had barely fallen asleep when a sharp noise from the chicken coop woke him up. Bill shot the raccoon and was very proud that he had been successful so quickly. However, a few days later, more chickens were lost. After doing a careful examination of the hay mow, Bill discovered a whole colony of raccoons living in the barn. He cleared them out and decided it was not a good idea to keep chickens in the barn. Instead, it was decided to put up a secure chicken coop.

To build it he hired a friend, Mose Shetler, known as "Wild Mose" because he was a bit wild for an Amish man and a nonstop talker. With Ellen working at the radio station every day and Bill in the middle of the busy season for his pottery shop in Chestertown, I was assigned the job of assisting Mose with the construction. His six-year-old son completed the crew, and I had a great time working with them. We talked about our different cultures, and I saw many similarities between my life on the farm in Baligham village and the way Amish people live in the North Country.

In most rural areas of Cameroon, including my village, people live without access to electricity, depending on kerosene lanterns for lighting as the Amish do. For farmers in my village, there is no money to purchase agricultural equipment, like tractors. As a result, most of them depend solely on manual labor to cultivate the land, as do the Amish. For economic reasons, most children from poor families don't have the opportunity to continue their education beyond primary school. For the Amish, schooling ends at eighth grade. Although the Amish do not practice polygamy, they too have many children, as is the case in Cameroon. This isn't surprising—in farming communities without mechanized equipment and power tools, children provide the manpower required to get the work done.

Learning about the Amish lifestyle reminded me so much of my years growing up and schooling in Baligham. However, I didn't really understand why the Amish chose to live with such simplicity in the midst of American wealth. On the other hand, the Amish people I met seemed happy and content with their way of living, and the tranquility of their culture really impressed me.

While we worked on the coop, I had the opportunity to ask Mose questions about being Amish.

"Don't you envy the luxurious lifestyle of English people?"

"I do," he answered. "But it's too complicated for me."

"What would you want to do if you were English?"

"I'd love to be an auctioneer," he replied.

I was expecting him to say something like a lawyer or doctor. Then Mose demonstrated how he would preside over an auction, and he sounded as good as a professional.

By the time the chicken coop was completed, I had learned a great deal about Amish culture. I had heard some negative remarks about them from "English" people I knew at school, but I realized they had never had an opportunity to get to know any of the Amish.

Among the things I learned from Wild Mose, one phrase stuck with me. Every time I drove a nail smoothly, he complimented me by saying, "You got it right on the pink nipple." I couldn't believe he would say something like that in front of his six-year-old son, but like people in my village, farmers are earthy people. In any case, this phrase became one of our favorites on the farm.

From my experience working with and getting to know a number of Amish people, I had some very positive takeaways. They are hard-working; they have deeply held religious beliefs but never push these on other people; and they are able to overcome their own fears and prejudices—like learning to like a black man from Cameroon—in order to live in harmony with people from other cultures.

One of the many benefits of living with Ellen was the opportunity to meet people she knew across the region, in part because of her job as manager of the radio station. Throughout the summer, she and Bill took me to potlucks and pool parties where there was abundant food and drink, and many new people to meet.

Since it was summer, students from the four colleges located in towns near the farm were away for a few months. I often found myself the only black person at the parties we attended. It didn't matter to me, but I wondered why black families didn't settle in this part of the country. Could it be because of the cold? I had no idea.

The most frequent question I was asked by people who heard me speak for the first time was, "Where are you from?" My thick accent made it obvious that I was a foreigner. I was glad that people asked because it gave me the opportunity to talk about my homeland. Except for those aware of well-known soccer players from my

221

country, few people knew anything about Cameroon. Many students on campus had no idea where it was located on the map. I found myself talking about Cameroon like I had never done before. I never thought I could come up with so many positive things to say about it—until I was in the United States.

When I arrived in America, I knew no one. Now, while living on the farm, I met so many people through Ellen and Bill. She had friends from out of the area who would sometimes come and spend a few days with us. My favorite person who visited during the summer of 2011 was one of Ellen's oldest friends, Laurie, who brought her grandsons, Asher and Ezra.

"We've been friends for over forty years," Ellen said. "Can you believe it?"

"Wow, that's awesome," I replied.

"These days, it's unusual for people in the United States to have friends for that long. People move around so much," Laurie said.

When I first arrived on the farm, I was not comfortable addressing Ellen simply by her first name, so I took to calling her Mama Ellen. Now I faced the same problem with Laurie, another older woman, so I called her Aunt Laurie. I wasn't used to the American custom of addressing everyone by their first names. In Cameroon, older people are given a title to reflect respect for them.

With Ezra and Asher, about six and eight at the time, creating a lot of noise around the house, it reminded me a little bit of home, where there were always lots of children playing and talking. Initially they held their distance from me, watching, just like the Amish kids. Then we went outside to play and throw crabapples at each other.

"Can I touch your hand?" Ezra asked.

"Sure," I said, and extended my arm toward him. "What do you think?" I asked Ezra after he felt my skin.

"It feels the same as mine."

"Well, I won't know until I touch your hand, too."

Ezra was happy to extend his hand to me, which I touched and confirmed that it did indeed feel the same. Then I asked if I could feel his other hand, and he was again happy to extend it toward me. This time I teasingly pinched him, and he yelled, "What did you do that for?" Then we went back to our crabapple game. Ezra became one of my favorite American kids, and I told his grandma Laurie that I was going to adopt him.

It's good for cross-cultural understanding when people, especially kids, ask questions about my cultural background instead of believing stereotypes, or making assumptions based on little to no accurate information passed from one person to another. As a kid growing up in a very black country, I believed that all white people were born rich, and that whites had fragile, delicate skin. My perception of white people started changing when I was in secondary school and met a group of white tourists who were visiting Lake Awing in the Northwest Region of Cameroon. Like Ezra, I had asked to touch the white people's skin. But back then I still believed there weren't any poor white people in the world. That changed when I came to the United States.

One of Ellen's guests at the farm in August was Gary Knell, then CEO of NPR. I couldn't believe that a high-ranking public personality would make time to visit the farm and mingle with ordinary people—without having a political motive. Ministers, governors, and even low-ranking government officials in Cameroon didn't interact with ordinary citizens. I wondered, how can the CEO of NPR be driving himself around? In my home country, even minor civil servants and retired government officials had personal drivers and people who wiped their shoes. The principal of my high school had a personal chauffeur who drove him to school every day and opened the car door for him to enter or leave the vehicle.

During that first summer I was in the US, a different perspective was revealed to me. Several of the very wealthy people I met at events Ellen took me to were major donors to the radio station. I learned that it was possible to be rich and still be down-to-earth with people who are not wealthy.

During the early part of the summer, I kept telling Ellen and Bill that farm work in America was a lot easier than what we did in Cameroon. Aside from helping Ellen in the garden, most of the work

With Gary E. Knell, former president and CEO of NPR

I did on the farm was done with power tools, like using the tractor and wagon to move around heavy loads rather than carrying them on my head.

"Wait until we start haying," Bill always replied when I talked about how easy the farm work was in the US. When I arrived at the farm, I had no idea what haying was. Growing up in Cameroon, all the livestock owners I knew were nomads who moved their cattle from pasture to pasture, depending on whether it was the dry or rainy season. They did not have to store feed for the winter because there isn't any winter that close to the equator.

*   *   *   *   *

When we finally had a string of clear-weather days after a long stretch of off-and-on rain, we began the haying process. Bill was in charge of cutting the fields, while I rode on the side of the tractor to learn how he operated the hay mower, which was hitched to the tractor. After cutting, we gave the hay two days to dry. Baling it the old-fashioned way—in small square bales—was the most demanding part of the process. On the day we expected to bale, Bill invited several of his friends to come to the farm and help. At about eleven in the morning, once the dew had dried from the field, Bill taught me how to operate the rotary windrower rake. This machine fluffs the hay and moves it into parallel lines, or windrows. After I made three passes around the field and windrowed the outermost hay into nice, neat lines, Bill started following behind me with the baler, and our helpers moved the finished bales into big piles.

When I was done windrowing, Ellen took over running the baler, and Bill joined the others in loading bales onto wagons. These were then pulled back to the barn, where an electric-motor-powered hay elevator was used to move the hay to the upstairs section, or mow, of the barn. I was in charge of stacking the bales in the mow, and the hayloft was hot as hell. People kept telling me I must be happy with the hot weather and the heat in the mow. This was not true—I wasn't used to the humidity. The dry heat in Cameroon is very different and much more pleasant. I really hated the humid heat of the North Country summer.

By the end of our first day of haying, I was wishing for night so we could get out of the field and barn. But summer in the North Country means long days—it didn't get dark until about ten o'clock. With rainfall forecast for the next day, Bill was worried about leaving bales in the field. Wet bales mean rotten hay or, worse, the possibility of spontaneous combustion leading to barn fires. When we finally got back to the house, everyone was exhausted. I took a shower and went right to bed. I didn't even have the energy to eat. I dreamt all night that I was out in the field haying, which was too much work to be doing in my sleep, too! At this point, I officially declared haying the hardest job on the farm. You don't know the meaning of hard work until you've worked in the fields baling and storing hay.

Our next round of haying was fun. The second cut, usually late in the summer, produces the highest quality feed. I windrowed for hours one day in the front field, which was still soggy from a long rainy period. The forecast for sunny skies proved to be wrong. Mid-afternoon, a dark cloud moved over the fields and heavy winds dispersed my nicely windrowed hay. Then it started pouring, and we struggled to load the baled hay onto the wagon. Bill was upset about hay getting wet, but I was imagining how the whole event would make a great YouTube video.

Despite occasional problems caused mostly by weather, we successfully filled the hayloft with over 3,000 dry bales, enough to feed the sheep flock through the winter, and lots left over to provide bedding for the chicken and turkey coops.

30

Summer 2011: Part Two

While I was busy enjoying summer vacation and learning about small-farm practices in America, a lot of things were happening in terms of my status at SUNY Canton for the upcoming fall semester. First, I received an update on my international grant from the admissions counselor, Erin Lassial: "You did very well in school this year; great job! Because of this, I am happy to report that you will be receiving $3,000 per semester in international grant money for next year. As long as you maintain your grades, this will equal a yearly total of $2,000 more than you were receiving before."

This was great news and I was very appreciative, especially since college costs for international students were about double what state residents were charged. While working on the farm and hoping for miracles regarding my return to college, there was more good news: SUNY Canton's director of tutoring services asked if I was still interested in a position. I accepted without hesitation, even though I was enrolled in seven courses and had a very densely packed schedule.

Before leaving campus back at the start of summer, I was told by Rev. Mike to stay calm while he worked with Ellen and SUNY Canton staff to explore possible financial solutions for my fall semester costs. Soon after, he made a case for me in his monthly newsletter, "The Pastor's Report," sharing my story and financial situation. I can't find the words to describe how I felt after reading it. It turned out *he* was better at explaining my financial problem than I was. If I ended up returning to Cameroon without completing my college education, I'd still be grateful to Rev. Mike for all he did on my behalf. Here's the church newsletter article he wrote.

The Pastor's Report

Plea For Pierre...

Folks, a young man from Cameroon (Africa), Pierre Nzuah, has come into the life of our church this past spring. He is a charming young man (26 years old) who got a 3.8 GPA in the spring term (that's three As and two B+s), and is a kind and hope-filled soul. Unfortunately, the funding for his schooling has evaporated (family misfortune) and finds himself facing a mighty steep climb to remain in this country to continue attending SUNY Canton (studying computer technology).

Currently, for the summer, Pierre is working at a local farm for room and board, but faces the prospect of having to return to Cameroon (and the associated lack of opportunities there) unless, quite literally, a miracle happens in his life.

I have been in communication with the office of International Students at the college and they are tremendously supportive and deserious of Pierre continuing his studies. The problem, though, is money. In choosing to write about Pierre's situation, I'm "putting this out there" to our church community with the thought that the Spirit might move some folks to want to support him financially in providing him the opportunity to fulfill his dreams and in frankest terms, have a life.

Now, this is a VERY tall order, and to be clear I'm not doing any arm twisting here. But I do believe that miracles happen, if the need is

known. **So here is the reality of the need: $13,000 a year for the next three years, a place to live in town (ideally where he could fix his own meals).**

I know, that is *staggering*. It staggers me so much that I feel a bit foolish in even writing about this. In the end though, three things persuaded me to do so.

First, and most importantly, ours is a profoundly compassionate, loving and miraculous God. I don't think we should ever underestimate what God, can and might do. So, in defiance of the odds, I feel called to simply make this need be known.

Second, Pierre is a wonderfully bright, hard working, and kind young man. He was raised a Presbyterian in Cameroon. He has touched my heart, as he as done with each person who has met him. As "good causes" good, he is the poster child.

Third, through our work with folks in Malwai, I understand the need in so many African countries is simply beyond our ability to comprehend; both is range and depth of need. So much so that it becomes quite easy to tune it out, throw up one's hands, and say, "what possible difference can we make?" Well, with respect to Pierre, we could make ALL the difference.

Finally, I would simply ask all of us to keep Pierre in our prayers and let's see what God will do. - Rev. Mike

Jesus looked at them and said, "For mortals it is impossible, but not for God; for God all things are possible."
- Matthew 10:27

The newsletter reached Presbyterian congregations around the United States, which is how many in the church came to know my story. After reading it, former church member Carolyn Nevaldine called the SUNY Canton president to see if a scholarship fund that had been established to honor her late husband could be used to help me. Peter Nevaldine had founded and taught the first technical electrical engineering program at the college, and the engineering building on campus was named in his honor.

I learned that I had been awarded this $1,000 scholarship in an email from Rev. Mike, who asked if I would be so kind as to send a thank-you note to Mrs. Nevaldine. Indeed! Sending a thank-you letter was the least I could do to express my gratitude.

It seemed unreal that people who never met me were working hard to make a once-in-a-lifetime opportunity possible—the pursuit of my academic dreams. Growing up in a place where poor people struggle on a daily basis just to get by, and rich people closely guard their wealth, I had never seen prosperous folks use their own resources to help others reach their goals. Living on the farm with Ellen, I learned a lot about philanthropy because much of her work involved developing relationships with affluent donors. She said studies have shown that wealthy people who give money to charity and who help with the work of those charities tend to live much happier lives than rich people who don't engage in acts of generosity. As the person on the receiving end, I was very grateful for the moneyed people who were so giving.

When I was growing up, my parents always told me that family isn't only a matter of blood relations. Living with Ellen and Bill turned out to be one of the best things that happened to me in the United States because they treated me like family. They "adopted" me as their son and were actually easier on me than my biological parents. The love and care I received from Ellen and Bill helped me to quickly get over the difficulties of my first semester. Their place in the country became my home away from home.

Not long after I moved out to the farm, Ellen started writing occasional blog entries, focusing on my experiences in America.

Soon, people across the region knew about me, and each time I showed up at a party with Ellen and Bill, I was asked questions about my life and Cameroon as if we had already met. Ellen's first blog entry introduced me to people who read it.

Saving the World

When I was 20, I thought I could save the world. That's the beauty of being 20. I have more-modest aspirations now. Maybe I can do some good where I live. I think I have a positive impact because I say "yes" to unlikely or unexpected situations. Opportunity. You seize the chances that cross your path.

Don't get me wrong, it's very much a two-way street. Pierre joined us at the farm when he finished his first semester at SUNY Canton and needed a place to stay and work this summer. He joined us as a farm apprentice a few days ago. We're trying to help him figure out how to continue at SUNY Canton. If we can help him even a little bit, it will make me feel really good ... because Pierre, who is 26, has been trying to get a college education ever since he finished high school in Cameroon. Finally, he made it to Canton for the spring semester.

I think Pierre would say he is grateful for the opportunity to come to Canton, and to stay at the farm. I am incredibly grateful to get to know Pierre. Listen to this: within three days of being with us, he has driven a tractor for the first time, driven a car for the first time, used tools like a weed-eater and lawn mower for the first time, eaten his first asparagus (Cameroon, of course, is an equatorial country ... no asparagus). He may think it's fun to drive a tractor, but do you know how much fun it is to see someone learning a skill like this? Holy cow.

Pierre driving, Billy McNamara escorting

Billy McNamara, who just received his degree from St. Lawrence University, is also spending a month with us. He had the pleasure (it was a pleasure, Billy, wasn't it?) of giving Pierre his first car-driving lesson.

The things we take for granted: cars, college, lawn mowers ... asparagus. I'll keep you posted on Pierre's farm escapades ... oh, by the way, Pierre did not much care for asparagus, but he LOVED driving a car.

Ellen Rocco

Ellen made me famous through her regular blog posts about having me on the farm. She reached out by phone to family and friends in search of financial assistance to get me through the fall 2011 semester. On one occasion, she was talking to her friend, Cali Brooks, CEO of the Adirondack Foundation, which serves the Adirondack community by "inspiring donors, building partnerships, and mobilizing resources to strengthen community through philanthropy" (according to the organization's website).

231

"I have a Cameroonian student staying with Bill and me for the summer," Ellen told Cali. "I consider myself Pierre's American mom, so I can boast about his academic achievements. We're trying to figure out how to pay his college tuition in the fall so he can continue his studies and avoid deportation."

"Don't you know Annette Plante?" Cali asked, after she'd thought about the situation. "Annette is always interested in helping students who want to pursue studies in science and medicine. Maybe she could help Pierre."

Annette Plante was a retired teacher who had taught the basics and beauty of the French language and culture for 26 years at SUNY Potsdam. Ellen knew Annette because she had been a supporter of North Country Public Radio for years.

"Annette, do you have a moment to listen to a story about a young man I know?" Ellen asked on the phone.

"Of course, dear."

She shared my family and academic background, and my financial problem. It was amazing how quickly Ellen, like Rev. Mike, had learned my story and was able to tell it in a more compelling way than even I could.

"Oh, Ellen, David Wells is the dean of engineering at SUNY Canton, and he is my friend and next-door neighbor. I'll talk to him."

A few days later, Ellen took a call from Dr. Wells. I remember I was sitting at the kitchen table, eating a slice of apple pie and drinking a cup of coffee mixed with milk and lots of sugar.

"I don't know what you said, Ellen," Dr. Wells said on the phone. "Annette has offered to make a generous contribution toward Pierre's fall semester tuition, and a friend of hers who lives in Florida is going to make a contribution as well."

"My son, you're all set for the fall," Ellen said to me at the end of the phone conversation. "Annette and another donor are going to pay your remaining tuition costs."

"Oh, my God—I can't believe this!"

No words could explain how exciting this news was to me. I thought I would have a heart attack from joy. I went to my room and cried, feeling incredibly blessed and grateful. Annette's generosity was definitely one of the critical breakthrough moments in my academic journey.

Later in the summer, Ellen arranged with Dr. Wells for me to meet with Annette so that I could thank her in person for lifting a giant burden off my shoulders. It was surreal to me that Annette had only heard my story on the phone and responded by contributing a large sum of money to help me.

It was my utmost pleasure to meet her. We spoke French for a little while before switching to English so everyone in the room could talk to each other. I called Annette "my quiet angel" because I deeply believed God had sent her to rescue me. She had just pledged thousands of dollars to help with my college costs, and said she was delighted that Ellen had reached out to her with my story. She was so happy to help, and promised to assist me financially through the rest of my college career as long as I kept taking my education seriously.

Really, there are good people in this world, and I am forever indebted to Annette, who came through for me at a moment when I was beginning to despair.

31

Fall Semester 2011

At the end of a productive summer of learning new farming skills and having fun at lots of parties with endless food and beer, the most important outcome was that I now had new parents, Ellen Rocco and Bill Knoble. It was a summer I will never forget. My upstairs room was officially named, "Pierre's room." Bill and Ellen told me to consider their home my home, and that I was welcome to come back to the farm anytime I wanted, with or without letting them know. Back in my village, I never had the opportunity to have my own room, but here in the US I had one totally my own. This was so cool.

For my back-to-school preparation, Ellen helped me open a checking account at a local bank, and then she and Bill loaded it with enough money to purchase textbooks, which they suggested I could find more cheaply online rather than going to the campus store. I was set to return to school one week before the start of the semester in order to serve as an orientation leader for entering freshmen.

On August 14, Bill gave me a ride back to campus and helped move my belongings into my dorm room. For the record, this was the first time in my life that someone accompanied me to school at the beginning of an academic year—and helped me with my luggage! So, I say, thank you, Bill.

On campus, I joined more than twenty other orientation

leaders. As the sole international student on the orientation crew, I was selected to lead out-of-state and international students through information sessions. During orientation, I had the privilege to meet students from other parts of the world, some of whom were eager to know about my experiences during my first semester away from home. I only shared positive things because I didn't want to scare any of the newcomers.

During the nights of orientation week, we went from residence hall to residence hall, presenting a variety of skits to entertain and welcome new students. Sometimes I heard "you've got a cute accent" whispered from the audience. This made me start to realize my strange accent could be an asset. Perhaps one of my most interesting and embarrassing moments was an exchange with a very pretty and funny girl on the orientation crew, Sammie Lee. I had a crush on her and finally gathered the courage to ask her out.

"Pierre, I don't like men," Sammie said, with a nice smile.

Rehearsing a sketch with fellow orientation leaders.
(L-R) Pierre Nzuah, Nafeesa Johnson, Sammie Lee,
Jullian Phipps, Danesha Williams.

"What did men do to you?"

She started laughing so hard, and I had no idea what was so funny. To make things worse, she told other nearby students and they joined in laughing at me. Not exactly understanding what the joke was, I decided to ask a follow-up question.

"What is wrong with all of you?" I asked.

"Sammie is gay," crazy Danesha explained. "She only has sex with girls."

Now I understood why they were laughing, and I started laughing as well. But I wasn't ready to give up just yet.

"Well, Sammie can change just for me," I said.

"You don't just change from gay to straight," Danesha said.

Well, I had unintentionally created a comedy scene and made a fool of myself. I was still pretty new to the US, and guessing people's sexual orientation from the way they dressed or acted wasn't something I could do easily.

Being an orientation leader turned out to be one of the best decisions I made during my first semester. By the time classes began, I really felt like I was part of the SUNY Canton community. Beside the stipend and the number of friends I made, it was fun—which is why I told other international students that applying to be orientation leaders was a good way to integrate into the campus community.

Orientation brought out a mix of emotions. I saw parents weeping as they waved goodbye to their children; I saw students get emotional and cry as they watched their parents drive away. On the other hand, some students were excited to get away from home and started enjoying college life from day one. One young woman we helped move into her dorm room changed her mind about attending SUNY Canton just as her parents were about to drive away, so they talked with the director of Residence Life, and we helped move her baggage back into her parents' car. I'm sure she had her reasons, but I was shocked that a student with the opportunity to attend college would decide to withdraw at the last minute. They say America is the land of opportunity, so perhaps this student had other options.

* * * * *

I started my electrical engineering program in the fall semester and was quite satisfied with my course load. As a foreign student, I found everything challenging at first. Most of the technical courses had lab sections, and students were required to work in pairs. When instructors told us to pair up, most people quickly did so with friends or people they knew from high school. I was lucky that Andrew Squire, who gave me a warm reception on my very first day of college, had decided to continue with the four-year electrical engineering program after graduating with an associate degree in applied psychology. He and I became lab partners in all technical courses with lab sections. We worked great as a team because he turned out to be just as much of an overachiever as I am. Compared to some younger students who didn't seem to know exactly why they were in college, Andrew was my age-mate and we both put a lot of value on our education.

It happened that he was transferred as resident assistant on the north side of Heritage Hall to the south side, and moved into the room adjacent to mine. This wing was crazy, with students inviting me to play beer pong and other drinking games on weeknights. Andrew was the perfect RA for this section because he didn't take crap from anyone, and having adjacent rooms worked out well for us because we were enrolled in the same classes. We collaborated on homework and other class assignments, and a special benefit for me was that he didn't write me up for playing loud music.

Because of such a tight schedule, I could only fit in five hours of tutoring time each week at the Math and Science Center. From my meeting with the director, Johanna Lee, I was a little skeptical about tutoring because of the politeness level required of the tutors. She advised me to treat students so well that they would feel encouraged and welcome to come back. That wasn't hard to do, but the tutoring center had an open-door policy, so I didn't understand why students had to be treated with kid gloves as motivation to return for help.

During the first few weeks of the semester, few students sought help from the tutoring center. As classes got deeper into the semester, a lot of students started showing up for help with homework, but not from me. At first I thought it was because I was a new tutor, but that didn't make sense because I was at the tutors' table with a large sign announcing that I was there to help. Then I thought the problem might be that I was the only black instructor. While I was sitting at the table, students would come up to ask me for the other tutors: "Where is Jason?" or "Where is Dylan?" Both of them were very good, but I was frustrated: I wasn't hired to sit there and direct students to other tutors. When a young woman came up to me one day and asked for Dylan, I replied with a couple of questions.

"Why can't you ask for help from me?" I asked. "Is it because I'm black?"

"No, no, no," she said, denying the implication and taking a seat at a nearby table.

A few minutes later she asked me for help with algebra, so I thought the same approach I tried with her might be the solution to my problem. For a while, I kept using this question each time a student came to the tutoring center and didn't ask for help from me. This was going well until I asked a Caucasian student, "Is it because I'm black?" and a group of black students started laughing.

"What's funny?" I asked.

"Some students might find that offensive," one of them said.

Transitioning into a new culture can really be a hassle. When I first arrived in the US, I thought people were ignorant for thinking that Africa is a country, or for asking questions about what kind of clothes we wear in Cameroon. Or, how many times have you run into lions? Do you have your own currency? As time passed, I realized I was learning about American culture by asking a lot of dumb questions, too, or, questions that made people feel uncomfortable.

"Why am I the only black student in your class?" I remember asking my advisor, Dr. Frempong.

"You tell me," he replied, laughing.

SUNY Canton has a large black student population, and I simply couldn't understand why some weren't in my engineering classes. At the tutoring center, I began asking black students about their majors and why they hadn't chosen any of the engineering degrees.

"That shit is too hard," one student told me.

I was still having trouble getting students to come to me for help, so I decided to walk around and—based on their facial expressions—ask if they needed some assistance. That approach worked well because some students who came to the tutoring center were actually too shy to ask for help. On the other hand, I annoyed those who were there simply because it was a quiet place to study. Gradually, I became known at the tutoring center and students repeatedly asked for my help.

Tutoring at the Math and Science Center

In my first semester, I learned that class participation is required to get good grades. So, beginning in the fall semester, I sat in the front row of my classes and engaged all the time. I didn't want to be one of those annoying students who always jumped at an opportunity to answer a question, so I waited until no one was willing to offer an answer before raising my hand. Seeing me do that, classmates asked for my tutoring schedule and often joined me at the center for help in understanding the classwork, or with homework. As time progressed, I was so busy at the tutoring center that I sometimes wished I had just sat quietly instead of trying to make myself known to students who wanted help.

The most remarkable outcome from working at the tutoring center was gaining a little brother. One afternoon a little boy came running in, and students were talking about how cute he was, but I was playing my role as tutor and had to keep him from distracting those who were studying.

"Can you come here for a minute?" I asked, trying to stop the boy from running around. "What's your name?"

"I'm Rylan," he said.

"I'm Pierre. Do you like watching funny YouTube videos?"

"Yes."

I had put myself in a tricky spot because I didn't know what was considered appropriate for a four-year-old kid to watch. From my years of watching western movies and television, I knew families in America were very selective about what was appropriate for young children. I asked Rylan for help.

"What would you like to watch?"

"Angry Birds!"

"Yeah ... uh, let's watch Angry Birds."

This was the first I'd ever heard of Angry Birds, so I had no idea what he was talking about. Using one of the desktop computers at the tutoring center, I accessed YouTube, plugged in my earphones, and shared one with Rylan. As we watch the videos, he taught me everything I could ever want to know about Angry Birds, not that any of the information stayed with me. I was just happy to keep him away from disturbing his mother and the students.

"Can you be my brother, please?" Rylan asked.

"Of course. I'd like to be your brother," I answered, somewhat surprised by his request.

As soon as I agreed to be Rylan's brother, he ran off to break the news to his mother, Johanna, the director of tutoring services. A few minutes later he came back, grabbed my hand, and led me to his mother's office.

"Mommy, mommy, this is him," he said excitedly.

Me and Rylan at the Massena Mall

"Rylan told me he had found a big brother," Johanna said. "I thought he was kidding."

From that day forward, Rylan Easton Lee-Powell believed I was his big brother and that we had the same mother. I wondered, of course, why he would believe we were brothers from the same mother: he was white and I am black as charcoal. Nonetheless, Rylan had his mother bring him to campus regularly so he could hang out with me. Whenever Johanna was taking Rylan to a special recreational event, he insisted that I be invited to come along, sometimes threatening not to go unless I did. Because of Rylan, Johanna became a mother figure and mentor to me, both on and off campus.

* * * * *

Soon it was Thanksgiving break, and I was delighted to get away from the books to celebrate my first Thanksgiving in America. I knew exactly where I was going to spend the week because, a month earlier, I had received an invitation from Ellen.

A day after I was back on the farm, Ellen's only son, Jacob (Jake) Rotundo, arrived from Brooklyn for the holiday. I felt as if I already knew Jake because Ellen had told me a lot about him, including the number of parking tickets he had in college and the three years he had spent in Japan teaching English.

It so happened that Jake was exactly two weeks younger than me, even though he had already graduated from college. When Ellen told us that we were her two sons, I insisted I was the big brother. Jake insisted two weeks wasn't enough to make me his big brother. One thing led to another and we had a serious wrestling match on the kitchen floor. This was how Jake and I officially became brothers.

Thanksgiving at the farm was a big deal. Ellen's closest friend, Laurie, drove up from New Paltz with her family to celebrate and stay with us. Ellen also invited neighbors and friends, and the door was always open for those who had no other place to go for the holiday. During our Thanksgiving dinner there were more than twenty people around the table. All the traditional foods were served: turkey, stuffing, mashed potatoes and gravy, plus wine. My new favorite American dish became mashed potatoes and gravy, although stuffing and turkey—and wine—were right up there, too.

While spending time with Jake, I discovered we were both fans of the BBC news service, and we both followed reports from journalists stationed in remote places around the world where people spoke little or no English. At the end of the Thanksgiving dinner, we decided to entertain the gathering with some BBC reporting of our own. Jake didn't understand a word of my dialect, but that didn't stop him from playing the role of interpreter. I began saying random things in my dialect, Ngemba, and Jake translated in a "foreign" accent. We have assumed these roles many times since that first Thanksgiving—making fun of ourselves and the expected tone of BBC journalists.

The week went by quickly and I was soon back in school. At the start of my college education, I didn't quite understand the American system of grading. I simply worked hard and aimed for the best possible score in every subject. It was at the end of my first semester that I learned about things like the President's Honors List, Dean's Honors List, no list, and academic probation, all based on a student's grade-point average (GPA). My goal for the fall 2011 semester was to make the president's list again, but with a much better GPA. And I wanted to make a positive impression on all the people who were helping me get a college education.

Initially, I liked the American system of college grading because there was no ranking and I didn't have to compete with other students for the top position. In most of my classes, a score of 90/100 was enough to get an A, which was the highest grade at SUNY Canton. All I wanted to do was get an average score of 90/100 in all my courses.

Some of my classmates, however, made me work harder than necessary. During the fall semester, I learned that some of them were good at celebrating their class performance by bragging about it in a way I had never seen—and it drove me nuts! Throughout my academic journey, I believed students should not blow their own horns. If you let your performance do the talking, people will blow your horn for you. Because of my bragging classmates, I decided to work as hard as I could in order to get the highest scores in homework, tests, quizzes, and exams. Even though I succeeded in silencing the offensive students on several occasions, I was angry that they made me work so hard for it!

There were times when I wished I was a braggart so my boastful classmates could feel the pain they put other students through by making a big deal of their own performance. Bragging just isn't in my DNA. Back in Cameroon, I had experienced some boastfulness among my classmates, but none of them came close to the level of bragging here in America. On the upside, competition has always been my best incentive in the learning process, so my bragging classmates may have brought out the best in me. My conclusion: American students know how to be boastful when they're doing well.

As finals week approached, there was a lot of traffic in the math and science tutoring center. Some students were working hard to improve their grades from B to A, while others were simply trying to pass. I spent a lot of time calculating the scores individual students needed to have on their final exams in order to pass their courses.

During the fall semester I applied for the RA position, which carried with it the benefit of free housing. I was hoping to get the job and eliminate dorm-room costs, which were a considerable portion of my college expenses, but I was not selected. It was only my second semester, and I understood that maybe more experience was needed to secure an RA position.

Overall, the fall semester went very well. I received a total of $3,000 in meritorious scholarships, and Annette Plante sent a check to cover the remainder of my costs. I was very blessed. Also, I was inducted into the Phi Theta Kappa (PTK) Honor Society, and was accepted again onto the orientation team for the spring semester. It felt so good to look at my transcript and see straight As. And I knew that my transition into the American community had improved tremendously—I was able to figure out most of the bleeped words on TV, and could differentiate between the funny vs. pain-inflicting uses of profanity.

I returned to the farm to spend my first Christmas in America with Ellen and Bill. She was going to just buy a tree from one of the local Christmas-tree farms, but Bill insisted we use one from their own property. A few days before Christmas, he cut down the best Scotch pine we could find. Unfortunately, it had far fewer branches than the typical full tree. I made fun of it by standing on one side and asking Bill if he could see me from the opposite side—but he had a plan. We went back out, cut additional branches, and screwed them into the trunk to fill in the gaps. Ellen laughed when she got home from work, thinking at first that it was a new tree. However, we had to take it easy on the decorations so the extra limbs wouldn't fall off.

On Christmas Eve, Ellen baked several batches of bread and Bill made his famous Christmas sugar cookies. On Christmas Day, we drove around the neighborhood, wishing happy holidays to neighbors and giving them homemade bread. It was new to me to hear "happy holidays" instead of Merry Christmas. Sending Christmas cards to friends and family was new to me as well. The kitchen table was covered with cards Ellen and Bill had received.

My favorite part of American Christmas was opening presents. In addition to the gifts I received from the First Presbyterian congregation, there were piles of presents from Ellen and Bill. With winter approaching and temperatures dropping, they had bought me everything needed to keep myself warm.

"Getting through winter is a matter of staying warm and not worrying about how you look," Bill said. He was one hundred percent correct—I remembered the previous winter when I had almost frozen to death after arriving in Syracuse.

32

Spring Semester 2012

At the beginning of the spring semester, I joined the Collegiate Science and Technology Entry Program (CSTEP), which addresses the under-representation of minorities in scientific, technical, engineering, math, health-related, and licensed professions. I joined primarily to find students who might hire me as a one-on-one tutor, but discovered all kinds of positives including free school supplies, enrichment workshops, and a textbook-loaning program.

With all the benefits CSTEP offers, and only one requirement—attending at least two enrichment workshops per semester—I thought the program would be overwhelmed with applications. In fact, they had to persuade students to join. With the connections I had made through my tutoring job, I started collaborating with CSTEP staff to attract more students.

Everything went well in the early weeks of the semester until I received an email from Ellen. Annette Plante had passed away at the age of ninety-one.

A week later, Ellen picked me up on campus and we attended the funeral in Massena. Listening to the tributes to Annette, I wondered why kind-hearted people can't live forever. The almighty God will continue to rest her gentle soul in perfect peace.

With Annette's passing, I hoped for another miracle that would allow my college education to continue for another semester. My student account was blocked, I had no access to course and other student information, and risked being expelled for failure to pay required fees. I went to the Student Service Center and pleaded with the director of financial aid, Kerrie Cooper, who agreed to put me on academic deferment. Rev. Mike beseeched the First Presbyterian congregation to help me. Ellen called family members and friends to ask for any aid they could offer.

In addition to the help I received from the congregation, I will never forget a surprising contribution from Linda Nevaldine, a former church member now living in Baltimore. This was the second time a member of the Nevaldine family came through for me, even though we'd never met. By the time donations stopped coming in, I had only $1,900 left to pay on my semester costs. I felt so indebted to Rev. Mike and Ellen for doing everything possible to keep me in college.

When Ellen had exhausted her list of friends and relatives, she began looking for advice on how to find more financial help. Most sources advised seeking scholarships designed to keep minority students in college. Unfortunately, because of my international status, I wasn't eligible for those awards, even though I had fewer resources than any other student at the college.

The phone call that changed the course of my academic journey was the one Ellen made to Lee Keet, a philanthropist and businessman known for his history of contributing to local causes and charitable organizations. Calling for his advice, she told him my story and explained the current situation.

"It is a miracle that against all odds, Pierre made it to the United States," she told Lee. Ellen and Rev. Mike had come to know me very well and were great at telling my story. "There are no undergraduate scholarships for international students. Most of them come from very wealthy families who can afford to pay tuition. Pierre is an anomaly among international students in this country."

In fact, all the international students I knew at SUNY Canton had their tuition paid through scholarships from their home countries or by their families. Many of the teachers and staff wanted to keep me on campus, but at public colleges like SUNY Canton, funding was very scarce for international students, and the tuition was much higher than for state residents.

"We have to keep students like Pierre in our community," Lee said. He suggested Ellen talk with the president of the college to determine the cost for me to complete a four-year program in electrical engineering. He made two other suggestions: establish a charitable fund that could accept contributions so that donors received a tax break, and tell everyone she knew to contribute to the fund.

Ellen loved this advice. "Pierre might be the first student to benefit from this fund, but there are other students, particularly from Asia and Africa, who could use this support. And it is a real enrichment opportunity for our local students to study with people from other countries."

At the end of their long conversation, Ellen wondered out loud what to call the fund.

"You said Pierre arrived in the US against all odds. That's a great name," Lee suggested.

"Against All Odds it is!"

At the end of the conversation, Lee and Nancy Keet said they would write a check for what I still owed for the spring 2012 semester and pledged to contribute regularly to the Against All Odds fund.

Ellen met with Joseph Kennedy, then president of SUNY Canton, to talk about creating a scholarship fund for financially needy students from Asian and African countries. He was pleased to have the fund established as a way to increase campus diversity.

* * * * *

With financial troubles behind me for another semester, I was happy to return to the farm for the winter break. Even though there wasn't that much outdoor work to do in the winter, I still helped Bill repair fences, take care of the sheep flock, and plow snow. Most interesting at this time—it was the beginning of lambing season, which came with a lot of responsibilities and entertainment.

We often brought the sheep outside to wander in the pasture between the house and barn, but had to check them periodically

Hanging out with sheep

because lambs **born** outside on a cold day in the North Country faced serious survival challenges. Just like there are some bad human mothers, there **are**, I soon learned, bad moms in the sheep family, too. Some of them, especially if they were first-time mothers, abandoned their newborn lambs.

One night, a ewe gave birth to twins and did just that. We were all inside watching the UK version of *House of Cards*. By the time we went outside to check the sheep, one of the twins had died and the other one was near death, barely breathing. Bill brought him inside, where we took turns massaging and warming him next to the wood cookstove. Miraculously, this ram lamb came back to life. However, every attempt to reconnect him with his mother failed.

We set up a small pen in the workshop, where we kept the young ram and bottle fed him lamb-milk replacer and electrolytes. We named him Togo because he was the tiniest of the lambs on the farm and reminded me of the small country, Togo, in West Africa. Eventually, we ended up with four bottle-fed lambs who preferred people over other sheep. As a result, we were able to sell one to a woman in a nearby town who wanted it as a pet. Watching lambs bounce and jump around a snowy hillside would make anyone smile.

During that winter we had heavy snow cover, and Bill suggested we go snowshoeing. Of course, I had never been on snowshoes before and had no idea what he was talking about. After strapping on a pair of long ones, I asked Bill and Ellen how they expected me to walk on these contraptions. "If you can walk, you can snowshoe," they said together. And as soon as I was on the snow, I discovered snowshoeing really wasn't as difficult as I had imagined.

Snowshoeing with Bill Knoble

I realized that my problem with winter the previous year wasn't so much the snow as the cold. In my second winter, gradually transitioning through late summer into fall and then cold weather was very different than arriving from 80°F weather one day into -20F the next.

Winter break takeaway: snow can be fun.

* * * * *

Back on campus, I was very busy. Midterm exams came early in the semester and I was taking eight courses—nineteen credits—besides tutoring for twenty hours a week. A large portion of my tutoring hours were devoted to one-on-one work with students in academic support programs. I enjoyed working with those who were determined to do well. On the other hand, it was painful to work with students who had been forced by their advisors or parents to get help but who had no personal motivation to succeed. I had begun to notice that many of them struggling with math and with succeeding in college blamed their high school teachers for their difficulties. Some students said their college teachers were too demanding. Others suggested that high school was too easy and didn't provide adequate preparation for college. I found out that some high schools advanced students through the grades even without a passing performance. This was a big surprise to me because in Cameroon, failing students had to repeat grades until they achieved passing marks.

I noticed that college students who were living away from their parents for the first time often struggled with time management. Some freshmen were easily distracted by all the fun things to do on campus and forgot that their primary goal was to get an education. Through my work as a peer tutor, I realized there were students on campus who could do much better in their schoolwork if they dedicated more time to studying rather than partaking in other activities. Seems obvious, I know. I was amazed at how many students found themselves on academic probation with GPAs of 1.0 or less. Considering the cost of college in the United States and the number of free academic support services available, I believed most students, with a little more work, could achieve a 2.0 GPA.

After midterm grades were published, we had a week of spring break in early April. My friend Monti, originally from Senegal, invited me to spend spring break with him and his family in Flatbush, in Brooklyn. I had been hoping to visit New York City since my arrival in the US, so I was glad to accept. I loved living in Canton, but it didn't look like the America I had seen on TV and in the movies when I was growing up.

On Friday, April 6, 2012, we took a bus from Canton to the Syracuse station, where we sat and talked in the terminal while waiting for our bus connection to New York City. Out of nowhere, a uniformed officer appeared and started asking me all sorts of questions. I still don't know why he singled me out—maybe because I was speaking too loudly? I really don't know.

"Are you a citizen?" the officer asked.

"Yes, sir," I replied without hesitation.

"Can I see your ID, please?" he requested.

"Sure." I reached inside my wallet and gave him my Cameroonian ID card.

"You told me you're a citizen!"

"Yes, sir, I'm a citizen of Cameroon."

People around me started laughing, but the officer was not amused. He thought I was trying to be funny, perhaps at his expense. This was the first time someone had ever asked me if I was a citizen, and I supposed that I was a citizen of some place, particularly since he hadn't specified a country.

As requested, I showed my passport to the officer and that was the end of the story. Later, I tried to joke about the encounter, but Monti advised me to never mess around with a uniformed officer or official.

We arrived in New York City after a seven-hour bus trip. Finally, I saw the America I had imagined. We walked to the subway station and Monti gave me a quick lesson on how to use a Metro card. When we boarded the train, the interior of the subway car was neither as fancy nor clean as I thought a train in the US would be.

When I met Monti's family in their Flatbush apartment, I was warmly welcomed and instantly felt at home. It was almost like when I returned to the village at the end of a school term in Cameroon. Besides Monti's younger niece and nephew, everyone in the room was born in either Senegal or Cameroon before moving to the US. We all spoke in a variety of thick accents—and for once, I didn't have to repeat myself over and over during conversations because we all seemed to understand each other very well. We had so much to talk about—mainly the vast differences between the American lifestyle and African culture. Since French and English are the official languages of Cameroon, and French is the official language of Senegal, all of us in the room were bilingual.

We talked a lot about food, one of my favorite subjects. For the nearly fifteen months I'd been in the US, all my time was spent in northern New York, where foreign cuisines are hard to come by.

"What do you think about American food?" Monti's mother asked.

"Campus food is too sweet, but I'm getting used to it."

"I'll make *ceebu jen* for you boys on Sunday."

I never got to know Monti's mother's name because she was introduced to me as *la mère de Monti* (the mother of Monti), which was a respectful way of addressing an older person, as we would do in Cameroon. This was something I had noticed shortly after arriving in the US: for older people and those in positions of responsibility or authority, I had a tough time addressing them directly by their names. Although I had learned to use most people's first names, I still couldn't speak to any of my teachers without using either professor or doctor.

On Saturday, we started exploring the city: Times Square, the Empire State Building, Central Park, and Rockefeller Center. No offense to Canton, but being in the city for the first time finally gave me the opportunity to take pictures for my Facebook page to show family and friends back home I was having a great time in the US.

Sunday evening, after hours of exploring the city, we returned to Flatbush, where Monti's mom was preparing the special Senegalese dish, ceebu jen (pronounced as che-boo-jen), comprised of rice, fish, vegetables, and a mixture of spices and ingredients that I don't know. We could smell the aroma as we entered the apartment, and when it was time to eat, we sat on the floor around a tray loaded with ceebu jen. Together with his two brothers, we devoured two trays of food. Monti's mother tried to force us to eat more, but we were stuffed. I can't describe how delicious the dish was, but I urge you to try ceebu jen if you ever have the opportunity.

On Sunday night, as we were wandering around the city, I was shocked at the number of beggars and homeless people we saw on the streets and in the subways. Growing up in Cameroon, I thought hardship and suffering was only a problem in developing countries. Nobody could have convinced me there would be so many people starving and seeking shelter in the US. I wondered why parents admonished their children about wastefulness by saying, "there are many kids starving in Africa," when the problem also exists so widely in developed countries.

About halfway through spring break, I suggested we go to DC, and vowed to stay awake for the entire ride because I didn't want to miss anything along the way. We had breakfast there and then headed for Pennsylvania Avenue. I couldn't believe I was actually standing in front of the White House. I hoped Barack Obama would come out of the Oval Office and wave, but he never did.

In front of the White House

By the time we reached the Washington Monument, Monti and Dyna were exhausted and didn't want to go any further. With all the financial troubles I was having at school, I thought it would be a disaster if I got deported back to Cameroon without enough photographic evidence of famous tourist attractions to prove to my people that I had been in the United States. Leaving Monti and Dyna at the Washington Monument, I visited the Korean War Memorial and the Lincoln Memorial. When I got back from my solo adventure, we proceeded to the Smithsonian museums before taking the bus back to New York.

As we prepared to return to SUNY Canton, Monti's mother told me to feel free to visit again. I owe a debt of gratitude to my friend and his family for hosting me. They were so hospitable and I had such a great time being with them.

* * * * *

Shortly after spring break, the Institute of Electrical and Electronics Engineers (IEEE) club organized a field trip to NASA at Cape Canaveral in Florida, and I wasted no time in signing up. As a foreigner with limited means, I was always looking for opportunities to travel. SUNY Canton provided us with a school bus, and all we had to do was raise money for gas.

We stayed at a very nice Marriott Suites hotel near SeaWorld in Orlando, and it was great to have this luxury without having to pay for it. I enjoyed touring the Kennedy Space Center and the US Astronaut Hall of Fame. Plus, I learned to play miniature golf. It turned out I was good at it, and I wondered if I could have played golf seriously if I'd been introduced to it at a young age. At night, we would all gather in one of the rooms to drink beer and talk, which gave me an opportunity to bond with members of the group who were already in their junior or senior year at college.

After our trip to NASA, it was close to final-exam time. This was my third semester at SUNY Canton, and I was learning how to reduce the pressure during finals. Early in the semester, when my brain was still fresh and teachers hadn't yet covered a lot of material, I studied hard and scored well on homework, quizzes, tests, and

SUNY Canton IEEE Club at Kennedy Space Center

midterms. So, by finals week, I didn't have to panic about studying—I already knew a lot of the material and had established good grades. In most of my courses, the final exam only made up about 30 percent of the overall grade.

Once again, tutoring was a good experience for me. As finals week approached, I signed up for evening sessions as a way to make some extra money. After having proved myself an effective tutor to both students and supervisors, I could be myself and students put up with it. Unlike some of my fellow peer tutors, I was able to openly criticize students for being too lazy or not taking their studies seriously. They simply accepted my honest criticism. During the semester, I often warned students that if they came to the tutoring center without their notes, I wouldn't help them. I didn't really mean this, but it made them do their part in the process. Some students, each time they arrived at the tutoring center, immediately said to me, "I brought my notes." Tutoring them from their notes was important because different professors had different approaches to problems, and some teachers didn't like it when other methods were used. Not necessarily reasonable, but a fact of the classrooms.

By the time final exams were over, I was completely exhausted, not only from preparing for my own tests, but from helping so many students prepare for theirs.

Near the end of the spring term, the college announced that tuition for international students was being increased by $3,000 per semester. With other miscellaneous increases, my cost would rise from $11,120 to $14,340 for the fall semester. This was very worrisome—how was I going to find the money to return to school in the fall? In an attempt to obtain some funding, I applied for the resident assistant job again, but just like the previous year, I didn't get it. On the bright side, the Residence Life staff thought my experience as a tutor would serve them well for the peer-mentoring program they were planning to start in the fall. While it didn't carry the same benefits as the RA position, my goal in college was to embrace every opportunity that came my way.

In addition to being offered the peer-mentoring job, other good things happened to me at the end of the spring semester. I was selected to work as an orientation leader for the third time; I reapplied for the $1,000 housing scholarship and received it; and during the college's annual student award ceremony, I received the Phoenix Award "in recognition of a student who, despite the odds, has succeeded as a student at SUNY Canton."

Also, I joined a group of students at the 2012 Honors Convocation Ceremony, where we were recognized for academic excellence and achievement. I was honored for having one of the highest cumulative GPAs in my class and was presented with the $1,000 Peter Nevaldine scholarship. Being rewarded for my hard work made studying in the US feel special, and I appreciated the recognition.

Even though my future as an undergraduate student was in limbo, I was living my dream. If I had to return to Cameroon at this point, I had a lot of experience and stories to share about America—in local bars, where I would be bought all the beer I wanted. Of course, the future of my family was in my hands and I couldn't afford

At the Honors Convocation, May 2, 2012, with the three main professors from the Electrical Engineering Department. (L-R) Dr. Stephen Frempong, Pierre Nzuah, Prof. Rashid Aidun, Prof. Robert Jennings.

to return home as a failed bushfaller (one who seeks their fortune far away, often in another country).

At the end of the semester, I was very happy to receive a grade of A in each of my eight courses. I was humbled by the number of text and Facebook messages from students I had tutored who had passed their courses and done well. There is something special about knowing you have helped someone succeed.

I was happy to have no worries about where to stay during the summer. Because of my SUNY Canton connections, my church family, and my practice of attending many events across the community, I was known by a lot of people around the region. Some farmers in the area heard about my farming skills and offered me free housing to come work for them. Some offered to pay me at the end of the summer. However, I had established a great relationship with Ellen and Bill, and their home was my home. Instead of asking whether I wanted to spend the summer on the farm, Bill asked when I wanted to be picked up from the residence hall.

33

Summer 2012

Once I was back on the farm, it hit me that I had successfully completed three semesters. I was incredulous. The first thing I did was take time to write thank-you notes to the good people who had helped me get this far. Included with every letter was a copy of my transcript to let my benefactors know that I was working hard to earn their support. Everyone who helped me—financially or spiritually—will forever have a special place in my humble heart.

There was another young man on the farm who planned to stay for the whole summer. I'm going to just call him Mike because things didn't go well between him and Bill, as you will see. A couple of years later, things did not go well between him and me either. Mike had just earned a bachelor's degree in forestry, and Ellen offered him a place to stay while he figured out where to get a job. He was raised in upstate New York, and it was good having him on the farm because he could drive. I wasn't licensed yet, so Mike could handle quick trips to town when Bill and Ellen were away from the farm.

My not being able to drive placed an extra burden on them. On Sundays, one of them would give me a ride to church and attend the service with me, even though Ellen is Jewish and Bill practiced no religion. Nonetheless, with Rev. Mike's charming style of preaching and his sense of community within the congregation, they enjoyed going to church with me. After a while, it became a tradition for us to go to church on Sunday whenever possible. If I was exhausted from farm work—like haying—and didn't want to go to church, I still got a knock on my door on Sunday morning.

"Get your ass up, young, man," Bill would say. "We're gonna be late for church."

Suddenly, church attendance wasn't optional for me anymore. Bill, in spite of his age, was enrolled at St. Lawrence University, taking one or two courses per semester in order to earn a bachelor's degree in geology. While Ellen knew almost everybody in the church congregation because of her connections through the radio station, Bill knew almost as many people as I did because of his SLU connection.

He was in his sixties, but Bill was one hell of a tough guy. Even though I'd grown up on a farm, it was hard work keeping up with him. One thing that bugged me was that he tried to do everything on the farm without ever asking for help. If I didn't get up early enough, he would have chores done before I was out of bed. I told him to wake me up in the morning, but he told me that wasn't going to happen—he wasn't in the business of waking anyone up. During my first summer on the farm, I would be upstairs talking with my friends in Cameroon, and by the time I came downstairs, Bill would have already mucked out the sheep and hauled wood he'd cut by himself. This made me feel very bad about myself.

So, during the second summer, I came up with a plan to get back at him. I figured out that he was usually up at about six in the morning to do chores. I started getting up at five and worked to get all the chores done before Bill came down from his bedroom. I did this until he started feeling as badly as I had the previous summer.

"You shouldn't be doing this all by yourself. You should have woke me up."

"I'm not gonna wake up a grown-ass man," I replied, using the same words he'd used at me.

"Okay, you got me."

Competing with him on the farm improved our relationship tremendously. After a while, I realized Bill wasn't very good at bossing people, which was why he just dove into projects by himself. So, I decided to adopt his ways. In my upstairs room, I kept my window open in order to track what Bill was doing. One of the things he liked to do before it got really hot in the middle of the day was cut brush from around the hayfields and pastures. But he never gave us a time for when he planned to start a project. Whenever I looked through my window and saw him on the tractor with the wagon hitched to it, I would rush outside and jump onto the wagon.

There was a problem with this partnership. Bill was so passionate about farm work that he'd go out to the back fields without bringing any food. On several occasions, we took chainsaws out to the fields and spend hours cutting and clearing on empty stomachs. As hunger set in, my stomach would start growling but I couldn't complain, so I came up with a solution. Ellen always kept a full jar of cookies on the kitchen table, and I decided to take advantage of that. Each time I rushed to join Bill as he headed to the fields, I would quickly grab a handful of cookies on my way out. One day, he loaded fencing equipment in the tractor bucket and started driving out without the wagon. When I hopped onto the mount bar at the back of the tractor, Bill noticed I was chewing something.

"What the hell are you eating?"

I looked at what it was—two white cookies with a black cookie in between.

"Cookie sandwich."

"You're so full of shit," Bill said, laughing.

Bill had come to understand me very well and we were treating each other like family. I didn't have to prove my worth anymore, and he didn't treat me like someone who was just helping out in exchange for food and shelter. As things improved between us, they got worse between him and Mike, who had been on the farm for about a month.

Mike wasn't a morning person and just couldn't seem to get himself out of bed before noon, which meant he never did chores. This didn't sit well with Bill, considering that most of the farm work was done in the morning. You can't really be a successful farmer if you can't get up early, especially if you have lots of chickens, turkeys, and sheep as we did. Ellen didn't really notice that anything was wrong because she was at work every day, but Bill was increasingly frustrated with Mike. In order to address the problem, Bill gave him two weeks to change his morning behavior. I tried to help by knocking at Mike's door every day when I got up early for chores, but he didn't like that too well. He would yell, "What?" and then fall right back to sleep.

When his habits didn't change, I suggested he have a one-on-one talk with Bill to explain that he wasn't a morning person, but that he would compensate by covering afternoon chores and work. Unfortunately, Mike wasn't willing to have that talk, so I tried to convince Bill about Mike's problem with getting up early.

"Are you his spokesman? Mike is an adult. He can speak for himself." Bill just wasn't buying any of it.

He started talking about asking Mike to leave the farm, but Ellen intervened, so Bill assigned him responsibility for taking care of the turkeys, while he and I were in charge of the other animals. Our turkeys were housed at night in a coop away from the house, at the far end of the front field. Well, Mike actually got up early for about two days to take care of the turkeys. But then he gave up. Because we got along well and I didn't want him to leave, I got up and took care of the turkeys for a few days, before Bill got up. I had no idea Bill knew what I was doing. One morning, as I rode my bicycle up to the turkey coop with a bucket of feed pellets, I ran into him.

"Ah ha!" Bill mocked me. "What do you think you're doing?"

"I don't know."

"Mike is a twenty-four-year-old college graduate and he's got to learn to take responsibilities seriously," Bill said.

He and Mike just weren't going to get along. Whenever we worked on group projects, Bill wanted things to be done one way and Mike wanted to do them his own way. I don't want to mention all the things that Mike did that drove Bill nuts, but the last straw was when Bill got up one morning and realized the turkeys hadn't been closed into their coop the previous night. He was furious because they were very vulnerable to raccoon, fox, and coyote attacks.

Bill asked Mike to leave the farm. I had a short chat with Mike and told him how sorry I was that he had to go. He actually admitted that it was his fault and took full responsibility, blaming no one else for what had happened.

When Mike came to the farm after graduation from college, he really didn't have any concrete plans for finding work, but after the falling out with Bill, he was forced to start looking. Luckily, he did find a job with a conservation group in downstate New York. This would help him start repaying his college loans. Maybe his departure wasn't so bad after all.

34

Fall Semester 2012

I started the new semester working as an orientation leader for the office of Advising & First Year Programs, helping new students transition into college. Then I began my work as a peer mentor, in addition to tutoring math, French, physics, and electrical engineering courses. As stipulated in the peer-mentoring job description, I was required to spend five hours per week in the main lounge of my dorm counseling residents, especially first-year students who needed help integrating into campus life. I had to organize social programs to get people out of their rooms so that they interacted and made friends with each other. Another requirement was working with them on time management and study tips.

With good turnout during my lounge hours, I used the opportunity to provide both tutoring services and some advice on how to have a great college experience. While tutoring, I asked students what they thought about SUNY Canton, how their classes were going, the challenges they faced living away from home for the first time, and about their overall experiences on campus. Few students knew about clubs or the free academic support services available. I shared with them my extensive knowledge about campus resources.

I met with students who were attending college simply because their parents wanted them to, and were just trying to make it through to please them. I told them about my background, and that

Peer mentoring/tutoring in Heritage Hall main lounge

they should feel lucky to be born in a country where their biggest problem was choosing between the many opportunities available. They seemed to get motivated when I used my personal story to encourage them to do better; it was much more effective than using rote tips I found through Google searches. Sometimes peer mentoring turned out to be a two-way street. Many students commended me for helping them with academic work, and I was learning so much about America through my conversations with them. Helping students smoothly transition from high school to college life strengthened my leadership skills and helped me connect with students from very different backgrounds.

Because of the positive feedback from three sources—as a peer mentor, from campus involvement, and from my main job as a peer tutor at the math/science tutoring center—I was optimistic that the Residence Life staff would see me as a good candidate for resident assistant. However, after applying and going through the interview process, I was turned down for a third time. The more I was turned down, the more I wanted the job.

* * * * *

At the end of the semester, I returned to the farm for Christmas break. When I called my siblings through Skype to wish them a Happy Christmas, my younger brother Festus said that our father was being harassed by members of his njangi contribution groups in the village. These were money clubs which my father borrowed from to pay his children's school fees. He was getting older and didn't have the energy to work enough to pay his debts, and worse yet, all the money he borrowed was accumulating interest, making payback even more difficult. Members of the njangi had been taunting him for not being able to pay his debts despite the fact that his son was in America. I felt so bad. I was reminded of all the times during my secondary and high school years when I pressed my father for school fees and rent money, so much so that he was obliged to borrow a lot of money from these groups.

Hoping to help with his problem, I called my brother Vincent in Douala. He told me that members of the njangis had seized my father's sewing machines and other valuable items from his tailoring workshop. All this had driven him into a depression. Instead of trying to repay his debts, he started drinking heavily, and according to Vincent, had even been in a bar fight. This was unreal to me—my father never drank in bars. If he wanted a beer, he sent one of his children to buy it and he drank at home with the family. The father I was hearing about wasn't the responsible parent who raised me, and I felt obliged to do something.

I told Vincent to go to the village and find out the total amount our father owed to the njangi contribution groups. By this time, I had accumulated some savings from my campus jobs to buy textbooks for the upcoming spring semester. I sent this money home and it covered most of my father's debts. For the remaining portion of what was owed, I told Vincent to discuss the situation with the rest of my siblings during the yearly family meeting and find a way to pay it off together.

I felt guilty sending money home to bail out my father while people in America were trying to raise money to get me through college. However, I felt the need to restore my father's dignity. After the New Year celebration, I called my brother Innocent, who travels regularly between the village and Douala, selling merchandise from each to the other location. He told me, "You put a smile back on our father's face." I was able to call and talk to my dad in the village and he seemed very happy, which was a big relief for me. He had cut down on his drinking and was doing well again. I couldn't believe that I was warning my father to be on his best behavior. It's crazy what poverty can do to people.

35

Spring Semester 2013

By winter break, I realized I was lagging behind in some classes and needed to do something different if I wanted to keep my grades up. I requested permission to remain on campus during the break to do some catch-up studying. Many of my peers wouldn't believe that I had to put in this kind of extra effort to maintain good grades. They were always telling me, "Oh, you're smart, you don't need to study." God knows, I couldn't get a 4.0 GPA without working my ass off.

I didn't want to eat Ramen noodles through the winter break as I had during my first semester. Luckily, my friends Amida Mumuni, an expert in making African food, and Kristy Tyson, who owned a car, were also staying on campus for the break. We didn't have a kitchen in our dorm, but our friend Araba Asamoah gave us the keys to her off-campus apartment before leaving for New York City.

However, I don't know if staying on campus helped me catch up on schoolwork. The three of us spent much of the break eating, gossiping, and watching movies. At the time, we had access to free streaming of Nigerian movies. Amida and I (born and raised in Ghana and Cameroon respectively) had no trouble following the movies, but Kristy, an African-American, had a hard time understanding the dialog. Often we had to do a Nigerian-English to American-English translation for her. We didn't get a lot of work done during the winter break, but we had a lot of fun.

During the spring break, Jake (Ellen's son) invited me to come and hang out with him in Brooklyn. On April 6, I was on the bus to New York City with Amida—it had been a crazy semester and a break from the books was welcome. I learned during the trip that I had somehow managed to miss the application deadline for the resident-assistant position for the fall semester.

"Did you apply for the RA job?" Amida asked.

"What? When did they send out the email notification?"

"Long time ago."

"Why didn't you tell me? You know how desperate I am for the RA job."

"Don't blame me. You should have been checking your email."

The deadline had passed, but I wasn't going to give up easily. As soon as I got to Brooklyn, I emailed the Residence Life director, but received an "out of office" response from him. I was so worried and impatient, I made my case to Troy Lassial, the associate director.

> Hi Troy,
>
> I was really looking forward to applying for the RA position, but I just heard today that the deadline was April 1st. Because most of my Electrical Engineering subjects are only offered in spring, I'm taking a lot of them this semester and I have been spending most of my time at Nevaldine, working on projects. I know I have myself to blame for not finding out about the application information, but it has always been my dream to be a Resident Assistant and if you give me the opportunity to apply, it would be like a dream come true.
>
> This is a very difficult favor I'm asking from you, but if you can use your high office to give me the opportunity to apply, I would really appreciate it. I sent an email to John, but he is out of office until April 14th. I'm anxiously waiting to hear from you.
>
> Best regards,
> Pierre

During spring break, Troy gave me an opportunity to submit an RA application electronically. As required, I wrote an essay listing activities and personal strengths that made me stand out as a good candidate for the RA position. With my application submitted, I was ready to enjoy spring break. This episode was typical of so much of my life: persist and pursue.

*   *   *   *   *

I took a night bus on April 11 to join other SUNY Canton students for a weekend event at the Sagamore Resort on Lake George in eastern New York. This was a Collegiate Science and Technology Entry Program (CSTEP) conference that brought together students from several New York State colleges and universities amid a setting with good food and nice lodgings. It was a serious conference and there was a lot happening. Professional guests presided over workshops, students shared posters and oral presentations, and representatives from top engineering and science schools from across the US populated a job fair. There were many networking opportunities. I met some great people, like Dr. James Duah-Agyeman from Ghana, the chief diversity officer at Syracuse University. I even got to meet another Cameroonian—my first in all the time I'd been in the US. She identified me by the Cameroonian soccer jersey I was wearing.

The educational part of the conference concluded on Saturday evening with a banquet at which students received awards for the best presentations, and the guest speaker delivered an inspirational talk. And, to my great delight, there was much good food. On Saturday night we had a sendoff party that lasted into the early hours of Sunday morning. This was the fun side of attending college in the US, and the outcome of being involved in the right kind of extracurricular activities.

Shortly after spring break, Johanna and Rylan (my American little brother) invited me to join them on a trip to Canada to attend a festival. I couldn't turn down the opportunity to visit another country, but had no idea that as an international student, I needed a visa to travel there, even though the border was just a half hour from the SUNY Canton campus.

Johanna and Rylan picked me up on campus and we drove to the border, where we were asked to present our passports. The other people in the car had theirs returned immediately, but mine was withheld and I was asked if I had a visa to travel to Canada. Of course, I did not. The border officer asked us to park our car and come inside for questioning. Little did I know what a long process we were going to be facing. I was asked all sorts of security questions to certify that I wasn't a terrorist trying to sneak into Canada. The fun part of this encounter was when the officer asked questions about my family.

"Do you have any siblings?"

"Yes."

"How many?"

"Sixteen."

"Would you mind naming them," the officer asked, in disbelief.

This was the first time in a long time that I had to name all my siblings. In an attempt to not miss anyone or make a mistake, I decided to recite the names from oldest to youngest. In the process of doing so, I realized that I was actually the eleventh of my father's seventeen children, instead of the tenth as I had always believed. My conversation with the border officer went well, at the end of which he gave me a list of instructions on how to apply for a visa the next time I wanted to visit Canada.

"I'm sorry, but we can't allow you to visit Canada at this time."

"But, I'm already in Canada."

"No, you're not," the officer replied, laughing.

I told Johanna and the others to go the festival and pick me up at the border on the way back, but they refused. The most interesting part of this excursion was yet to happen. We also had to go through the US border checkpoint, where we parked, went inside, and I presented my passport with the documents given to me by the Canadian border officer.

"Your visa has expired."

"Yes, it was only valid for six months when I got it in Cameroon over two years ago."

"I see that, but you can't re-enter the United States without a valid visa."

I tried explaining to the border officer that the visa I got from the US embassy in Cameroon doesn't have to be valid while I'm in the United States. The two critical documents that had to be up to date were the I-20 form and my Cameroonian passport.

"But you're coming from Canada, trying to enter the US without a valid visa."

"Oh, no, I wasn't allowed to enter Canada."

I was getting really confused. At the Canadian customs, I was told I couldn't enter Canada without a visa, and the officer said I wasn't in Canada. At the US customs, the officer said I was coming from Canada and wasn't on US soil either. If I wasn't in either Canada or the US, where was I exactly? I had no clue.

The US border officer didn't give me a chance to further explain my situation, and Johanna got really frustrated. Comparing my experience with the Canadian and US border guards, the Canadian officer gets an A and the US officer gets an F. It took us more than twice as much time at the US border than at the Canadian border to clarify my situation. Finally, I was warned to never attempt traveling to countries neighboring the US without a proper visa, and I was allowed back into the US ... if I wasn't already in the US.

To salvage what we could of the day, we visited Boldt Castle in the Thousand Islands, which is located on the US side of the St. Lawrence River—so no paperwork was required. From that day forward, each time Johanna invited me to go somewhere, she always asked, "Do you have your paperwork?"

The spring 2013 semester was one to remember. Early on, a student offered me $400 to take his online statistics class for him. I was glad that I was not tempted. My personal financial situation was less tenuous than it had been during earlier semesters, and I was earning money legitimately through tutoring. As a peer mentor, I educated incoming students about the consequences of cheating or other forms of academic dishonesty. I didn't have to think twice before turning down the offer.

I knew this student personally and he was no dummy, but math wasn't his thing. Once again, I didn't understand why he hadn't found the time and patience to utilize the free tutoring resources on campus. I offered to help him during my tutoring hours and even outside my official hours, but he didn't think that was a good idea. Despite the pressure he put on me, including increasing the amount of money he was willing to pay, I turned him down. Instead of hating me for it, he found a new respect for me. Every time we met on campus, he'd say, "When I grow up, I wanna be just like you."

This student graduated before me and got a full-time job on campus. One day, I showed up for an on-campus job interview and he was the lead interviewer. It occurred to me that he might take revenge by not choosing me, but I ended up getting hired and he was my supervisor. During one of our conversations, he joked about having passed the statistics class without my help, but said he still hated math. We became friends, and he told me that what I did was right, adding that he had come to understand the importance of doing one's own work, particularly after interacting with students and being involved in job recruitment.

Toward the end of the semester, I was in Nevaldine Hall doing an assignment for one of my engineering courses when I got a call from Javon Joslyn, the residence director of Mohawk Hall. I knew for sure it was about the RA job.

"I've got good news and bad news for you. Which do you want first?"

"Hmm, give me the good news first."

During the previous semester, I'd received a similar call and asked for the bad news first, which turned out to be that I hadn't gotten the RA position, while the good news was getting the peer mentoring job. This time, I opted for the reverse order.

"The good news is that you've been selected to be an RA."

"Yeah ... uh, thank you so much."

"The bad news is that you're going to be in the pet wing."

"I have no problem with that."

Some students applying to be RAs said they'd refuse the offer if they were assigned to the pet wing because of the additional responsibilities—working with both students and their pets. As for me, I was just happy to get the job at last. It came with free room and board, which was now worth about $5,000 per semester. This was the point where the odds of having the resources to graduate started shifting significantly in my favor.

When I shared the news about my RA job for the fall semester, some of my friends and veteran RAs warned me to watch my language once I started the job. When I arrived in the US, it took me forever to adjust to the new environment, but one thing that came to me with little effort was the use of profanity. I was amazed at the way Americans used profanity in casual conversations or in frustrating situations. I promised to work on my language before the start of the fall semester, but wasn't sure I'd succeed.

On May 1, at the Annual Honors Convocation, I was cited again for maintaining a high cumulative GPA. Most importantly, I also received the Canino Prize for Academic Excellence, in recognition of outstanding academic achievement in the Electrical Engineering Technology Program. The prize came with $1,000 applicable towards my college costs.

The spring 2013 semester was one for the record books, personally. I was inducted into the Tau Alpha Pi National Honor Society and the Golden Key International Honor Society. I was presented with the CSTEP Outstanding Student award for my personal academic achievements and contributions to the program. As if all that wasn't enough, at the May 7 annual Student Recognition Ceremony, I was presented with the Spirit of Success Award, given to a student who "demonstrated active citizenship in the college community" while maintaining a high GPA. I had never felt so humbled and honored for having my hard work appreciated. Concluding this semester with straight As, I couldn't ask for more.

36

Summer 2013

This summer was a bit different than the past two because Bill had officially closed his shop in Chestertown and moved his pottery studio to the farm. After about four decades as a full-time working potter, Bill seemed more interested in being a farmer. He was only doing pottery in the winter months.

I felt very comfortable living with Ellen and Bill because they treated me like one of their own. Without worrying about hurting my feelings, Bill was now comfortable knocking on my door early in the morning and saying, "Wake your ass up, young man." He was a lesson in the importance of doing more than one thing in a lifetime. His newfound love for farming, especially his connection with the animals, was out of this world. One time, when I hadn't seen Bill for a few hours, I walked up to the back field and found him napping on the ground, with sheep and lambs lying next to him, their heads resting on his chest.

Our sheep flock had expanded, and we expected the winter lambing season to see fifty to seventy-five new lambs, so Bill decided we needed to improve and expand our fencing system. We spent a lot of time that summer building fences with cedar posts and barbed wire. Our best work was the one we constructed along the roadside. Bill was so proud of it, he wanted to put a light on every fence post so people could see how perfect it was when they drove by at night.

He wanted to make the most of the 120 acres of land, so we also spent a lot of time cutting brush and making huge piles of it. When the weather brought a series of good days, we cut and baled hay. In addition to our own fields, we helped neighbors get their hay in as well. That summer the weather cooperated through two cuttings, which filled our barn with over 4,000 square bales. We also helped cut hay for Abe, our Amish friend and neighbor. Though the Amish don't use fuel-powered moving machinery, they helped us load bales onto the hay wagons. To my surprise, Abe let his two sons, John and Levy, ride the top of the full hay wagon, pulled by a tractor.

My favorite part of haying came at the end of the day. Since we were usually exhausted and nobody wanted to cook after long hours of hard work, Bill instituted a tradition of taking us to the Asian Buffet on heavy hay days. He loved the buffet, and so did I.

This was one of my busiest summers on the farm, and I learned how to use more tools. Bill hired Abe to help us replace the house roof and build a new porch in front of his workshop. This was a great learning project for me.

At the age of sixty-seven, Bill was on track to graduate with a degree in geology from St. Lawrence University in May 2015. His young classmates at SLU loved him because of his enthusiasm for school, and because he applied his pottery experience to make geology classes more interesting. Most people think I'm crazy about education, but Bill's passion about going back to school was on a whole other level. Although he was only taking one or two courses per semester, we had a small competition going to see who had a 4.0 GPA at the end of each term. Since we were both scheduled to graduate in the same year, we planned to have a joint graduation party.

With Ellen at work at the radio station, I often accompanied Bill to the geology lab during the summer. Aside from the research he was doing, he helped organize the slide collection for the geology department. We had farm responsibilities, so we were rarely able to stay at the lab as long as Bill might have liked. He arranged with his faculty advisor, teacher, and friend, Jeff Chiarenzelli, to bring a microscope home so he could do evening work on the cataloging project. Bill spent much of his free time at home studying rocks and cross-sections, and explained to me everything he was looking at. Although I looked through the microscope many times at his request, it all looked the same to me. Initially, I told him honestly that I couldn't see what he was seeing, but he wouldn't let me go until I pretended to see the things he was pointing out. Knowing that I was no good at using the microscope to see things, I developed a trick to keep Bill satisfied. Each time he looked through the microscope and said, "Look at this, isn't it fascinating?" I would take a look and say, "Wow, that is so cool."

I can't remember the number of times I had to prod him to leave the microscope so we could get back to farm work. It's hard to describe how deeply he loved the geology program. Life would be much easier for teachers if every student loved school as Bill did.

Despite all the geology lessons I got from him, the only one that stuck with me was guessing the age of rocks. Every time we were out walking, Bill would pick up rocks and tell us their estimated ages. "This rock is about 3.2 billion years old," or, "This rock is about 2.25 billion years old." I often wondered why he couldn't guess the estimated age of a rock in a whole number. Anyway, I started having fun estimating the age of rocks as well. When I was out in the field with him, I would grab a rock and say, "This rock must be about 1.75 billion years old." Bill would say "Bullshit!" and correct my estimate.

The summer of 2013 was when Bill and I cemented our bond and he became a real father to me. We completed so many farm projects and transformed the whole look of the place together. With two llamas wandering around in a pasture close to the road, a flock of chickens pecking in the front yard, turkeys foraging in the field across the road, and a flock of sheep pasturing nearby or being run up and down the road as we moved them from pasture to pasture, the farm became a tourist destination, with people frequently stopping to see our animals.

One night, shortly before I returned to college, Bill, Ellen, and I were playing a game of dominoes when we came up with a plan to travel to Cameroon after my May 2015 graduation. They were eager to meet my family, see how farming was done in my village, and see for themselves the country I had been talking about ever since I met them. As for me, I was missing my family and couldn't wait until the day I was able to return home. However, there were still two years to go to finish my degree, and there was no extra money at the present time for expensive trips.

37

Fall Semester 2013

On August 14, I returned to campus for a two-week resident-assistant training program. We engaged in a series of bonding activities and learned about RA responsibilities, including responding to emergencies, handling a variety of incidents, and, above all, how to help create a healthy living environment for all residents. At the end of the training, we were taken on a one-day adventure to Singer Castle on Dark Island in the St. Lawrence River.

During the training, some veteran RAs scared me about the challenges of overseeing the pet wing, and some said they'd quit if they were assigned there. I remembered visiting my friend Corinne Gentile in the wing before I became an RA—the entire floor was a mess and the smell of cat poop was unbearable.

Classes for the semester were set to begin on Monday, August 26. As directed by Residence Life, we organized a mandatory wing meeting on the evening of the first day to introduce ourselves to everyone. After being a resident for two years, living in the "party wing" of Heritage Hall, I was aware of most of the crazy things students did in residence halls. What was new was living in room 207 in the south wing of Mohawk Hall, where I had to be in charge of students *and* their pets. During our first meeting, my advice to residents was to treat their pets as if they were their babies and give them the utmost attention. I reminded them that SUNY Canton was one of the few pet-friendly campuses, and that there were several students on the waiting list, ready to move into the pet wing if someone screwed up.

At the end of the meeting, I contacted some returning students to inquire about past problems they experienced as residents of the pet wing. Then I contacted all the pet-wing residents and gave them an opportunity to tell me how they would like life to be in the hall. From their input and my own ideas, I created a list of rules that everyone in the pet wing had to obey.

I presented these rules during our next meeting and posted copies all over the pet wing. Together, we adopted a "three strikes and you're out" policy. Residents understood they'd be thrown out of the pet wing if they broke any of the rules three times. I wasn't a very strict RA, but I told them right at the start that being an RA was very important to me. During the first few weeks, I wrote up several residents who broke one of the rules they had helped develop. This was fun because they couldn't complain too much, having been part of the process that created the rules. It didn't take too long for me to develop good relationships with all the pet-wing residents, including those I busted for underage drinking and sent to counseling and boring rehab programs.

* * * * *

As I knew already, the cost of college for international students was more than twice the amount for in-state students. I thought I should make the most out of my very expensive opportunity, so I signed up for a minor in math. But I couldn't take one of the required math courses because of schedule conflicts, and because the school didn't offer advanced math courses every semester. Then I learned that students could cross-register for two courses per academic year at the other institutions in the Associated Colleges consortium—SUNY Potsdam, Clarkson University, St. Lawrence University (SLU), along with SUNY Canton—without any additional cost. I was happy to hear about this option, and quickly completed and submitted the cross-registration form to take Calculus-II at SLU, the closest to SUNY Canton. I purchased a $100 mountain bike at Walmart for transportation, and every so often, I got back to campus sweating like a Christmas goat. The morning weather could be nasty, and I looked pretty grumpy on my bike ride to SLU. On multiple occasions, it was raining.

As an elective for his bachelor's degree, Bill was taking an African art history course at the same time as my SLU math class. One morning, he saw me riding my bike to SLU and sent an email to confirm it was actually me. In our emails to each other, I signed off as "Black Son," but I never abbreviated with the initials BS for obvious reasons. Bill signed off his emails to me as WD, or "White Daddy." I was lucky to have him as my White Daddy and he was super proud of me. He bragged about me all the time, telling people about my journey and the academic accomplishments of his black son.

Since Bill refused to use a cell phone, we continued our communication via email. On Friday, September 13, we met for coffee early in the morning at the SLU bookstore before the start of our classes. Bill had regular coffee and I went for a cup of Chai tea. He updated me on everything going on around the farm, and I told him how my RA job was going. I complained to him about how the upper-level courses (300/400) were kicking my ass.

"You're a smart kid. You'll do just fine."

For most of our conversation, he lectured me about African art history and told me how much he was loving the class, which made me realize how little I knew about Africa in terms of the arts. Bill's class was being taught by a famous Nigerian painter, Prof. Obiora Udechukwu. I was delighted to hear that a course on African art was actually being taught by an African native.

I thank God for giving me the chance to have this chat with Bill because it turned out to be the last time we ever talked. On the night of September 23, a day before his sixty-eighth birthday, I was the RA on duty in Mohawk Hall. Shortly before eleven o'clock, I was sitting in the RA office doing my homework when I received a phone call from Sarah Harris, a former intern on the farm.

"Pierre, I'm sorry to be the one breaking this sad news to you, but Bill is dead."

"What? Which Bill are you talking about?"

"Our Bill, and I'm still in disbelief myself."

I just started crying in the RA office. This was one of those moments when I wished I were dreaming and would wake up. I decided to call Ellen to make sure the terrible news was true.

"Bill is no longer with us," Ellen confirmed from the hospital.

People who know me know I don't handle the loss of loved ones well. I had a breakdown in the RA office and was consoled by my fellow staff members. Residents were surprised to see me crying like a baby. It was so surreal that I had only recently enjoyed coffee with Bill, and just like that, I wasn't going to see him again.

I got a ride out to the farm very early the next morning, and I had to accept that Bill was no more. He had passed away from a sudden heart attack. There were no outward signs that this was going to happen—all summer he had worked long, hard hours with no problem, and he had been feeling great when I'd seen him for coffee. Bill's passing reminded me that we all need to make the most of every minute we're on mother earth because none of us know what tomorrow will bring.

Members of both Bill and Ellen's family arrived at the farm, including his two daughters, Jessy Knoble Gray and Naomi Knoble, who had embraced me as their brother. As we discussed where to hold the funeral service, Ellen suggested we contact Rev. Mike about having it at the First Presbyterian Church.

"My dad was never a church person," said Jessy, Bill's older daughter. "I don't think he'd like his funeral to take place in a church. No offense to you, Pierre."

Jessy had no idea that Bill had attended church with me on a regular basis and had come to enjoy Rev. Mike and the congregation. I kept my mouth shut because I didn't want to appear hurt if the service wasn't held at my church. Ellen explained Bill's relationship with the Presbyterian congregation, and everyone agreed we'd hold the service there. Saying he would be glad to officiate in any way we wanted, Rev. Mike graciously reserved the church for us.

Everywhere Bill went he made an impression, and attendance at his funeral was proof of the impact he had on this earth. Some of our Amish friends attended, and many people traveled long distances to be there. I was honored to have had Bill as a father figure in my life, and his death was devastating. If you met him just once, you'd never forget him. I know I'll never forget him. I don't have the right words to describe what kind of person he was, so the tribute Jeff Chiarenzelli wrote about his friend will give you a good sense of Bill. Jeff was both his teacher and friend, and had helped us in the hayfields during summers on the farm.

> Friendly and kind to everyone, full of curiosity, [Bill] had a remarkable capacity to engage others regardless of their age, ability, or viewpoint. He was extremely generous with his time and help, and I know many of our students relied on Bill to lead them through the difficult material crammed into a modern geology curriculum. My own memories of marching through the woods to look at remote outcrops; examining thin sections that held many mysteries; trying to keep up with Bill during the hay harvesting; admiring Bill's handmade ceramic treasures in wonderment; driving students to unique mineral localities with Bill as my right-hand man; and Bill showing up at the geology party we hosted last spring with two baby lambs in the back seat of his car. These memories I will cherish!
>
> Jeff Chiarenzelli

In addition to all the great things Jeff said about him, I know Bill had a great sense of humor and rarely exhibited sadness or anger, except when drivers sped past the farm and endangered our animals. After the funeral service and the gathering back at the farm, I thought things would be as they were in my village, where close family members come together and mourned the death of a relative for weeks. Nope! Two days after the funeral, everyone went back to their own homes, leaving Ellen alone. I couldn't believe it. She and I arranged to meet in Canton for dinner on a regular basis to comfort each other. Luckily, her longtime friend, Laurie Willow, made the five-hour drive from New Paltz to stay with Ellen almost every weekend during the first couple of months after Bill died.

Life on the farm was never going to be the same again. Before the end of the year, Ellen had sold the sheep because she worked full-time at the radio station and could not take care of them—and the soon-to-be born fifty or more lambs—alone. During lambing season, someone really had to be on the farm all the time. She gave the pair of llamas, Dolly and Daisy, to Sarah Harris and her fiancé, Joe Andriano. It was so sad to see all the animals go. I really wished I could have split my time between school and the farm, but that was just not possible.

* * * * *

During International Education Week in November, I was invited for the third time to give a presentation about my experiences growing up in Cameroon, and about the challenges I faced in order to get an education in the United States. Through this process, I found many positive things to talk about regarding Cameroon and my culture—much more so than when I was actually living there. Someone once said, "When overseas, you learn more about your own country than you do the place you're visiting." That is true about my experience.

When I was in Cameroon, I spent a lot time blaming the government for the lack of opportunities for ambitious young people. But when I had the amazing experience of being in America, I allowed Americans to complain about their own government, while I worked hard to make the best of every opportunity their country presented to me. If you're looking for positive things to say about your own country, consider visiting another land. I derived a lot of pleasure from the presentations I gave on my cultural background and academic journey because people always appreciated what I had to say.

After this presentation, I was asked if I'd be interested in delivering my talk to the retirees living at Partridge Knoll on the other side of Canton, where I had a great time sharing my story and eating pizza with them. It was unexpected that among the audience were members of my church, including some who had so generously and actively supported me. But my biggest surprise on this occasion was learning that many Partridge Knoll residents knew a lot about several African countries. Some were military veterans who had served on different parts of the continent. When I told these older people I was from Cameroon, they knew exactly what I was talking about, unlike students on campus who often asked, "Where the hell is that?"

The Partridge Knoll audience had many nice things to say about different parts of Africa they had visited when they were younger. They liked the simple life, traditional music and dance, the food, and so forth. Really, it was good to be in the midst of people who didn't perceive my home continent as a place where all the native people live with wild animals and dressed like the Kalahari Bushmen.

Of course, on campus, I knew the stereotypical perceptions about Africa weren't going to disappear anytime soon, so I started having fun with it. A student once asked me: "This might sound dumb, but have you ever seen a lion while walking down the street?"

"Those lions are everywhere," I said, "and as a rite of passage, I killed my first one at the age of twelve, with a spear."

"That's so cool!"

So surprised that he completely bought this story, I laughed until tears were running down my face, and finally told him I had made it up. Since it was funny to me that people believed I had killed a lion with a spear when I was twelve, I used this story whenever anyone made incorrect assumptions about wild animals in African nations. You'd be amazed at how many people believed it.

Watching TV, I had some understanding of why Americans didn't have any positive images about the daily lives of people in African countries. Most often, only the worst stories made it into the American media. On the other hand, I wondered why my fellow students didn't re-think some of these misconceptions, considering that I attend classes with them, tutored some of them, hung out with them, and was always number one in my classes. Other than my heavy accent, I didn't think there was a big difference between me and students who were born and raised in the US.

Late in the year, the Residence Life staff took all the RAs out to a nice restaurant for the end-of-semester banquet, celebrating our efforts. We were thanked for maintaining peace in the residence halls and were fed good food. At this event, my first RA banquet, I was presented with a Certificate of Excellence "for outstanding performance in being an outstanding, open-minded, and dedicated RA, especially for the pet wing."

"In the past, I couldn't spend a single minute in the pet wing," said Javon, "but Pierre has done an excellent job to change that."

Actually, one of the main reasons I did my utmost to keep the wing clean and odor-free was because I am allergic to dirty environments. I can't explain how, but I had established great relationships with all my residents. Together we had transformed the pet wing into a place where other students liked to hang out with the cats, hamsters, and chinchillas.

The most challenging part of the RA position was convincing students to attend RA programs, most of which were aimed at getting students out of their rooms and into an environment where they would interact with each other. Many students didn't want to attend, even though we provided free snacks. According to the Residence Life rules, each program had to have at least eight students in attendance or the event had to be rescheduled.

A few minutes before the start of each program, I would run around the residence hall, telling freshmen, "There's an RA program in the main lounge, and if you don't attend, you'll lose your financial aid." Before anyone realized I was making this up, it was close to the end of the semester. And students ended up having fun at our programs, so we did have some of the best turnouts compared to other residence halls.

Though it was challenging, being an RA was turning out to be one of my best college experiences. Through training, the whole campus-wide RA staff became like family. Beside the financial help I received with the free room and board, the position provided tremendous leadership experience. I always tell students who want to make a difference on campus to become RAs.

In early December, the weather turned bitterly cold and it was painful riding my bicycle to the calculus class at St. Lawrence University. It occurred to me that maybe it had been a bad idea to cross-register, but it was too late to give it up. When I signed up for the course, some of my friends had told me that SLU students claim to be smarter than the SUNY Canton students who take courses on the SLU campus. Part of my goal was to represent SUNY Canton and prove to my SLU "course-mates" that my school was a serious institution. I studied very hard, to the point that I was able to integrate some math problems in my head. I was a little obnoxious in class, trying to answer every question the instructor asked. Nonetheless, I won a monthly SLU math-puzzle contest that came with a ten-dollar gift card, which I used to purchase a pair of winter gloves.

Back home with Ellen for the Christmas break, life on the farm just wasn't the same. There were no more animals, which meant much less work to keep us busy, and she was still grieving Bill's death. The holiday season brought back a lot of fond memories of the three of us living together on the farm, which made us sad. Neither Ellen nor I wanted to do a fancy holiday celebration. Instead, on Christmas Day, we volunteered at a local church, where we helped prepare and serve dinner to people in the community who needed a place to be or some food to enjoy at this special time of year.

During the final week of Christmas break, I told Ellen I wanted to meet Lee and Nancy Keet, who had been supporting me every semester with my tuition costs. I wanted to thank them in person for giving me the opportunity of a lifetime to continue my education in the United States. Lee and Nancy split their time between Saranac Lake, New York City, and France. Ellen communicated with them and arranged a visit at their beautiful lakeside home in the Adirondack village of Saranac Lake. For several hours, the four of us sat at the dining table drinking coffee and talking about a variety of topics. Ellen explained how I ended up on her farm, and I recounted my journey from Cameroon to the United States. It amazed me that Lee and Nancy were just as happy to help as I was happy and grateful for their ongoing financial support. All philanthropic work is beneficial, but I particularly admire Lee and Nancy, who have dedicated part of their philanthropy toward changing the lives of underprivileged people like me.

During our conversation, Ellen mentioned that she was worried about coping with the summer farm work without me. I needed to do a summer internship in my field of study, and the two companies that were interested in having me were located in Oswego and Syracuse, far from the farm. Lee told us that his friend, Mark Dzwonczyk, the president and CEO of SLIC Network Solutions in Nicholville, about an hour's drive from the farm, might have an internship opportunity for me. He promised to contact Mark to find out if there were any summer positions.

A few days after our visit in Saranac Lake, Lee contacted Mark and connected the two of us. I met with him for an interview on the campus of Clarkson University in Potsdam, about halfway between the farm and Nicholville, and was hired for a summer internship with SLIC. I had done some background research on Mark before meeting with him, and he had a history of building new tech businesses. When I told him about my aspirations in the STEM field, he said to contact him whenever I needed to, and that he had connections with some tech companies in Silicon Valley.

As a foreign student who grew up in a culture where bribery is the norm, I am always grateful when people offer to help without expecting to be paid.

38

Spring Semester 2014

One condition for my upcoming summer internship at SLIC was that I had to have a driver's license. There was no way I could get to work forty-five miles from the farm without driving myself; a bicycle just wasn't going to work. I was actually eager to get my license, and envied all the teenagers who were already out on the roads. In northern New York, there is almost no public transportation, so driving is essential for getting around. Ellen tried to give me lessons using her stick-shift Toyota Yaris, but it was very frustrating, particularly for parallel parking or starting up on a hill.

When I told my peer-tutoring supervisor, Johanna Lee, I had secured an internship with SLIC, her first question after congratulating me was, "How are you going to get there?"

"That's the problem. I have a learner's permit but I can't drive."

"I can give you driving lessons after work," she said.

So we began lessons about three times a week, using her automatic transmission car, much easier to drive than Ellen's manual transmission. I owe Johanna for taking the time to teach me how to drive. After failing the road test twice, I finally passed, had a license, and was ready for my summer internship.

As an international student, I was required to keep my identification documents up to date at all times. My passport was going to expire in May 2014, so I had to get it renewed as soon as possible.

The closest place to do that was the High Commission of Cameroon in Ottawa, Canada, about 90 minutes' drive from Canton. I thought it would be easier and more economical to renew my passport in Canada rather than making the long, expensive trip to the embassy in Washington, DC. Before trying to cross the border this time, I applied for and obtained an entry visa to Canada.

For weeks, I repeatedly called the Cameroon High Commission office in Ottawa to schedule an appointment for a passport renewal. No one ever picked up the phone. Ellen called a number of times and she, too, could not reach anyone in the embassy. Her friend Laurie happened to visit the farm and suggested we just drive to Ottawa without making an appointment. The three of us went together, and when we entered the High Commission office, we were met by a receptionist who was not happy about me showing up without an appointment.

"You can't just come here without making an appointment."

"I called many times but nobody picked up the phone."

"Look, I'm the only one here, and you can't expect me to answer every call and take care of everyone who comes in here," the receptionist said, pointing to an area with one person waiting.

"It's not his fault that you're short-staffed," Ellen said, reacting to the woman's rude and angry tone.

The receptionist, even madder now, launched into a rant about how hard her job was and the difficulties of dealing with all the demands on her time. I wasn't surprised because I was used to this type of poor customer service back home. Ellen and Laurie really didn't help the situation by trying to debate with her.

"We wouldn't be going through this if you'd just picked up the phone," Ellen said.

"You're the official representative of Cameroon; who else should he seek help from?" Laurie added.

"Why couldn't he go to the embassy in Washington?" the receptionist responded.

I was laughing inside as I listened to Ellen and Laurie debate with her. Laurie got so upset that she left the building, knowing she'd explode if she kept going. I took Ellen aside and told her to stop arguing because it wasn't going to change anything. The reception-ist left the room without further comment and we didn't know if she was going to come back. When she did return, she opened an appointment ledger and scheduled me to return in November. It was currently January, and the earliest appointment she had available was almost a year away.

"But my passport expires in May and I won't be allowed to enter Canada in November."

"We operate on a first-come, first-served basis. If someone cancels, we can move up your appointment."

"This is unbelievable," Ellen said, and walked outside to join Laurie in the car.

I took the November appointment and pleaded with the recep-tionist to call me if there was a cancellation. When I joined Ellen and Laurie in the car, they couldn't stop talking about what had hap-pened.

"It's a miracle that you made it to the United States," Ellen said.

"There are so many little things we Americans take for granted," Laurie said. "If someone treated me like this at a store, I'd call the manager."

Even though the receptionist's behavior was no surprise to me, it was sad to see that my country was represented in this way to strangers. I had been painting a good image of Cameroon and the Cameroonian people to Laurie and Ellen, but it took just a few minutes with this government bureaucrat to undo everything. As soon as we got back home, I called the Cameroonian embassy in Washington and scheduled an appointment to renew my passport during spring break.

Laurie volunteered to give me a ride to Washington, bringing along her grandsons, Asher and Ezra, for the drive. She let me drive much of the way, which was the first time I'd driven on a high-speed major highway—a risky move, but Laurie is unique.

When I arrived for my appointment at the embassy, I was expecting the same lousy service and response I'd received in Ottawa.

Instead, the staff in Washington was very professional. I was particularly impressed with the person who checked my passport application documents. He received three applicants at the same time and took a phone call—unlike the Ottawa receptionist. When I was done at the embassy, I went back into his office and thanked him for his excellent customer service, and for representing our country in such a positive light. Even though he said he was only doing his job, the comparison with the Ottawa staff person made me appreciate and respect his excellent service.

Laurie was surprised at how quickly the embassy had handled my case—in and out in just a few hours. This gave us time to visit the Smithsonian Institution Traveling Exhibition Services (SITES) before starting the long drive back to her home in New Paltz. I am so grateful to Laurie for helping with this excursion and covering all the travel expenses.

Shortly after spring break, along with other SUNY Canton students, I attended the 22nd Annual CSTEP Statewide Student Conference at the Sagamore on Lake George. This time I was more than just an attendee. I did a presentation entitled, "The Challenges of Education in Developing Countries," using my academic journey as a case study. At the end of the presentation, some students thanked me personally for sharing my story, and some said listening to my narrative made them feel ashamed of all the things they took for granted as Americans.

Renee Butterfield, the associate director of CSTEP at SUNY Canton, was impressed with my presentation. As coordinator of programs for middle school and high school students, she asked if I would share my story at St. Lawrence County sites. When I completed my PowerPoint materials, I had Renee check every slide because I didn't know what was acceptable and appropriate for a presentation to the intended audience. Then she took me to schools across the county, where I talked with students about growing up on the farm in Baligham village, and leaving my parents to attend the equivalent of middle school in a nearby town. Some of the students couldn't believe I had left home to attend middle school at a young age.

My favorite part of doing the presentations was answering students' questions on a range of topics. Even though I included photographs of myself in slides, they still asked me about the kind of clothing and shoes worn in Cameroon. Some asked questions about food, our sources of water, and what it felt like growing up without access to electricity or the internet. I can't remember all the questions I was asked, but I came away feeling that these American students did not have a good picture of life in African countries. I was happy for the opportunity to dispel some of the inaccurate information and long-held stereotypes.

From doing these presentations, I also learned about some of the things I had missed as a child growing up in Cameroon. I remember one student asking me, "What is your favorite band?" It left me tongue-tied because I knew nothing about bands when I was a child. However, I told the students that we had some of the best traditional dance groups in my village. When I tried to explain traditional dance, I hit a brick wall—American students did not really know what this meant.

During the talks, I didn't just dwell on the issues that economically challenged students in Cameroon faced on their education path. I dedicated some time to sharing information about my cultural background, and said that my friends back home in Cameroon would jump and touch the sky if they had access to half the opportunities available to American children.

Presenting at Gouverneur Central School, Gouverneur, New York

Considering how much I had learned during my time in the United States, I encouraged all the students to take advantage of any opportunity to visit other countries. As I tell my American friends, spending time in a European country is a great learning experience, but spending time in an African country is a life-changing experience. It isn't easy to paint an accurate picture of Africa to Americans who have never traveled outside of their comfort zone. I was delighted when some of the public-school students expressed an interest in visiting Cameroon someday.

* * * * *

With about one year remaining in my undergraduate education, I had to start thinking ahead about what would follow. Part of being an international student is that you do not have time to waste. Since it appeared that I would actually be completing college, I started thinking about graduate school. My hope was to remain in northern New York because I didn't want to have to start making connections and friends all over again. Luckily, Clarkson University is also located in St. Lawrence County and has an excellent graduate program in electrical engineering.

Attending graduate school was a priority for me. I didn't want to visit Clarkson by myself, so I scheduled a meeting with the former dean of the SUNY Canton Engineering Department, Dr. David Wells, to discuss my future. He was one of the people strongly encouraging me to continue my education through the PhD level. We met at a downtown restaurant and talked for hours. Afterward, Dr. Wells contacted the Department of Electrical and Computer Engineering at Clarkson University and secured a date for us to visit the campus. He and Ellen accompanied me as we met with several faculty members in the engineering program and toured some of the research labs.

When we were finished, I ranked Clarkson as my first choice for graduate school based on two main factors: besides a good academic reputation, it also had an excellent track record for placing its graduates in jobs. At that point, my next step was to start thinking about the application process.

At the end of a busy semester, I had aced all my courses and was ready to start my summer internship. In addition to receiving the CSTEP Outstanding Student Award, I was recognized at the SUNY Canton Annual Honors Convocation for having the highest cumulative GPA in the electrical engineering program. During the Annual Specialty Student Awards Ceremony, I was presented with the Leaders of Tomorrow Award: "This student is a leader of a team, group, or organization whose combined effort provided exceptional team accomplishment." I received the Spirit of Success Award, which is self-explanatory, and at our end-of-semester RA banquet, I was awarded a Certificate of Achievement for my outstanding job as an RA in Mohawk Hall.

During my early semesters in college, when I was going through so much financial trouble, I sat in my dorm room crying and asking, "Why me, Lord?" Now that things were going well and I was receiving so many honors, I felt extremely blessed, and grateful to all the people who had supported me in getting this far. I had come a long way to where I was truly loving and enjoying college life.

39

Summer 2014

When I arrived at the farm for the summer, I found Ellen had brought in two recent St. Lawrence University graduates who needed a place to stay for a short time, Danny Lobo and Joshin Atone. They were on the farm for a month or so and helped out here and there with jobs, including a complete exterior house painting Ellen had started.

At the beginning of summer, I gave myself two weeks to relax before starting my internship. In need of a cheap car for driving to work, I found an old $800 vehicle on Craigslist. When I told Ellen about it, she said I could use Bill's 2008 Toyota Corolla if I figured out how to drive a manual transmission. The car had been sitting in front of the workshop since Bill passed away. I watched YouTube videos and practiced shifting gears out in the front meadow, including stopping and starting on the hill.

When I started my internship with SLIC Network Solutions, I had an agreement with my supervisors that I could miss work whenever we had to bale hay on the farm. Though we only needed a little bit of hay now that the large animals were gone, we still had to cut and bale on all the fields to keep them in good shape. I knew how to operate the tractor and haying equipment, but I wasn't much good at fixing machines. Our Amish friend Abe was going to buy all the extra hay and, in spite of not using motorized machinery himself, he was a mechanical whiz. In exchange for a reduced price for the hay, he agreed to work with us in the hayfields.

When the weather cooperated, I cut as much hay as I could. Then I windrowed it with the rotary mower rake while Ellen followed with the baler. As soon as I was done windrowing, I detached the mower and hitched the hay wagon to the smaller tractor. After we loaded hay bales onto the wagon, our friend Jochen hitched it to his pickup truck for the trip to Abe's home about ten miles away, where Abe's children unloaded and stacked the hay in their barn. Considering the amount of energy involved in haying, I was glad that I didn't have to put any away in our barn. Ellen and Abe were very proud of me for successfully running our haying operation. As for me, I had a lot of fun bossing people around.

Haying wasn't the only farm work to be done that summer. Ellen still used wood as the primary heating fuel, with an oil boiler only there for backup. I had to ensure that there was enough wood stacked for the coming winter season. Since I was busy with my internship most weekdays—traveling the region to install TV, telephone, and high-speed internet for SLIC customers—I cut wood on the weekends. While Danny and Joshin were still on the farm, they helped me load logs onto the wagon after I felled and bucked up trees. I taught them how to use the wood splitter so they could run it on weekdays while I was at work. I don't like to blow my own horn, but I was the master wood stacker on the farm. I loved making nice stacks along the fence line between the house and barn, giving people something to look at as they drove by.

James (Jimmy) Vanornum, an older disabled man who lived about a quarter mile down the road, was one of my favorite people. As a teenager, he had survived a house fire that killed his entire family except for one sister. Later, he was in a car accident, and during the rescue process, the responders dropped an engine on his head. He had mental disabilities, but he was a hard worker and spent most of his time helping neighbors with a variety of jobs. Jimmy liked me because I always spent time with him—talking and laughing—when he walked down the road to visit us on a daily basis.

Felling and bucking trees

As for my internship, I found it boring during the first few weeks because I was sitting at a desk doing drafting work all day. But as soon as I joined the construction and installation crew, it was a lot of fun and I learned a great deal. It gave me a chance to travel around the region and get to know more about the places and people of northern New York.

My internship with SLIC ended about two weeks before the start of the fall 2014 semester. I spent this time clearing brush from our fields and helped Ellen finish painting the farmhouse and barn. During the last weekend before I returned to college, we had one of our traditional suppers with our Amish friend Abe and his family, including his wife, Lizzy, and their ten children. This was a "sweet and salty" supper consisting of cake, jams, huge bowls of freshly popped corn, and a selection of various ice creams that we contributed to the meal.

Danny and Joshin had left the farm midsummer to work in Massachusetts and New York City, respectively. However, Mike, the young man Bill had kicked off the farm two years earlier, was back, having lost his job because he couldn't get along with his boss. Ellen allowed him to return so he could figure out what to do for the long term. She's one of those people who can't say no.

40

Fall Semester 2014

Ellen had given me Bill's Toyota to use at school, so I could now drive myself back to campus. It was exciting that I no longer had to ask friends for rides to the stores, which was a big change. And as for my belongings, I realized they had more than quadrupled since my first semester. Rewinding back to the day I left Cameroon, and comparing it to the current state of my academic career, I had to agree with what Ellen and Rev. Mike had been telling me: I had come a long way. In spite of all the obstacles to overcome along my path, I was enjoying every moment of my life at this point.

When the semester officially began on August 25, I was sad to hear that Dr. Joseph Hoffman had returned to SUNY Maritime College after serving for a year as acting president at SUNY Canton. When Dr. Hoffman had first arrived, Ellen and I both explained my financial situation to him, and he agreed to put me on academic deferment while Ellen and Rev. Mike searched for the money needed to cover my costs. As I got to know Dr. Hoffman through my participation in many events—especially those that involved free food—he became one of my favorite people on campus.

The new SUNY Canton leader, Dr. Zvi Szafran, turned out to be a very good president, too. During my first week of classes, Ellen and I went to talk with him about how I needed tuition deferment because I couldn't pull together the costs of a semester all at once.

This was now the fourth president of the college Ellen had talked with about my situation. To my great surprise, it turned out that Dr. Szafran had been to Cameroon and understood the challenges of getting an education in that part of the world. He was also full of praise for the food and cultural experiences he enjoyed in my home country. Most importantly, he agreed to contact the financial aid office to have them put me on academic deferment. By this time, in addition to the money I saved by being an RA, I had a few merit scholarships. There was far less to cover financially, and I wasn't scared about getting kicked out of school anymore.

Because I had overloaded myself with so many courses in previous years, I only had to sign up for twelve credits in fall 2014. This worked out well, allowing some time for me to enjoy my senior year. My favorite events were the biweekly student-faculty mixers. There was always plenty of finger food, and those of us old enough to drink could enjoy up to two beers. (I might bring another older student with me who didn't drink so I could have some extra beers.) Kudos to the person who created these events, where the atmosphere allowed students to have casual conversations with faculty and staff, and everyone talked about things other than schoolwork.

During this semester, two faculty members from PKFokam Institute in Yaoundé, Cameroon, paid a visit to SUNY Canton, and I was invited by the president's office to meet them. It was a pleasure to mingle with people from my homeland for the first time since my departure. I gave them a tour of our labs and other interesting locations on campus.

"How much does it cost to attend PKFokam?" I asked.

"About 2.5 million FCFA."

"Oh. That's why I didn't know about the school."

We all laughed. The beauty of growing up poor is that you learn to ignore things you can't afford and only embrace goals that are within your reach. Even these two faculty members of PKFokam admitted that the institution wasn't affordable for an average Cameroonian family. It crossed my mind that if I were still in Cameroon, I wouldn't have the privilege of spending time with two individuals of their stature. In any case, they were visiting to develop a partnership between the two schools so that some PKFokam students could spend their senior year of college on the SUNY Canton campus.

As the semester progressed, another faculty member from PKFokam visited our campus. I had a one-on-one conversation with him and agreed to be a contact person for any students at his school who wanted more information about life at SUNY Canton. He asked if I would be willing to return to Cameroon to teach at PKFokam if they paid for my graduate studies. I told him that if his offer had come when I was still in Cameroon, or even at the beginning of my college studies in the US when I was under great financial stress, I would have accepted his generous offer wholeheartedly, but at this point I had to turn it down. From my perspective, it had taken my entire family and many people in America to get me through my college education. I didn't want anyone from Cameroon to step in near the end of that effort and take credit for my success.

As a resident assistant, I was obliged to host high school students who visited the campus and spent a weekend exploring SUNY Canton. The purpose of their stay was to experience a little bit of college life and help them decide if they wanted to attend this school. I was surprised at how hard colleges worked to attract high school students. When I spent time hanging out in my dorm room with them, I realized that the prospects of having fun and enjoying lots of parties were among the main reasons for students to choose a particular college. I had come to love partying on the weekends, so I understood why having fun was important to these youngsters. However, I envied them—they were fortunate to be born in a country where one of their major problems was choosing from a list of colleges. Meanwhile, high school students in other parts of the world simply dreamed of having a chance to attend *any* college.

I convinced the four students I had entertained in my room to make SUNY Canton their first choice among the available options. After returning to the city, they called and had me talk with their parents. I was successful in persuading pretty much any undecided student to choose SUNY Canton.

I was honored when Stacia Dutton and Renee Butterfield, CSTEP staff members, asked me to be their annual guest speaker. Given how close I was to graduation, they thought it would be a good idea for me to share my story with the entire campus community. Some people didn't really believe the things I told them about my life in Cameroon and making it to America. I put together a PowerPoint presentation with photographs to illustrate my talking points, and delivered it at the Kingston Theater on campus.

Among those attending were students, faculty, staff, and President Szafran. In my younger days, never would I have imagined finding myself in America, speaking to a full-house audience about my life. Most people on campus had come to know me as just Pierre the Peer Tutor, or Pierre the RA. Through my presentation, people learned much more about the real me.

* * * * *

In addition to schoolwork and extracurricular activities, I began working on my application package for graduate school. I studied for about two months and then took the GRE general test. The next step was to write a personal statement or application essay. I spent much time online researching tips on how to write a good graduate school application essay. There were lots of good hints but plenty of conflicting advice.

After much thought, I decided to write a personal statement based on my academic journey all the way from Cameroon to the United States. It was easy for me to write it because I have very clear memories of everything I did educationally since my first days in primary school. I took the draft essay to the Career Service Center and had Katie Kennedy edit it. With all her corrections and suggestions, it was much smoother and was shortened from three pages to two. I was glad that Clarkson University didn't place a limit on the page count.

I submitted my online application, including the essay, in December for an early admission response. That way, if I was turned down by Clarkson, there was still time left for applying to other graduate schools.

The final step of my graduate school application process was to get three letters of reference. Even though most of the faculty and staff on campus were willing to put in a good word for me—something I greatly appreciated—I wanted a diverse group of references, including someone who knew my academic background. Such a person could vouch for my achievements and my motivation to pursue an advanced degree.

With that in mind, I chose my advisor, Dr. Frempong, to write one of the reference letters. In addition to being my advisor for four years, he knew and understood my struggles and my determination to get an education. I looked up to Dr. Frempong as a father figure; he had even purchased textbooks for the classes I took with him.

I chose Johanna Lee, my peer-tutoring supervisor, to write one of the letters. Johanna had also known me since my first semester, when she had initially turned me down for a job in the tutoring center. Her son Rylan had adopted me as his big brother, so Johanna had become a mother figure for me. The role she played in easing my transition from Cameroon to America can never be overestimated. She was one of the few people who knew about my academic performance and work ethic.

For the third letter, I wanted someone outside of my campus life. I contacted Mark Dzwonczyk, the president and CEO of SLIC, where I had done my summer internship. While working there, I had spoken with Mark about my future aspirations, and he offered to help whenever I needed his support. In addition, he was on the Clarkson University Board of Trustees.

At the end of the fall semester, I had completed the admissions application documentation, submitted everything to Clarkson University, and was waiting anxiously for the outcome.

41

Spring Semester 2015: Part One

As the New Year began, I started planning for a trip back home to see my family before starting graduate studies in the United States. More than four years of being away from home was tough, and I couldn't wait to reunite with them. After talking with Ellen during the Christmas break about a trip to Cameroon, I thought it was the right time to realize one of my long-held dreams: to create a nonprofit organization which could provide scholarships and supplies to students and schools in my village.

During my years at Canton, Ellen and I had talked about creating an NGO (nongovernmental organization; a nonprofit), an idea that came to me when I received my first paycheck of $68 from my first campus job. Getting paid at the rate of $7.50/hour at the time, I imagined how an hour or two of my time and money could pay the yearly school fee of a primary-school student back home. Because so many people had supported me throughout my undergraduate years—without expecting anything in return—it was time for me to start giving something back to the community.

By simply sharing my story, I knew I could inspire American students to make the best out of the abundant opportunities available to them. As for students back in Cameroon, I knew it would take more than just inspirational words: they needed financial and material support in order to make it through school. I knew that twenty dollars could put a child through a year of school in Cameroon, or purchase a classroom bench, or buy a box of chalk. That seemed like an appealing way to encourage people to contribute to an NGO—to help children who did not have access to free public schools or even the most basic learning supplies. For families in my village, paying twenty dollars for a child to attend school is a huge and often impossible financial burden.

I drafted a mission statement for the NGO, and Ellen helped with the paperwork to register with New York State as a nonprofit named Against All Odds: Outreach for Learning (AAOOL). One of her radio-station colleagues, Bill Haenel, helped us create a website free of charge. Finally, we set up a GoFundMe page with an initial target of $7,000, enough money for fifty to seventy scholarships plus the purchase of some basic classroom supplies. This seemed like a good way to launch the NGO during my return visit to Baligham.

From the first week of classes, I had a feeling my final undergraduate semester was going to be remarkable. Clarkson University confirmed in late January that I had been accepted into their Electrical Engineering MS program. I was so happy and relieved. This meant I didn't have to research and apply to other graduate schools across the United States. Although I was only offered a partial scholarship, I was still pleased because Clarkson is located just ten miles from Canton and about thirty miles from the farm. Ellen and Laurie offered to pay the remaining portion of my graduate-school costs, with the understanding that I would pay them back, interest free, once I was out in the work force.

* * * * *

Johanna invited me to speak to her First Year Experience Program (FYEP) students. The FYEP had helped ease my own transition into the college environment. I prepared a short PowerPoint presentation to accompany my remarks to her students, but had no idea that I would have a real impact on them. I learned later that the students had written "reflection" essays after my talk, and these were being circulated around campus. Some were as inspirational as my presentation to the students who wrote them.

Reflection Essay #1: Darian Hines

Last Tuesday morning at 11:50, I walked out of your class feeling astronomically inspired and completely dedicatel. I learned [from] Pierre that if you want a better life for yourself, you have to make sacrifices and not excuses. His will to pursue his education is so commendable. How he faced all setbacks and factors that made it difficult and extremely challenging to get to SUNY Canton, a place that is often looked down on and made fun of because of misconceptions about the learning level provided by the institution.

However, a place like this doesn't sound bad to a person coming from a poor village in Cameroon, Africa. The will and ambition Pierre kept throughout his journey to bettering his life is taken for granted and simply not used by most young people in modern America because of things like federal aid to funding public school systems. So kids grow up thinking it's an obligation rather than a chance to establish yourself as a successful contributor to the world around you and close and abroad.

So you ask me what changes I will make after hearing this man's story? I will stop finding little excuses to not do things that ultimately hold great value to bettering my everyday life. I will stop taking all the chances that I have for bettering my everyday life for granted. I will use the inspiration and motivation I gained from Pierre to go forth and establish a better living for me, my family I have now and to come, and the world around me.

What I like about Pierre's presentation is that, throughout his presentation he was never seeking any sympathy or pity. He carried himself with an attitude of knowing what needs to be done for himself and doing it without question. Almost as if there wasn't an alternative option. This reflects on me personally, because of the same background that includes little financial opportunities to take the steps to better life. I grew up with two other siblings with one parent who worked day and night and barely made a 5-digit salary. I fell into the wrong crowd at a young age, but I watched the people around me as we were growing up and the decisions they made, the same decisions I was also making and the consequences from those decisions. They range from living off your parents in your twenties and sometimes thirties to spending life in and out of somebody's correctional facility. Nowhere in the middle were "gaining an education" or "making a better life for yourself and others around you."

So this is where I had to drop a lot of friends, become a different person, and do the right thing. All by myself. With no excuses I knew it was what I had to do.

Reflection Essay #2: Hannah Hill

I'd like to start off by saying I really enjoy your class. Already I have learned so much about things to do, places to find things in the library, and that I can make it through college. Moving into the dorms has been a really hard transition for me. I haven't really had a stable home in the past year, and now I'm living with a complete stranger.

After sitting in on Pierre's presentation, I realized I've had everything handed to me and done for me my whole life. College really is the first thing I've ever done for myself, and this is going to reflect on where I go and what I do in the future. I now see people who have had it much harder, in not only everyday life tasks, but in living conditions too. Pierre didn't live in a big beautiful house, he lived in a little house, being one of 17 children; they didn't even have good drinking water. The teachers weren't really teachers, and the schools were made of mud-bricks. I can't believe I used to think my school was bad.

I guess now after listening to this presentation I know I need to and have already been taking school very seriously. Some people don't have the privilege to go to school. Some people in this world don't even have "the right" to go to school. I used to hate school, and just thought college was something you had to do after high school and it would all just be the same drama and a different location. I was totally wrong, and Pierre opened my eyes to see that teachers here can be your friends if you let them, and students won't bother you if you don't bother them. I actually enjoy doing my homework now more knowing Pierre had to sneak to school in the morning, and use his brother's old uniform.

I really hope you have someone similar to Pierre in future classes, though I don't think you'll be able to find someone with a story as touching as Pierre's story. I really enjoyed this presentation. It most definitely wasn't a presentation you walked away from with nothing. I walked away with a better attitude toward my family, my schoolwork, and my everyday life. I hope SUNY Canton never decides to get rid of this class. I know it's going to be so helpful to me. I hope others walk away with as much knowledge that I feel I'm going to from attending this class.

Reflection Essay #3: Jessica Casper

I chose to write my first event paper on Pierre Nzuah's presentation. I really enjoyed him taking time to come speak with us about his country and experiences. I think it's important for people to see and hear about other people's culture, especially one so very different from our society. Sometimes it's very easy to take for granted small things that others would give their life for. I learned a lot about his culture and country and was fascinated by how different it is than America. They have to work hard for everything they have, so they appreciate things that we as a society just have handed to us.

I think that he is a great asset to Canton because he can offer knowledge that others can't. He taught me to make the best of every experience and the opportunities offered here at college and in life. He is a great inspiration to me and think it is great he's trying to help other people in his country to succeed also. Pierre is a great example of how just one person can make an impact on many things and it's better to make the best of every situation instead of only seeing the negative. When he was denied school by his own family, he fought for what he wanted because he knew it was the right thing to do in the end.

I will always think about him and how far he came when I feel like I can't accomplish something, or people tell me I can't do it.

I have included some of these essays because they inspired so many students at SUNY Canton, and they might be motivational for readers of this text. Soon after my presentation, students started coming to me to ask questions about my country, culture, and educational experiences. President Szafran wrote about my FYEP presentation in his weekly blog, "From the Pouch."

Pierre Speaks at FYEP—Students Listen

Lots of our first-year students at SUNY-Canton are participating in the First Year Experience Program (FYEP), which focuses on how to make a successful beginning in your studies. Johanna Lee, one of the FYEP section teachers, invited Pierre Nzuah to come in and tell about his own experiences at Canton.

Pierre is a student from the Cameroons in West Africa, where life is considerably different than in the US. He is part of a large (but very poor) family, living in a mud-brick house in a small village there. I've heard him speak before—how he had to live on his own (subsisting on just a dollar a day) while going to high school on the other side of the country, how he came to the US and when he first came to Canton, didn't have a coat because he hadn't heard about our winters, and how he's had to work, scrimp, save, and get help from others to be able to afford to keep going to college.

Along the way, he has participated in everything on campus, made friends with essentially everyone— the whole campus and town all know him! It's a remarkable story of determination, perseverance, and ultimately, success, because Pierre will be graduating this year, and I'll be proud and humbled to shake his hand as he does so.

The most recent time I saw Pierre was at the hockey game on Friday, where he was sporting a very thick white fur hat and looking every bit the North Country regular.

I've had a chance to see essays that some of the FYEP students wrote about Pierre's talk, and they were remarkable too. Many of the students commented on how they thought their lives had been hard until they heard about Pierre's far more challenging path. They realized that they were lucky to have gotten the opportunity to get an education, and were now more determined to take advantage of that opportunity, and not let the small things stop them.

Those are pretty important insights, which we'd all do well to remember.

Dr. Zvi Szafran

I never expected praise from SUNY Canton because the school had given me so much, more than I had ever expected. The love that I received from staff and faculty, especially those in the Residence Life and International Programs offices, was simply too much. Though I thought I would be attending college in a place like New York City when I left Cameroon, ending up in Canton, New York, turned out to be the best thing that could have happened to me. I don't think I would have been able to complete college if I had found myself in a big city. After visiting New York City and seeing how people didn't even know their neighbors, it seemed that I was lucky to have ended up in a remote area where I had the opportunity to easily integrate and become a part of the community.

* * * * *

Now, back to life on campus during my last semester. I was doing an hourly tour around the residence hall during one of my weekend shifts when I came across a group of students hanging out in the pet wing and making a lot of noise. I wasn't a big fan of weekend shifts because this was when students were most likely to get into crazy behavior. This was my last semester, and during the weekends I wanted to be somewhere having fun myself. In any case, I told these students, a group of more than ten, to keep the noise down. During my subsequent round, the noise level had increased and some of the other residents were starting to complain. I gave the noisy group a second warning and said that, as much as I liked to see them chilling with friends, I'd have to kick them out of the lounge if they continued to be so noisy.

As I was climbing the stairs to the third floor, one of the students yelled at me: "Go back to Africa!"

That really hurt. For the four years that I had been in America, no one had ever said something like that to me. I walked back into the lounge and couldn't control my emotions.

"Whoever the f*ck you are, you do not dare to tell me where to go. Ignorant students like you tarnish the reputation of this school. Say one more f*cking word and we'll see who will be leaving this campus...."

Everyone was quiet as I ranted, using profanity that I had been specifically trained to not use as an RA. I walked away and went back to the RA office, where it occurred to me that I was supposed to write up the student for saying what he said to me, but I had yelled at the whole group without asking which individual had said those words. The truth is, I had no regrets about my reaction because I would have felt worse if I hadn't gotten the rage out of me.

This incident got me thinking. I was actually born in an African country, but still was offended when a white student told me to go back to Africa. How painful is it for millions of Americans who are often treated like second-class citizens in their own country, and even told to go back to Africa when they have no connection to any place but America?

Back on the positive track, I was walking along after leaving the dining hall one day, talking with Julia Wais, and we ended up in the Habitat for Humanity (HFH) Club meeting in Payson Hall. I was warmly welcomed into the club by the advisor, Joanne Fassinger, and by others in the meeting. They didn't know I had kind of inadvertently ended up there, but I joined on the spot because Mrs. Fassinger was one of my favorite people on campus and I didn't want to disappoint her.

It turned out I knew everyone in the club, and I liked the work they were doing to help the campus become more "green." On a weekly basis, members went around to each of the residence halls, collecting returnable bottles and cans to fundraise for the spring-break trip, which took them to places where they could work with HFH affiliates on building affordable houses for low-income families. Unfortunately, I couldn't join the weekly bottle-collection work because it conflicted with my nightly tutoring schedule. However, once the bottles had been collected, I helped to sort and bag them on Saturdays.

Our biggest collection campaign was a drive in the village of Canton. The first step was to advertise our campaign by handing out flyers to local residents and asking them to hold onto their bottles and cans for our collection day a week later.

One cold, winter Saturday, members were dropped off at various locations around Canton to pass out the flyers explaining that we were raising money to work with HFH in Florida during our spring break. Julia Wais and I were in charge of the same street, each taking one side—and something strange happened. Every time I knocked on a door, someone would open it and then close it in my face. People would crack their door open and talk to me. I showed my Habitat for Humanity badge to prove I was a SUNY Canton student, and then I introduced myself.

"Hi, my name is Pierre Nzuah and I am a member of the SUNY Canton Habitat for Humanity club. I'm here to advertise our community bottle-and-can drive next Saturday."

Although there were a few exceptions, most people refused to take the flyer from me. Someone flatly said, "I don't have any bottles for you, sir." When I responded that the collection day was still a week away, this person reiterated, "I said I don't have any bottles for you, sir."

This kind of hostile reception continued for a while, and I started feeling uncomfortable because I was making other people uncomfortable. I had been in America long enough to know that the use of "sir" in this context was unwelcoming or reflected fear.

I didn't really know how to explain to Julia what was happening. Maybe it was okay or normal for people to be afraid when a black man dressed in winter gear showed up at their door, but this was the first time this had happened to me and I found it hard to understand. I called Julia over from the other side of the street and asked if she'd be willing to do a few houses with me.

I made her stand to the side with the flyers while I knocked on the doors and did the introduction. After a few buildings, Julia couldn't believe what she'd seen.

"What's going on?" she asked.

"What?" I pretended I didn't know what she was talking about.

"Don't you see how they keep slamming the door in your face?"

"That's exactly what I wanted you to see. I didn't know how to explain it to you."

"Oh my god, I can't believe this is happening."

I switched with Julia: she did the door knocking, while I stayed back and handed the flyers to her. This worked and everything went smoothly. During my time in America, I had really only interacted with friendly people and audiences, like the members of my church, or students on campus, or attending events and parties with my farm family. I don't want to make too much of this incident, but it gave me a better understanding about the racial stories I heard from my black friends who grew up in the city.

When Julia told Mrs. Fassinger about what had happened, she was furious. She apologized to me but I told her it was okay. On our collection days, she assigned me to students' apartment complexes. This turned out to be a great idea. I came across places where students held a lot of parties, which meant I was able to collect hundreds of bottles and cans.

I was sorry I hadn't joined Habitat for Humanity Club earlier in my college career. It was a well-organized and well-run group. During spring break, fourteen students and three advisors traveled to Florida to help HFH of South Palm Beach build homes.

Habitat for Humanity Club in Florida

We arrived in Florida on a Friday and were put up at a church in Boca Raton. The following day, we cleaned and sorted used merchandise at a Habitat ReStore in Boca Raton before moving to a church house in South Palm Beach, where we would be based for the rest of our stay. This was a nice, one-story house with an outdoor pool—where I almost drowned. I thought I could just dive into the pool and start swimming like little kids do. It turned out I was wrong and drank a lot of pool water before being rescued by Antonio Ortiz, who had thought I was playing a joke at first.

For a week, we worked on two homes in Delray Beach and Boynton Beach. We painted, helped put up ceilings, and worked hard on the project—typically from around eight in the morning until three in the afternoon—before spending the rest of our time at the beach and sightseeing. I had made two field trips to Florida with the IEEE club, but that wasn't nearly as fulfilling as the trip with HFH, where our work directly benefited someone who needed help. I was especially touched by the story of an immigrant woman from Brazil. She was so grateful to HFH for giving her the opportunity to own a home. Like me, she had come a long way.

On two occasions, SUNY Canton alumni took us to fancy restaurants, which made me realize that you can be connected to your college for your whole life. We finished our work on Friday and spent Saturday, our one day off, visiting Lion Country Safari and Loxahatchee National Wildlife Refuge before boarding a plane back to cold and wintry northern New York State.

* * * * *

Knowing that I would be the first person in my family to graduate with a college degree, I thought it would be so joyful to have two of my siblings from Cameroon come to America to watch me walk across the graduation stage. The cost wasn't a problem because Ellen's sister-in-law, Nancy Knoble (who referred to me as her nephew), had offered to pay for a round-trip ticket for one of my brothers as a graduation gift. I had saved enough money from my campus jobs to fund the other ticket. I chose my cousin Samuel because I had lived with him in Yaoundé for over three years before traveling to the US.

From the day I was accepted into SUNY Canton, his dream was to be present at my graduation. I chose my brother Vincent as the second person because he was the eldest son, and everyone looked up to him as a father figure. He was equally excited to attend my graduation ceremony.

We knew that getting visitor visas from the US embassy in Cameroon wasn't going to be easy. I contacted the president's office at SUNY Canton, and invitation letters were prepared for Samuel and Vincent. Ellen wrote one of them and included a bank statement that demonstrated her financial capacity to pay for my family members during their visit. Both letters were mailed, but sadly, despite many attempts, neither Samuel nor Vincent were granted visas.

If my siblings were rich and had big bank accounts to prove it, they would have easily been granted visas. It's said that money can't buy everything, but as someone who was born into poverty, I know how money can make life so much easier for people. Instead of having my siblings at the graduation ceremony, I promised to post as many photographs as possible to Facebook.

On a positive note, I received a letter from the office of the chancellor of SUNY. I had been selected to attend a ceremony at the Egg Performing Arts Center in Albany to receive the Chancellor's Award for Student Excellence. I invited Johanna Lee and my little American brother, Rylan, to be my guests at the ceremony.

I don't know if I deserved this award more than some of the other graduating seniors, but I was incredibly honored. The road to this successful moment hadn't been easy, but all the hard work and determination were gradually paying off. I believe I accepted the honor for all the poor kids around the world struggling to get a basic education and thinking all hope is lost. I often doubted this quote, but it would come to mind when life was roughing me up: "Don't ever give up, because the boulders that you face today will be the same ones that build your castle tomorrow."

I didn't enjoy growing up poor, but the constant battle to overcome economic hardship had helped me learn how to become independent and develop a fighting spirit that pushed me past adversity.

(L-R) Johanna Lee and Rylan Easton Lee-Powell with Pierre, recipient of the SUNY Chancellor's Award for Student Excellence

I don't think I would be the strong person I am today if I were born with a silver spoon in my mouth. In other words, I want to tell all the underprivileged kids in the world that hard work and resilience are the keys to success, and it's possible to fight past the economic circumstances we are born into.

42

Spring Semester 2015: Part Two

Towards the end of the semester, an email was sent out inviting students to participate in the Dr. James M. Payson Speaking Prize Competition. It was scheduled to mark the official inauguration of President Zvi Szafran around the theme of "Always Moving Forward," and competitors were asked to discuss how they could incorporate the theme into their own lives. The intimidating part of this competition was that the winner would present his or her speech during the inauguration ceremony.

At first I wasn't interested in the competition, but then I learned that the winner would receive a prize of $250. There was no chance I was going to let that amount of money slide by without giving it a shot. I quickly put together a two-page speech and had Melissa Manchester from the Writing Center edit it.

> Chancellor Zimpher,
> Dignitaries and honored guests,
> Dr. Szafran and family,
> Faculty and fellow students:
>
> I started my college studies in Electrical Technology at SUNY Canton in January 2011 when the four-year electrical technology program was still new. Just four years later, I am proud to say that I will be gradu-

ating from an ABET Accredited program. During my stay at SUNY Canton, the international student population has increased. Every year, I meet more and more students from Sri Lanka, China, and Canada. Even the number of students from my home country, Cameroon, has recently increased from one to three.

During my studies, I have watched SUNY Canton move through challenges. But you know what? SUNY Canton takes these challenges and embraces them as opportunities.

We are always moving forward, and never backwards. That is the spirit of the SUNY Canton I am talking about! "Always moving forward!" This sounds like a perfect phrase to describe my educational journey. I grew up in a small village in a rural area of Cameroon where my parents were subsistence farmers and lived without access to electricity. I was the eleventh of seventeen children, so my parents had me stay at home to take care of my younger siblings while they went to the farm.

With no free education in my country, my father did not want to send me to school because my two older siblings who graduated from high school did not get jobs to pay back his money as he had anticipated. But I was determined to get an education.

At the age of eight, I started going to primary school without my father's knowledge. When he found out, he was angry and said he would only pay for my school attendance costs if I was the first in my class. The first semester I was the fifth, BUT in the third semester I was first! And he paid for my school costs.

From an early age, I have been driven by an eagerness to learn. While I did not realize it at the time, my experiences growing up in a village without electricity fostered in me a desire to attain an education, pursue undergraduate and graduate study in the field of electrical engineering, and ultimately give back to my community.

In the fall, I will be starting my graduate studies at Clarkson University, and I have already created a non-profit organization through which I will be helping underprivileged children back in Cameroon.

SUNY Canton has definitely made my dreams come true. As I graduate in May, I foresee SUNY Canton as the internet of colleges:

➤ A global village where you can meet faculty and students from all over the world
➤ A college of continual progress
➤ The most successful distance learning college in the world
➤ A school that makes the dream of even an underprivileged student like me from a rural area of Cameroon come true

A college that is not only welcoming and friendly-looking, but one that is fiercely competitive and always thrives for success because we are the Kangaroos.

Let's go Roos!

If you are wondering why I used "kangaroo" in my speech, here's the explanation. As I learned from the campus website, "SUNY Canton has adopted the kangaroo as its nickname, logo, and mascot" as of 2007 "because the marsupial can only move forward, reflecting the college's progress and mission." If you attend a SUNY Canton hockey game, "Let's go Roos" is the common chant. Well, the explanation sound pretty good, but I have always questioned the choice of a kangaroo, considering that the college is located in Canton, in northernmost New York State—more of a deer and coyote place.

I delivered my speech in front of a panel of judges, only taking an occasional peek at my script because I had it memorized. I won the competition.

Pierre Nzuah and Dr. Svi Szafran

After receiving a framed copy of my address and a check for $250, I presented the speech at President Zvi Szafran's inauguration. Among those in the audience was Dr. Anthony (Tony) Collins, the president of Clarkson University, where I was heading next for my graduate studies. I later met him at an event on the Clarkson campus, and he recalled listening to my speech at the inauguration ceremony.

"I told my wife the best student from SUNY Canton is coming to Clarkson."

When I received my speaking prize, I didn't want to spend it on pizza. I wanted to invest the money in something that would keep the memory and meaning of the competition alive. I thought about my brother, Ntinwa Job, who had some physical disabilities and who had completed primary school several years ago. However, my parents couldn't afford to send him to secondary school. I considered Job the smartest person in my family and I hated to see him without any educational opportunity. I called him and asked if he would be interested in attending FLEXCOM Institute in Bamenda, the computer training institution I had attended after high school. He embraced the idea, so I immediately contacted the director at FLEXCOM, Mr. Khan Felix, via Facebook. I negotiated a price for my brother's tuition, which reflected a small discount because I was an alumnus.

Job enrolled at FLEXCOM, and I used the speaking prize money to pay for his tuition. Then I used some money I had saved from my on-campus jobs to purchase a cheap laptop he needed for his studies. I also paid for his house rent and provided him with some extra cash for pocket money because I didn't want my parents to have to take on any financial burden.

Before I came up with this idea, Job had been living in Douala with my first younger brother, Festus, who told me that Job had been on the verge of getting married, but when he was given the opportunity to go back to school he immediately called it off. I wasn't against him getting married, but I wondered how he was going to provide for a family without having any direct source of income. Job told me he had begun to believe that nobody in the family cared about his well-being. He was very grateful for the opportunity to pursue some kind of education.

I had accomplished so much during my time at college, but spring 2015 was truly remarkable. I was recognized for the fourth consecutive time at the SUNY Canton Annual Honor Convocation Ceremony for having the highest GPA in my class. During this same ceremony, I was presented with the prestigious David R. Maynard Student Activities Award. It is given each year to honor a member of the graduating class who has demonstrated superior citizenship, outstanding leadership, and dedication to extracurricular activities.

Aside from my willingness to do so, I engaged in a lot of extra-curricular activities because I was limited to only twenty hours of work-study per week. My American classmates, on the other hand, could work more hours on or off campus. The preferential treatment for citizens is understandable, but I think foreign students should be allowed to work as many hours as they need or want to. I under-

State University
of New York
at Canton

David R. Maynard
Student Activities
Award

Pierre Nzuah

2015

Student Activities Award

stand that the primary goal for international students is to gain an education, but I believe that before coming to college, many foreign students like me have already learned to balance education and work time. Every semester, there were more students than I was allowed to help who wanted me as their one-on-one tutor; I had the time, but couldn't go beyond the maximum of twenty hours of work each week. It would have been a win-win situation if I had been allowed to tutor for as many hours as I thought possible, making money for myself while helping students who needed my assistance.

* * * * *

In preparation for a much-anticipated trip back home, I was working on raising money and supplies for our NGO, Against All Odds: Outreach for Learning (AAOOL). I received donations from several people on campus, from the First Presbyterian congregation, and from others across northern New York. The SUNY Canton Early Childhood Club on campus wanted to help, but they weren't allowed to make monetary contributions. Instead, they ran a pen-and-pencil drive through which they collected thousands for us to bring to Cameroon. The effort was coordinated by Dr. Maureen Maiocco and Mrs. Rhonda Rodriguez. I was so thankful to the club. Those pens and pencils would be much appreciated by the students and schools in my village.

On April 12, I was asked by Rajiv Narula to speak about our nonprofit organization to members of the United University Professions (UUP) at their end-of-semester gathering. I gave a short speech about the goals of Against All Odds and drank wine with the UUP members, after which they raised a total of $268 to go to the NGO. This was much appreciated.

On April 28, I was invited to share my experiences and talk about the importance of education at the Boys & Girls Club in Massena, a town about thirty miles northeast of Canton. After talking and going through a Q&A session with these boys and girls,

Early Childhood Club donates pencils and pens to AAOOL

I met and shook hands with the mayor of Massena, Tim Currier. This would have been an incredibly big deal in Cameroon, but it seemed normal in America for a person of his stature to mingle with the common people. Before I left Massena, two members of the club presented me with a check for twenty-five dollars to benefit Against All Odds. These children were making a big difference with their gift, enabling a child in my village to attend school for a full year. This donation would have covered my fees for five of the seven years I was in primary school, back when it cost about five dollars per year. Remember the trouble I had getting my father to provide even this modest amount each year for my fees.

As the big day approached, I still didn't believe I was finally going to be a college graduate. I knew it was time to leave SUNY Canton because almost everyone there knew me by name. As an admissions concierge, I could talk about almost any school program on campus—like International Relations, Career Services, CSTEP, or Habitat for Humanity—during open-house events designed to attract students and their parents to campus.

In preparation for my graduation party, I sent out invitations to everyone who had supported me morally or financially during my college years. My friend, Marsha Osei, agreed to prepare several African dishes for the celebration. She is a great cook!

On commencement day, May 9, 2015, I put on my robe, honor cords, and the six honor medals I had received during my undergraduate years. As I looked at myself in the mirror, it seemed like a dream, and I felt proud for what I had accomplished. I thought back to the day at the end of my very first semester, watching graduating seniors walking in their robes to the commencement ceremony. I remember wishing at the time I was one of them, but thinking I would never get to this moment. It seemed like ages since then, but I was finally going to have a sweet ending to my improbable quest to obtain a college education.

Throughout my undergraduate studies, I had received a total of twenty-two awards and academic honors. After a series of straight As, I had improved my GPA from a mere 3.75/4.0 during my first semester to 3.92, and was graduating with highest honors. I had taken every advanced math course offered at SUNY Canton, and worked with Mr. Fred Saburro to develop a curriculum for a graph theory course. God knows, I counted my lucky stars and felt like the most blessed person in the world. Most important among all those accomplishments: I had made long-lasting friends and found myself a new family in America.

All attempts to bring two of my family members from Cameroon had failed, so they would not see me walk across the graduation stage, but I wasn't left without supporters at commencement. Aside from Ellen, my American mother who was obliged to attend, Nancy and Kate Knoble, Bill's two sisters, traveled from Oregon and Pennsylvania, respectively, to be at my graduation. Laurie Willow, my American aunt, came from New Paltz to celebrate this special moment with me. Our farm neighbors, Uncle Phil Harnden and his wife, M. J. Heisey, were present. Since I was the recipient of both the Chancellor's Award and the Maynard Award, all my guests were granted VIP seats at the front of the hall. I cannot translate into words my feelings on graduation day.

After doing interviews with college and local media, I joined other graduating seniors lining up in the hockey ring. I was one of only four students graduating with a bachelor's degree in electrical engineering technology. This reminded me of something Prof. Robert Jennings had said during my freshman year to a group of about forty students in a Digital Fundamentals & Systems class: "Take a look at the person sitting on your right; then, take a look at the person sitting on your left. Odds are that they won't be graduating with you in four years."

It turned out he was right. While some students graduated with two-year associate degrees and decided to go to work instead of coming back to pursue their bachelor's degrees, many switched to other programs because they found electrical engineering too challenging.

The surreal moment came when my name was called. The audience applauded and I could hear my name being yelled from mul-

Proud graduate

tiple places throughout the hall. While walking across the stage, I raised two fingers towards the sky to thank God above for guiding me through an interesting college career. After shaking hands with the dean of the engineering department (Mr. Michael Newtown), the president (Dr. Szafran), and receiving my diploma, I took the Cameroonian flag from my back pocket and waved it as I walked away from the stage. My graduation from college will forever be a high point of my academic career.

As promised, I started posting photographs to Facebook right from the moment I dressed in my robe to give relatives back home a feel for what was going on. Since none of them were at work on the day of my graduation, they all gathered at Vincent's house, drinking beer and following my updates on Facebook.

At the end of the official ceremony, I went around the reception area and thanked some of the amazing staff and faculty for their fervent support throughout my time at college. I didn't forget to thank the dining staff for being very kind to me and helping me gain over fifty pounds during my college years.

Despite wanting to stay a little longer, I had to get back home for my graduation party. Picking up Marsha from her off-campus apartment—plus all the African food she had prepared for this special occasion—I drove to the farm. By the time we arrived, cars were lined up as if there were a funeral going on for a rich man. Among those present were several people from my church congregation; staff and professors from SUNY Canton, including President Szafran; and many members of my American family. I was humbled that Lee and Nancy Keet, who had invested thousands of dollars in my education, drove all the way from Saranac Lake to celebrate with me. My good friend Bob Sauter, who worked at the radio station, had made sure there was a setup for blasting music.

The day after graduation, I sat at the kitchen table with Ellen, Laurie, Nancy, and Kate, eating French toast with maple syrup and opening my graduation cards. Besides all the warm, congratulatory messages, a total of about $3,000 had been donated to benefit our NGO.

One of the saddest moments came while packing all my belongings in the residence hall for the last time, and realizing I would not be returning to SUNY Canton in the fall. My next adventure would be at a university just down the road, but it was still hard to bid farewell to SUNY Canton because it had become a home for me, rich with memories.

The opportunity to attend college in the United States was one of the best things that ever happened to me. When I first arrived with just a single piece of luggage, I had no money and knew no one. Nonetheless, people who came to know me, as well as some I never met, helped me have a taste of the American dream. Along the way—through peer tutoring, club memberships, peer mentoring, serving as an RA, and being an admissions concierge—I had a lot of fun, made a number of friends, and helped other students achieve success. Now, with the college experience behind me, I could see a path into a successful future.

And this can not be emphasized enough: I owe a debt of deep gratitude to Ellen Rocco and Rev. Mike for doing everything possible to get me through college. My life in the United States would have been a disaster if I hadn't met these two awesome and kindhearted individuals.

43

Summer 2015,
the Journey Home: Part One

In preparation for our trip to Cameroon, Ellen, Laurie, Jake (Ellen's son), and Mike (her farmhand) had completed their visa applications and mailed them to my country's embassy in Washington, DC, along with their passports and processing fees. In less than two weeks, without appearing there in person, they were issued visas to travel to Cameroon. I was envious that they didn't have to go through the same tedious process I endured in order to obtain a visa from the US embassy in Yaoundé, back when I was leaving home for the US to start college.

For all the years I was away from my village, when I attended school and worked in Cameroon, I can't remember ever saying I missed members of my family. But after four and a half years in the US, I was very excited about reuniting with each and every one of them. We had tickets on Turkish Airlines, which permitted two check-through suitcases per person, plus a carry on. We filled ten pieces of luggage with school supplies, Against All Odds logo items like t-shirts and Frisbees, and all kinds of gifts for dozens of family members. We held off buying many school supplies like chalk and notebooks that were less expensive if purchased in Cameroon.

A few days prior to our departure, Dr. Thomas Ortmeyer, who directed the electrical engineering program at Clarkson University, told me he had secured full funding for my graduate research assistantship studies, except for about $2,500 for health insurance. And as it turned out, Ellen offered to pay this health insurance fee! With Dr. Ortmeyer as my supervisor, I would be working with him on a microgrid project being studied for possible construction in Potsdam, New York. This was great news to take back home to my family in Cameroon.

Arriving at Douala International Airport on May 20, I knew we were in Cameroon because, just before we landed, I saw primary-school students outside playing soccer.

At Douala International Airport

We were received at the airport by a number of family members who resided in Douala, the commercial capital of Cameroon. Getting ten heavy suitcases to JFK airport had been a bit of a logistical challenge, but getting them out of the Douala airport was even trickier because people kept trying to help us with the luggage in exchange for money. I had to use my mean voice to keep them away so my family members could take care of our bags.

Making the situation worse was the presence of "my" white people, which made strangers think they could make a lot of money from the "rich tourists."

We spent the first evening at the home of my eldest brother, Vincent, and his wife, Bernadette. After several years of telling my American family about fufu and *njama njama*, water fufu and *eru*, and other delicious traditional dishes, we finally had a chance to feast on some of them, along with domestic beer. There was a lot of laughter, hugging, and storytelling. I can't even remember making introductions because there were simply too many relatives crammed into my brother's house.

We headed to the bus station after dinner, accompanied by my brothers Festus, Job, and Innocent, and my dear cousin Samuel, for an overnight ride to Yaoundé, the governmental capital, where I was expected at the US embassy for a visa interview appointment. I had to get a visa as soon as possible to make sure I could return to the United States at the end of our two-week trip. The road between Douala and Yaoundé was terrible, made worse every couple of miles by speed bumps designed to slow down traffic. The bus driver rode over these as if he was on a smooth road. For the safety of our American guests, my brothers yelled at the driver to slow the hell down whenever he sped over the bumps. Bus drivers go extremely fast on our terrible roads.

While other passengers fell asleep during the trip, I stayed up most of the night talking with my brothers because there was so much to catch up on. We finally arrived at Samuel's house in Yaoundé at about three in the morning. This is where I had lived for about three years prior to leaving for the United States.

Early in the morning, on day two of our trip, I took a bucket shower for the first time in a long time. Nonetheless, I had no problem going back to my childhood practice of scooping water from a bucket with my hands and releasing it all over my body. It felt like home.

I went to the US embassy in Yaoundé for my visa interview and everything went smoothly. Compared to my first one almost five years earlier, there were far fewer questions. I was told to come back the next day to pick up my visa, but I was eager to see my family in the village, so I planned to pick it up on the way back from there later in our visit.

When I returned to Samuel's after the embassy visit, my brother Innocent told me that my sister in the village had lost her eleven-year-old son two days before we arrived in Cameroon. When nobody else was at home, he had fallen out of an orange tree and died. My family knew me as a very emotional person, so they didn't want to break the bad news to me before the embassy visit. Knowing about it now, I was even more anxious to be with everyone in the village, but also had to pull myself together to make sure my American family had a good time.

At about nine that night, we left my cousin's house for the bus station at Carrefour Carrière. While waiting for our eleven o'clock departure, we tried a variety of street food. This included roasted fish (called *poisson braisé*), roasted pork, *miondo* (made from fermented cassava), and plantains. I sat with my brothers and my American family on a street bench and we all ate together, spending less than thirty dollars to feed everyone a lot of food. With so much time still on our hands, Jake went on a mission to sample every type of street food he hadn't yet tasted. He tried several breads and beignets from a boulangerie next to the bus station, Congo meat (sautéed snails), kola nuts, and more. Considering Jake's appetite, I have always wondered why he is not fat.

We embarked on the eight-hour ride at about midnight in a bus that was hot and very crowded. Our plan to travel overnight gave us an early morning arrival in the village, which is how most of my family travels. After a few hours, the bus stopped for passengers to relieve themselves. No restrooms—just a ditch alongside the road that men and women used. My American family didn't hesitate to join the others.

About halfway into the trip, Jake got sick—very sick. We assumed he had food poisoning from the excess of foods he had tried at the bus station. We were all sad because he usually kept everyone laughing. Ellen was worried; he had a high fever and was delirious.

Early in the morning on May 22, we pulled into the bus depot in Mbouda, a small town in the Western Region, about an hour from my village. Here we were met by more family members who had traveled on motorcycles from the village to welcome us, including my brother Vincent (Pa Meldrick) and my sister Marie, or Mama Marie. Vincent is called Pa Meldrick because his eldest son is named Meldrick, and it is a custom of respect to add "Pa" to the name of an older person's eldest child. Anything less than this would be considered impolite. As for my sister, we addressed her as Mama Marie because she is a mother figure to her younger siblings. In fact, wherever she goes, she is called this because of her motherly instincts and her stature.

In Mbouda, we purchased more gifts for my family and our neighbors, including rice and soap. Jake was too sick to travel with us to the village, so Ellen and Laurie took a room in a shabby hotel to let him rest until medication made him feel better. From my American crew, only Mike made the initial trip to the village with me.

Our first stop in Baligham was at my sister's compound, where most of my relatives from across the region had gathered to mourn the death of her son. This wasn't the way I wanted to reunite with my family, but I joined them in crying my eyes out. As much as I wanted to stay to console my sister, our time in Cameroon was limited. I had to make sure we stayed on schedule so that we accomplished everything we planned on doing.

I bought a crate of beer to add to the whiskey I had purchased in Yaoundé, and we headed to the village palace with my entourage to meet with the Chief. It isn't unusual for people from the dias-

341

(L-R) Mama Laurie, Mama Ellen, and Mama Marie

pora to sit down with him and discuss how their experiences can make a difference in the village. At the palace, we were well-received by the Chief and his *Chindas*—village notables. I told him about our new nonprofit organization, Against All Odds, and its mission to provide support to all the nursery and primary schools in the village. I explained that we expected to make gifts of school supplies and equipment, as well as offering scholarships to meritorious and underprivileged students at the start of every academic year. The Chief thought it was a great idea.

"Thank you for not forgetting where you come from. It is good that you are using your experience from the white-man's country to help your village."

While drinking beer and talking with the Chief, I told him about our plans to visit each school in the village to launch the mission of Against All Odds. He promised to send a messenger to all the schools to announce our upcoming visits.

From the palace, we drove down to my family's compound where I was born and raised. Since all my brothers and sisters were in the village, we decided to have an impromptu family meeting. Starting with my father, family members gave joyful speeches, thanking God for taking good care of me and bringing me safely back home. I wish I had the right words to describe the joy on the faces of my family members, especially my father, who openly said he was proud of me—something he had never said publicly before. In a way, my presence in the village eased the pain a little that my family was experiencing after my nephew's death.

Later in the evening, Mike and I returned to Mbouda to reunite with the rest of our American crew and hopefully alleviate our concerns about how Jake was feeling. Mbouda is predominantly French-speaking, and I needed to be there to help with translations. Jake seemed to be doing a lot better by the time we arrived at the so-called "hotel," where electric power was on and off and there was no running water. The hotel staff provided us with water in buckets for flushing toilets and washing.

* * * * *

On day four, May 23, we decided to move from Mbouda to Bamenda (commonly known as Abakwa), which is the capital city of the Northwest Region. We hired a small bus for the trip, and gave a lift to an old woman we met who needed a ride there. She sat next to Jake in the front row, and his attempt to speak French was cracking her up. Out of nowhere, when we stopped and fueled up at a gas station, her son appeared on a motorcycle. He was surprised to see his mother in our bus.

"Mama, qu'est-ce que vous faites avec le blanc," he asked, wondering what his mother was doing with a white man.

Motorcycle taxi drivers, aka Okada men, are some of the funniest and most entertaining people in Cameroon.

The forty-five-minute journey from Mbouda to Bamenda was an exciting escapade on a road that was rougher than it was good. However, the countryside and farmland offered amazing and beautiful views.

In Bamenda we stayed on Cow Street, Nkwen, at the Top Star Hotel, a decent place with running water, electricity, and a small store called a "supermarket." The hotel's location was very convenient because the five of us could take a taxi for about two dollars to reach major parts of the city. Ellen wasn't happy that we were staying in Bamenda because she wanted to spend time with my family and stay with them in the village. Unfortunately, after my day there, it was obvious that my presence—not to mention that of my white American family—was bringing too many people into the family compound. Keeping a room in Bamenda gave us an escape from the crowd in the evenings. I told Ellen she would understand once she had spent a day in the village.

During this whirlwind trip, I wanted to see most of my close family members, and moving from one city to another helped accomplish this. On our first day in Bamenda, we spent time visiting those who live and work there.

There are virtually no food regulations in Cameroon, so people set up food stands everywhere. This made it easy for us to try different types of food common to the Northwest Region. With over 200 tribes in Cameroon, it is noteworthy to experience the variety of cuisines from region to region. Everywhere you go, the food reflects the locality.

After exploring Bamenda, including Commercial Avenue and the Food Market, we returned to our hotel. My uncle Matthew and his wife, Stella, visited us there, and we took them to a nearby bar for conversation and drinks. Cameroon is a beer haven—Cameroonians love their beer like Americans love their pizza—and as much as people complain about poverty in Cameroon, somehow there is always money for beer. As we sat at the bar drinking and buying beer for everyone, Ellen and Laurie split a single bottle of Guinness, and both of them became a bit tipsy—Cameroonian beer comes in much larger bottles and has a much higher alcohol content than the average beer in America.

Later that night, Jake and I decided to go out. I called some of my friends and we met up in a bar at Hospital Roundabout, which is next to the Bamenda General Hospital. Before leaving the United States, I had told Jake that most of the beer in Cameroon is brewed in the country, but he found that hard to believe. When we arrived in Cameroon, he learned that Les Brasseries du Cameroon was one of the biggest companies in the country, brewing almost all the traditional brands of beer we were drinking. The standard bottle is over twenty ounces and costs about one dollar.

Ah, but most importantly, we arrived at a time when there was a promotion going on, so drinkers were given a chance to easily win free beers. On the inside of each bottle cap was a message indicating if you were a winner—and this happened frequently. At one point I won three freebies in a row, but Jake really got carried away with it. He bought lots of bottles for everyone just to collect a bunch of "free beer" caps as souvenirs.

Before I left Cameroon back in 2011, a bottle of beer was about a dollar. Coincidentally, the standard price—or bribe—for settling with police at roadside control points was also about a dollar. On this return trip four years later, the price of beer had increased to a dollar twenty. As a result (so I was told by a taxi driver), the police had rounded up the cost of settlement to two dollars. According to my brother-in-law, who was a taxi driver in Bamenda, he had been driving for decades without a driver's license; all he had to do was pay the required charge at control points. The Cameroonian police refer to the tradition of taking money from taxi and bus drivers as *l'avantage de service*.

The police feel entitled to collect money from drivers, and back in the office, their bosses expect a commission on whatever they've collected while on the road. For drivers who make an effort to present papers, they are often asked by the police, with sarcasm, "Est-ce qu'on va manger vos papier?" (Are we going to *eat* your papers?) It's almost a waste of time: whether or not the driver has papers, they'll still find a reason to collect money. The level of corruption within the Cameroonian police is extensive. As for those free-beer caps, drivers said they could actually settle with some officers at control points by giving them some of the caps.

While we sat at the bar drinking, a twelve-year-old boy walked in with a bucket of boiled eggs on his head. It looked like a normal thing to me, but Jake couldn't believe that parents would allow such a young child to be out on the streets so late at night. He talked to the kid, who told us he had to go to school in the morning. There was another young boy in front of the bar roasting and selling meat known as *le soya*. Jake bought some roasted meat from him before telling him it was way past his bedtime. It is eye-opening to witness what young children in Cameroon go through to help support themselves and their families.

All in all, it was a fun night with friends and family. Even though our large group had a lot to drink, we spent less than $200. Giving beer to people is something that is expected from every bushfaller, or anyone who returns home from abroad. I had to do what I had to do.

On the fifth day of our trip, May 24, we set out early in the morning for the village, which is less than a two-hour drive from Bamenda. When we were stopped by the police in Akum village, Jake started yelling, "1,000 francs police," as the driver was in the process of negotiating a settlement price with the officers. I thought the police would try to make a good impression on the white people in the bus by not asking for money. Instead, they wanted the driver to pay more than the standard two dollars since he had white passengers on board.

When we arrived in Santa, I showed my American family where I had lived and attended secondary school. Then we made the turn onto the dirt road leading to my village. As we drove through hairpin turns and went up and down hills, I vividly recalled how I used to carry a bag of raw food on my head as I walked this uphill path to school. The drive took us through amazing landscapes: sheep and cattle grazing on green hills, small farms in the lowlands cultivated with a variety of crops, and lovely scenery punctuated with tall eucalyptus trees—which produced some of the nicest long branches used by teachers to beat the hell out of us in primary school. Coming home after my years abroad, I found myself appreciating the beautiful landscape as I never had before.

Ellen Rocco and Pierre in the highlands outside Baligham village

When we entered the village, my American family wanted to see my mother's largest farm. I knew there would be many people awaiting our arrival at the compound, so I decided we'd visit the farm first. We drove to the biggest plot, located two or three miles away on the outskirts of the village. On the way, we hit a patch of road with huge, water-filled potholes. We all got out of the car as the driver used a piece of stick to measure the depth of each pothole, and we only got back in after he had carefully driven through the rough section.

In the United States, I had struggled to explain the size and style of farming practiced in my village. This was the chance for my American family to see it all for themselves. First, we walked through our cassava plantings, the mainstay product for farmers in Baligham village. Jake wasn't satisfied to just look at the above-ground portion of the cassava. He also wanted to see the underground tuber that was used for food, so I gave him permission to pull out one of the plants.

It was only a year old but already had a good-sized cassava. When we got to the companion planting section of the farm, where we grew corn, groundnuts (peanuts), beans, squash, and other vegetables, he pulled out a few groundnut plants because he wanted to see how they grew. I showed everyone the difference between plantains and bananas, both of which were available on our farm in abundance.

We had fun climbing mango trees and eating fresh fruit right off the branches. I had told Jake that in Cameroon we have over ten categories of mangoes, simply labeled as Number One, Number Two, and so forth based on their taste, with Number One being the best. He wanted to try them all, but after everyone had eaten many Number One mangoes, I asked Jake if he was ready to try Number Twos or Number Threes. "F*ck Number Two mango," he said.

Eating Number Ones in Cameroon will ruin your appetite for any lesser mango. I remember my first summer on the farm, when Ellen brought home some grocery-store fruit that looked like what we call Number Three mangoes. I tasted one and it was terrible because it had been picked green and ripened off the tree. Now, eating Number Ones in Cameroon, she understood why I didn't buy grocery-store mangoes in America.

Driving to my family compound after our farm adventure, we were welcomed by brothers, sisters, cousins, uncles, aunts, neighbors, and many children. Some of these kids had been born shortly before I left for America and were already attending school.

This was where I grew up. On one side of the compound was my mother's mud-brick house with an open doorway. A bit of indirect sunlight filtered into the front room, and a pot bubbled on an open fire in the second room. On the facing side of the compound, my stepmom, Mami Suzanne, had an identical mud-brick house, and she was cooking a fufu corn and *njama njama* meal for us. On the side of the compound between the two mothers' houses was my father's old house, and behind that was an outdoor toilet consisting of a large hole with slabs of wood across it.

One of the most emotional moments of the trip was when I introduced my American mother, Ellen, to my Cameroonian

Tiny cross-section of relatives in front of my mother's mud-brick house

mother, Odette (whom we call Mama Bar). Many people called her that because my neighborhood had so many bars (small stands set up in front of peoples' houses), and she is like a mother figure to everyone in the area. I wondered how I was going to introduce the two of them since my mother only speaks pidgin English and dialect, and Ellen speaks English. But things sorted themselves out when my mother rushed out of her house and gave Ellen a hug, shouting "Mama Pierre," referring to Ellen as my mother.

"No, you're the mama," Ellen said.

"No, you're the mama," my mother said.

They went back and forth debating who Pierre's mother was. As I watched both of them crying, I was so happy for the simple miracle of their finally meeting each other. Since my mother spoke very little English, she asked me in dialect to translate.

"Tell Ellen that for what she has done for you, I don't deserve to be your mother."

"Are you kidding me?" Ellen said. "Tell her I'm honored to have you in my life."

The two of them started making me uncomfortable, talking back and forth, appreciating each other. I left them and walked away.

Within a few minutes of our arrival, the compound filled up with neighbors and friends who wanted to see me and the four white people who had accompanied me to the village. All of us were lost in a sea of love and laughter.

After a lot of hugging, we sat down for a meal of many traditional dishes: *achu* and yellow soup, rice and groundnut soup, and, of course, fufu corn and *njama njama* greens. I waited for my American family to begin, and when one of them started eating the *achu* and yellow soup with a spoon, I burst into laughter because the tradition is to eat the dish with the index finger or two fingers. In dialect, my mother told me to be nice to my people.

When we were done eating, Jake took his (portable) guitar outside and started entertaining the crowd. Off the top of his head, he improvised a song: "Eating fufu and *njama njama* in Baligham." Everyone was having fun when my father arrived with five liters of locally tapped palm wine for us to drink. This palm wine had already undergone some fermentation, and the alcohol content was pretty high. Palm wine is best enjoyed with some kola nuts, which are bitter and complement the sweetness of the wine.

Before we had finished the wine, my parents called us into the house for a brief meeting. My father, mom and stepmom, my favorite aunt Manyi Jacqueline, eldest brother Vincent, and other close family relatives came forward in the middle of the room to thank my American family for going the extra mile to accompany me home to Cameroon. Praises were lavished on Ellen for "adopting" me as her son and helping me get a college education. She gave a speech thanking my Cameroonian family for their hospitality, and saying that she had received so much—by meeting me and knowing them—that it was a two-way street. Nonetheless, we all know by now that without the golden opportunity of meeting Ellen, the trajectory of my life would have been totally different.

When the speeches were done, Ellen was presented with a live rooster, the equivalent of a medal of honor for her humanitarian will-

Drinking palm wine (aka *matango*) in Baligham village

ingness to pave the way to a brighter future for me. Unfortunately, we were pretty sure we couldn't get a live rooster out of the country and into the United States. I felt so honored that Ellen, Laurie, Jake, and Mike had accompanied me to Cameroon because, at the end of this large and special gathering, it was clear to me that we had all become one big family.

In order to get a break from the huge crowd, we decided to visit some of my relatives who lived nearby. Our first stop was at Uncle Moses' compound. When we saw his pineapple and pawpaw in the backyard, one of my brothers used a bamboo stick to harvest a pawpaw, which dropped on Jake's head. He said the f-word but happily accepted the fruit. We were followed by a multitude of kids everywhere we went. I asked Ellen if she still wanted to spend all her time, including sleeping, in the village.

"Maybe not, but don't get me wrong; I love your family."

I didn't want to spend the night in the village either—the crowd at our family compound was too much and we needed to return to Bamenda to cool off. We had to go back there anyway to prepare for the next day, when we planned to visit all the village schools. With rain on the horizon, we hurriedly left the village because our driver warned us that if it began falling, he might not be able to get us out on the already tricky dirt road. Driving on country roads in Cameroon requires special skills. Although many of these drivers have never had a license, none of us from the United States could have driven us out of the village.

*　*　*　*　*

On the sixth day, May 25, we hired a small bus in Bamenda and loaded it with all the supplies we had brought from the US, plus school materials we had purchased in Cameroon. By the time we arrived at the compound, several family members and elders in the neighborhood had donned the green Against All Odds t-shirts and were ready for our tour around the village.

As the bus led the way, several motorcycle riders and many people on foot followed us. Our first stop was at the Government School (G.S.) Gahdiwala. When we arrived, the school bell rang for all the primary-school students to come out of their classrooms. Responding without hesitation, they lined up on the assembly ground according to their respective classes.

Government School Gahdiwala; students lined up on the assembly ground

"Hands on the shoulders, please," a teacher said.

"And go backward," the students responded, as they put their hands on the shoulders of the student in front of them and stretched backward to create perfect lines.

"Clap one, clap two," a teacher said, pausing for the students to clap. "Now, be quiet and listen to our brother from America."

There was perfect silence. This whole routine reminded me of my days in primary school. Everyone was dressed in uniforms, each had a low haircut, and mango trees grew around the assembly ground.

Standing in front of these students, I delivered a simple message.

"I was born and raised here in Baligham just like you. I also attended primary school in mud-brick classrooms. Now I have a bachelor's degree in electrical engineering from an American university and will be started my master's-degree program very soon. If I could do it, you can do it, too...."

There were times during my academic journey, especially in secondary school, when I had wished someone was there to assure me that everything was going to be all right. I wanted these students to know that with hard work and persistence, they could achieve success despite the economic status of their parents. Although they were at the beginning of their academic pursuits, I hoped some of them could look up to me and keep me in mind when they faced challenging moments on their academic journey. From my experience growing up in the village, most children have no inspirational role models. I hoped sharing my experiences from abroad could make a difference, and perhaps even make a life-changing impression on some of the students.

At the end of my speech, Ellen took over to explain the general mission of Against All Odds. She announced our scholarship program and introduced my brother Job as our coordinator in Cameroon. With Job's success in computer school and his innate intelligence, we had all agreed that he was the best person to manage the NGO activities. Sending him to computer school had turned out to be a very good idea.

Following Ellen's remarks, we delivered all the supplies we had brought for the school: chalk, notebooks, pens, pencils, soccer balls, handballs, and more. Giving thanks, the headmaster explained that the lack of teaching supplies was one of the major difficulties affecting both teachers and students. Expressing his appreciation for the scholarship program, he explained that children were often sent home because they could not pay their school fees. Politicians will say that primary school in Cameroon is free of charge for everyone. However, in practice, schools do not have enough teaching materials or teachers, so students are obliged to pay for their primary-school education with a levy.

This charge, overseen by the PTA organization, is used to hire teachers and buy basic teaching supplies. The gratitude expressed by the headmaster underscored how any assistance is so important to these village schools.

Our sixth and final stop of the day was at G.S. Mificat, where I attended primary school. Half of the mud-brick building that housed my last classroom had collapsed. The other half was still being used,

My former classroom building (when I was in Class 7)

but was on the verge of meeting the same fate. It was so unfortunate that years after my graduation from primary school, things had not improved, and sad to say, the situation was only getting worse. This made me even more eager to help my village's schools, which were so seriously in need of support.

At G.S. Mificat, I saw Mr. David, who had been my Class Six teacher. He had been teaching for years before I was born, and I couldn't believe he was still doing it. He called me aside and asked for cash, saying he had gone for months without being paid by the government. I had no reason to doubt him, for this was not unusual in Cameroon. Unlike Mr. David, who was working for the government, one of my favorite primary-school teachers, Mr. Peter, was a PTA-hired instructor who was no longer teaching at G.S. Mificat. During the time I was in primary school, his monthly salary was about thirty dollars. During our tour across the village, I met him at a different primary school, where he had transferred for a meager monthly salary increase.

"I knew you'd go places," Mr. Peter said to me.

Mr. Peter is one of the teachers who instilled the love of mathematics in me. It is crazy to think about how little he earns for his services, considering the impact he has had on pupils like me.

At the end of our visit, students in their blue uniforms lined up in the dirt schoolyard and sang a song of thanks, "If You're Happy and You Know It, Clap Your Hands." Even though everything I saw or heard was familiar to me, I still got emotional thinking about what these young students would have to go through to get an education.

As we left the last site and drove back to the family compound for dinner, a group of students ran after our bus. Visiting the schools in my village was a humbling experience that I will never forget. I hope the memory will always remind me of where I came from, and serve as inspiration to always give back to my community.

44

Summer 2015, the Journey Home: Part Two

We left Bamenda on the night of May 25, headed for the US embassy in Yaoundé to pick up my visa. As an international student in the United States, I had to go through the nonimmigrant visa process every time I paid a visit back home. The journey from Bamenda to Yaoundé was not pleasant. The driver of our bus took on more passengers along the way in order to make some extra money. As a result, a row of two passengers became a row of three, while the last row of four passengers became a row of five. By the time we arrived in Yaoundé, everyone was cranky. None of my brothers were with us at this moment, and we took out some frustrations on each other. We hired a taxi to take us to a hotel where everyone could relax and cool off.

On May 26, Laurie accompanied me to the embassy to pick up my passport and the new visa. Then we all went to a more reputable bus agency, Boca Voyage, and purchased tickets for our planned trip to Douala. I didn't want my companions complaining about the uncomfortable travel conditions, so I purchased VIP tickets.

We spent the rest of the day sightseeing in Yaoundé. We visited my cousin Samuel's welding workshop and the cyber cafés where I had worked before leaving for the US. With only one day in the city, it wasn't possible to see everyone in their homes, so I instead invited a number of my relatives and friends to have dinner with us in a restaurant. I had told Ellen and the others that I only had a few family members in Yaoundé. More than twenty people showed up for dinner with us.

My brother-in-law, Nestor, drove us to the bus station in his taxi early on the morning of May 27. I never thought we'd be spending so much time traveling. Before we boarded the Boca Voyage bus, we were offered beignets and beverages. I had no idea there were such comfortable, air-conditioned buses in Cameroon. The seats were more luxurious than those on buses I'd ridden in New York State. I was not used to this VIP style of travel. Passengers were dressed in business suits, reading morning newspapers. As a poor student in Cameroon, I had only experienced travel on buses for the common people, where the conversation often turns to complaining about the terrible living conditions in Cameroon.

In Douala, we rented two rooms at Hôtel des Amitiés at Quartier Bependa-Douala, close to where most of my family members lived. Each room had air-conditioning, running water, and a decent bathroom. The cost was thirty dollars a day for both rooms. Ellen and Laurie shared one, while Mike, Jake, and I shared the other, which was what we had been doing in all the hotels we stayed at. With the crowds of relatives and friends who wanted to see me and my American family, we once again thought it important to have a place we could escape to when we needed a break.

I had really hoped to spend most of the visit in my village, but many of my close relatives were now living in Douala and couldn't get away for much time. Instead, I asked my father, mother, Aunt Manyi, and others to travel from the village to spend time with us in Douala. After arriving in the city, we headed out for a meal at Vincent's compound, where most of my relatives were gathered. On the way, we stopped at the boulangerie from which Vincent bought the bread he delivered to retailers at the seaport. He was surprised when he pulled his motorcycle over and saw us sitting in front of the boulangerie, eating *gâteau*. I'm glad so few people in Cameroon bake their own bread or my brother wouldn't have a business.

In order to get to Vincent's house, Jake, Mike, and I—plus the driver—got on one motorcycle, while Ellen, Laurie, and their driver were on another motorcycle, or *bendskin*, as they are called locally. This was the easiest way to maneuver through the city because the motorcycles could get around traffic. As we headed to my brother's house, we heard strangers yelling at us, "Même les blancs bâche?" (Even white people get stacked [on motorbikes]?) They were surprised to see more than one white person on a single motorcycle. They thought we were being cheap, but really we were having fun. When these two *benskineurs* dropped us off at Petit Marché, a small outdoor food market near Vincent's house, we made their day by giving them a lot of extra money. Besides being appreciative, they insisted on giving us their cell-phone numbers so that we could call them whenever we needed rides.

As we walked through the narrow, muddy street running through Petit Marché, I heard people shouting *"les blancs"* or *"oyibo"* at my four white people. *Oyibo* is a Yoruba word for white people and it is used commonly in Cameroon because Cameroonians watch too many Nigerian movies. Nobody paid special attention to me because I looked like everyone else who lives in my country. Most people

Mama Laurie Willow and Mama Ellen Rocco

thought I was the tour guide for the white people. One business-woman in the market tried enticing us into buying her coco yams, telling us, "Depuis le martin, je n'ai rien vendu." (Since morning, I haven't sold anything.) Because we refused to buy anything, she asked us to at least take her picture to show the world her suffering.

We finally arrived at my brother's house. All the roosters that had been given to Ellen in the village had been brought to Douala and cooked. There was music playing, and the whole yard was filled with children and relatives. I sent my brothers out to buy crates of beer. For hours we talked, laughed, and drank a lot of beer. Some of my siblings whispered to me that they were having a tough time understanding what my white companions were saying because of their accents, and because they spoke too fast. Every now and then I had to play translator in both directions.

One of the surprising things for my American family was how politely they were addressed by my brothers and sisters. Ellen was always called Mama Ellen, Laurie was Mama Laurie, while Jake and Mike were called Tonton Jake and Tonton Mike. I was called Uncle Pierre. I referred to Ellen and Laurie as Mama Ellen and Mama Laurie, even though it sounded odd after years of just calling them by their first names.

I was happy to see how—without running water or reliable electricity, without extra money for fancy vacations, and with the ongoing headache of finding money to send children to school—my family members embraced life and each other. It was an unimaginable, amazing experience, watching my American and Cameroonian families naturally blend together, everyone just laughing and extending love without question. Late in the evening, we returned to our hotel to wash up before heading out for a little Douala nightlife.

On May 28, we visited my younger brother Festus at his welding workshop along the street of Axe-lourd Bependa. He now had eight apprentices under him. So, while I was working my ass off at college, younger brother Festus was already a boss, telling these apprentices what to do. The work he produced was of the highest quality, sought after by customers from Europe as well as in Cameroon.

We sat at the bar next to his workshop, talking, drinking, and giving away beer until noon, when we all got on motorcycles and went to his apartment for lunch. His wife, Vanessa Kimi, had prepared rice and plantains with a special Cameroonian black stew known as *mbongo chobi*. After this delicious meal, we went back to Vincent's home, where the rest of the family was gathered. While we were in Douala, we always ended up at Vincent's place because he had the largest home and a nice, tiled, outdoor area. My other siblings in the city were all renting shabby, timber-built apartments known as *kalabu*.

Sitting outside at Vincent's, I taught my family how to play dominoes with a set we had brought with us to Cameroon. Several kids started bugging me to buy them bonbons, so I made them work for it, offering an equivalent reward of one dollar to any child who could successfully sing the Cameroonian national anthem, either in French or English. These were mostly very young nieces and nephews. A few did a great job, but most of them had us all laughing as they mixed English and French versions of the anthem. Even the very little nursery-age children wanted to give it a try because of the money.

In the midst of all the family gatherings, I found time to have one-on-one conversations with every member of my family. For those still in school, I gave them advice about taking their studies seriously because I was not going to help anyone who was lazy. During a talk with my mom, she told me I should try to come home at least once every year. Then she told me I was getting really fat and asked about the food I was eating in America. When I told her she had hurt my feelings, she didn't seem to care—she laughed at me instead. Others in Cameroon saw my fatness as a sign that I was living a good life in America.

This brings me to a story my father had told me long ago. When I was born at the Baligham Health Center, I was a chubby kid with a big head, which wasn't surprising because my mother had carried me for more than nine months. When she was ready for release from the health center, my mother refused to go home until the doctors did something about my weight. My father conspired with the doctors to prescribe some kind of phony medicine that they told her would get rid of all my fat.

After being away from home for years, having a long conversation with my mother meant a lot to me. During the time when I had been pressuring my parents to pay for my schooling, she had always been my number-one supporter, even though she didn't see the point of attending school in Cameroon because most graduates ended up jobless. During our conversation, I jokingly asked if she had changed her mind about the importance of education. She certainly had, and the evidence left no room for doubt: she was personally sponsoring one of her granddaughter's education costs.

And there was one thing my mother said to me that day, something I will never forget: "You're not my child. You are a child of the world." This got me thinking about my life ever since I decided to leave the village to attend secondary school in a nearby town. I can't emphasize this enough: throughout my academic journey, I had always been fortunate to find people who were willing to help me over some of the toughest hurdles. Despite the fact that I was born into a large family and had a strong work ethic, it seemed as if it had taken support from the whole world for me to succeed.

On May 29, as the end of our stay grew closer, we decided to visit my brother at the Douala seaport, the largest facility of its kind in Central Africa. I expected the place to feel quite familiar since I had helped him deliver bread in this region during my secondary and high school years. However, most of the small shops that once lined the roadside had been bulldozed by the government to make more room for the big companies operating at the seaport. This meant my brother had lost more than half his customers.

After selecting freshly caught fish and shrimp that were roasted as we watched, we ate lunch right on the water's edge. This was by far our most expensive meal of the trip, but it was worth it. I've never met anyone who can roast seafood as well as those women at the Douala seaport. After lunch, we wandered around the district for a while. One of the things we hoped to see from a viewing spot right on the banks of the port was a giant ship. Unfortunately, two policemen stopped us and said we couldn't go that close. Of course, the policemen said they would make an exception for us if we gave them 10,000 FCFA—about twenty bucks.

"Ten thousand francs to see a ship," Laurie said. "I'll go and see a ship for free when we're back in New York."

We had all become used to police officers asking for bribes, but this was way too much. They wanted us to haggle over the price, but none of us was interested in bribing the police this time. I told them what they were doing was wrong, and if people weren't allowed near the ships, the restriction should apply to everybody, including us. They felt insulted and asked if I was keeping them from having a taste of the white people's money, adding that the white people would soon be leaving Cameroon—and leaving me in my same state of poverty. They had no idea I had been to the United States and was back home for a brief visit.

As someone who had worked in journalism most of her life, Ellen was always interested in talking to random people and asking questions. With the high unemployment rate, people complained to her everywhere we went about needing jobs. This was no surprise to me. In the village, where people are able to survive on what they grow and don't need or expect to make much money, people are poor but not impoverished. Village dwellers are only concerned about having enough to eat—they have shelter and a community. The same thing cannot be said about Douala, the economic capital, where poverty was evident everywhere we went.

On May 30, we went to one of the large, open-air city markets, Marche Congo, to buy souvenirs for friends and family back in the United States. Haggling wasn't as easy as I thought it would be. Sellers raised their prices as soon as they saw our group of white people. I was impressed with Jake, who successfully bargained the price of a *boubou agbada* (a locally made robe for men) from 20,000 FCFA down to 5,000 FCFA. But then he got angry with the merchant for trying to overcharge him, so he walked away without buying anything. Many of these small-business operators made the mistake of having an extremely high starting price when they were dealing with white people. Then, when it was bargained way down, their customers distrusted them and questioned the value and price of anything they were selling.

I was running out of money and couldn't afford to shop with my white family. Each time I saw something of interest, I separated from them and haggled the price alone. This was an interesting shopping expedition. One of us bought a piece of traditional jewelry for one price, and another bought the same item for half that price.

That evening we had a big gathering at Vincent's house, the last night we'd be in the country. While my American family thanked everyone for their hospitality, my Cameroonian family acknowledged the specialness of having them come to visit. Returning to Cameroon with my white family definitely elevated the status of my family. My mother was so grateful to meet the people who had embraced me as one of their own in America. She said she could sleep peacefully knowing that I was in the hands of good people. This was a very emotional evening as people stood to give short speeches and propose toasts.

As we all talked about our favorite moments of the trip, I knew mine was seeing my family for the first time in four years and seeing their reaction to me after my long absence.

"All of my preconceived notions about Africa have been totally dissipated," Laurie said.

"The beauty of the countryside was totally unexpected; the combination of open grassland, rolling hills, and beautiful farm fields was not what I imagined," Jake said.

The highlight of the evening was when Vincent's wife, Bernadette, an accomplished seamstress, presented Ellen and Laurie with *kabba* dresses, traditional garments that wrap around the body. Bernadette had completed tailoring training before she met Vincent, but never had the resources to open her own shop. With her treadle Singer sewing machine, she sewed clothes at home to sell to customers on special occasions, such as Women's Day. I thought to myself that I would like to help Bernadette open a shop once I completed my graduate studies.

While Ellen and Laurie were given dresses, Mike, Jake, and I were given locally woven bags made of fiber obtained from raffia palm plants.

Our last day in Cameroon was May 31. For the whole day, I was secretly hoping our flight would be canceled so I could spend more time with my family. The visit had gone too quickly. With our remaining money, we threw a big daytime party at Vincent's house.

In the evening, we were accompanied to the airport by an entourage of relatives. Jake and my younger brother Festus had become very close, like natural brothers. Jake wondered if it was possible to replace me with Festus.

"I wish it were possible to reduce Festus into a tiny creature and take him home to the States with us," Jake said.

After much picture-taking, hugging, and saying farewell to my parents and relatives, we walked through the airport. Looking back through the metal gate, I immediately missed the voices and smiles, the closeness of my big family, and all the great times we had spent together drinking beer and talking. Tears were running down my face. I just hoped I had brought some pride to them.

(L-R) Mama Laurie, Bernadette, and Mama Ellen

Our twenty-hour trip home, on Turkish Airlines from Douala to Istanbul's Ataturk Airport, brought us back to JFK International Airport. While all my American friends went through customs quickly, I had to wait in a long line. When I finally reached the customs officer and presented my documents, he told me that I had come back too early because my graduate program wasn't going to begin until late August. I tried to explain the guidelines to him—which I knew well—but he decided to send me to a detention room.

I had anticipated this possibility, so before we left for Cameroon, I had contacted the director of International Student & Scholar Services at Clarkson University. She had confirmed by email that I could come back to the United States anytime I chose because I was a continuing student rather than a new student. I printed the email and had it with me at the port of entry. The customs officer seemed like a stubborn man. I tried to tell him that only first-time foreign students weren't allowed to enter the country more than thirty days before their program began, but he wouldn't listen to me. He kept talking and not letting me explain myself. Then I presented the email from Clarkson University, but he made me stay in the detention room for a while longer before letting me go through.

Back home in the North Country, Ellen and I immediately went out into the garden, turned soil, and planted the red and black beans my village family had given us to take back to the United States. While doing this, we reminisced about the trip. Our neighbor, M. J. Heisey, happened to stop by while we were in the garden and asked us to tell her everything about our visit.

"Pierre had often talked about his family and country," Ellen said. "Seeing him with his people and in the Cameroonian landscape was like fitting the last piece into a puzzle."

With the $2,000 I had for spending money while in Cameroon, I had felt like a millionaire and people treated me like a celebrity. Everyone in Cameroon respected me and wanted to talk with me. Back in the US, I was just a regular person and people couldn't care less about taking a picture with me. A lesson I learned from my first trip back home was this: I came to America in search of a better life for my family and myself, but my aspirations had expanded to cover concerns for my entire village, Cameroon as a whole, and all the students in the US who looked up to me as a role model.

45

Back in the USA:
Graduate School Begins

I must take a moment to summarize one of the darkest periods in my American experience. When we returned from Cameroon, Mike, who had traveled with us, became increasingly antagonistic toward me. It had started in Cameroon, where he showed little interest in the trip and seemed to be very angry about being out of the United States. Of course, no one had forced him to travel with us. In fact, Ellen had paid his way.

The situation became worse and worse through the summer. We ignored each other, and we argued sometimes. I was careful to control myself because any incident that might come to the attention of the authorities could land me in immigration trouble. There were times when I actually feared for my life. Mike was very resentful about my success in school and my acceptance into Clarkson for graduate studies. Some of our exchanges left me feeling he was racist and xenophobic.

I mention this because it would be dishonest to ignore the bad times and just talk about the good times in America. I do not have to go into the details, but I will say that I was relieved when he left the farm in early fall 2015.

On August 17, 2015, I began my graduate studies at Clarkson University. Given the situation with Mike on the farm, I was relieved to be out of the house and back at school. Clarkson University is located in Potsdam, New York, about thirty miles from the farm. I had come to know several people in Potsdam, and some offered me free housing if I preferred not to commute. However, I chose to stay on the farm with my surrogate mom, Ellen. I appreciated all the housing offers, and knew if the weather was bad during the winter, I had places to stay closer to school.

The transition from living on campus during my undergraduate years to commuting every morning wasn't an easy one. My earliest class was at nine, so I had to get up at about seven in the morning to shower, dress, make breakfast, pack a lunch, and drive to school. Just a week into my graduate studies, I missed the good old days at SUNY Canton, when food was always available at the dining hall. In graduate school, I was so busy doing research between and after classes that there was no time to buy food. I had to have something with me or go hungry all day. It was wrong to think graduate school was going to be easier than college.

During the fall, we got more serious about AAOOL, our NGO. This was my first time being the manager of a nonprofit, so I had to improvise a lot. I had Ellen to back me up, and she had years of experience in the nonprofit world.

The first thing I did was create an announcement about the availability of scholarship money for primary-school children in my village. I sent this to my brother Job (our coordinator of AAOOL activities in Cameroon), and he printed enough copies to put around at public places. I also created a scholarship application form for prospective recipients. To my surprise, all 210 of the forms were completed. Job said people in the village had asked for more!

One of the questions on the application form was, "Why do you deserve this scholarship?" I was touched by the responses, more so because I knew some of the families applying and how poor they were. I was also moved by what some of the students wrote they hoped to be in the future. Here are some of the responses to the question about deserving the scholarship—some written by students' teachers, and some by the students themselves.

1. Mother has delivered five times and all are twins, making a total of ten children.

2. This child is handicapped and also an orphan.

3. Father abandoned the children with the mother.

4. Single mother with many children.

5. Parents are unable to pay fees on time and most of her brothers are loitering in the village.

6. The child's parents are epileptic patients.

7. Father is the only one taking care of my siblings and me, and he is only a [palm wine] tapper.

8. Parents can't send me to school but I like learning.

9. Father died many years ago. My mother is the only one caring for us and she is often sick in the hospital.

10. Mother is the only one caring for me and she is trying to go to school herself.

11. The child lost his parents in the Baligham vs. Awing tribal war. The grandmother is already old and weak.

12. My parents cannot send me to school like other children, so this scholarship will give me an opportunity to go school.

Ellen was overwhelmed as we went through the applications. She wished we had raised enough money to help all the applicants, but we were only able to assist eighty-eight students. I worried about the ones who would be disappointed about not receiving scholarships—I knew how it felt back in primary school when it was hard to find tuition every year. When you grow up in a family that is always struggling to make ends meet, your future is always uncertain, so it would be very painful to miss the AAOOL scholarship opportunity. But Ellen and I told each other this was just the first year of the program, and we would try to reach out to even more students in subsequent years.

After sending out these scholarships, we continued to promote AAOOL on our GoFundMe page. With the money raised, we were able to pay for the construction of 150 student benches to be divided among the seven primary schools. While this hardly took care of all the students in those schools who needed a good place to sit in class, the staff at the schools were very appreciative of the gesture. We had witnessed cramped classroom conditions so we knew every little bit would help.

Ntinwa Job, AAOOL Coordinator, delivering benches

When I was accepted at Clarkson University for the master's program, I thought I would pursue a PhD after that. But my trip back home made me realize it was time to conclude my academic career and start worrying about improving the living conditions of my family and my village, paying forward all the good that people had done for me through the years. A big advantage of being a research assistant was receiving a decent biweekly stipend. With this money, I was able to take care of my personal expenses—which were modest since I was living with Ellen—and have some left over to help my family on a regular basis. Unlike my mother, who sometimes needed a little help to buy cooking oil and lamp kerosene, my father always needed cash for his beer. If I passed up the occasional pizza, I could send twenty dollars to each of them to purchase what they needed or wanted.

Returning to Cameroon after four years had been an eye-opener. I thought about the rough relationship I had with my father when I was a youngster—always pestering him for money for my schooling. My conscience was now acting up as I remembered how much I harassed him for money—to the point that he had gone around the village borrowing what I needed. Though I was pushy because I wanted an education, I still felt so guilty for not having understood my father's financial stress.

I thought sending money to him on a regular basis would help me feel better, but that didn't really work. Deciding to write to my father, I emailed the message to Job, who printed it and sent it to him in the village.

Dear Father,

I hope you are doing well as far as health is concerned. I was happy that I had the chance to spend some time with you and the rest of the family during my short visit to Cameroon. People may say things about you, but I know that you are the best father any child could ever have. You loved education more than anybody in the village and that certainly reflects on all your children.

I'm sorry that I had to fight with you all the time about school fees and house rent. The truth is, you are my father and I could not go to anybody else. I just hope you are proud of me for my academic accomplishments, and as your son. As you can imagine, if I gave up on school, that might have been the end to the family dream about education. That is why I never gave up, because I wanted to succeed by all means so that the younger ones in the family could look up to me.

Dear father, I want you to be the happiest person because you have one of the most united and happy families in the whole world. I want you to take good care of yourself and live a long life. As soon as I complete my master's degree and start working, I want to make sure you live like a KING because you deserve it.

I would have loved to write more, but I have to go to the library and do some homework. Please take good care of yourself and the rest of the family.

Regards to all,
Pierre Nzuah

I had enjoyed spending time with my father during our trip to Cameroon, but we were so carried away by the excitement of seeing each other after such a long separation that we didn't really have time for a deep conversation. I felt much better after writing this personal letter to him and apologizing for my past behavior.

After receiving the letter, my father wrote back to me.

Pa Jean Mofor
N.W. Region
Mezam [Division]
15th December 2015

Dear son,

It is a privilege most greatest honour having a word from you again. I saw the letter you sent to me through Job and all the things you have been sending. Truly speaking I'm so proud of you my dear son. I really pray God should guide you in your master's program so that someday you can make me more prouder than now. My regard to your people, I mean your American family, and tell them that I love them so much. Stay blessed, son.

I love you so much.

Receiving this letter from him was the best Christmas present I could have asked for. My father saying "I love you so much" was pretty special to me. I couldn't remember him ever saying those words to any of his children or wives. I was ashamed that I hadn't ended my letter to him by telling him I love him. Although cell-phone service was still terrible in the village, I vowed to myself to call my father and mother on their cell phones on a regular basis.

By the end of the fall 2015 semester, I was exhausted from schoolwork. Even though I was signed up for only fifteen credits, the workload was substantially more demanding than when I took twenty credits a semester as an undergraduate. This first semester of graduate school was a bit overwhelming as I familiarized myself with what was expected of me.

I can't overemphasize the difference between my undergraduate and graduate experiences. Trying to complete class assignments and do my assistantship research, I found myself studying late into the night and all through the weekends. Sometimes I only saw daylight on my drive to school—I was inside studying and researching all through the short days of late fall—and drove home in the dark. The good thing about this situation was that I wasn't the only student putting in long hours. More often than not, I left the research lab at about ten at night—and I was the first graduate student to leave.

It is important to feel passionate about your graduate-school field of study. Otherwise, life in grad school is miserable. My love for electrical engineering, especially the field of power engineering, was one of the many reasons I didn't give up in spite of the tough start. But one thing I hated about grad school was that teachers didn't push me to work hard. I had to do all the pushing myself.

46

Spring Semester 2016

During the second semester, figuring out what to do and when to do it was no longer my biggest problem, replaced instead by the thirty-mile commute each way during the North Country winter. Much of the drive was on back roads that were often unplowed when I headed out in the morning or was returning at night.

On one occasion, a heavy storm delivered more than two feet of snow while I was inside all day working in the lab. Ellen texted me around nine o'clock and warned me to stay with a friend either in Canton or Potsdam. She said she had barely made it home from work—from Canton to the farm—and her car had all-wheel drive. Visibility was very poor, the highways were covered with snow, and cars were moving along at fifteen miles per hour. I had decided to try to make it home, but about five miles from the farm, when I made a turn from the state highway onto a county road, I immediately regretted that decision. The road had not been plowed and it was impossible to tell where it was, except where there were trees or houses close enough to the shoulders for guidance. I had to shovel my car out multiple times, but I made it home without having to abandon it in the snow, as many others had.

Overnight, the weather got worse, with more snow piling up and temperatures dropping. In the morning, I was relieved to find an email from Clarkson University canceling classes for the day. The thermometer read forty degrees below zero.

I put on four layers of shirts, two pairs of pants over my thermal underwear, a thick pair of gloves, my winter boots, topped it off with my fur hat, and headed out to plow around the house and barn. You know it is cold when you just step outside and it feels like someone is squeezing your face.

I slogged my way through the snow to the barn, plowed my way out on the larger Kubota tractor, and then cleared around the barn. It was so cold, I felt as if there was ice inside my gloves. After about an hour, Ellen came outside and told me I should come into the house to warm up before continuing. I refused, saying I just wanted to get the job done and over with.

After about two hours of plowing, our front yard looked nice, surrounded by the huge piles of cleared snow. When I went into the house and took off my gloves, I couldn't feel my fingers and don't think there was any blood flow into them. Washing my hands in warm water made my fingers turn red, and they were so painful that I almost cried. A few hours later, they finally felt normal except for my middle right finger. This episode taught me a new word: frostbite.

Despite the harsh winter weather conditions, everything was going well in graduate school. In just two semesters, I had learned much about power engineering—more than I had in my four years as an undergraduate. I was trying to complete my degree in eighteen months rather than two years, so I overloaded myself in order to complete all class requirements by the end of the second semester. For the third and final term, I could focus on research without the ongoing distraction of class assignments.

* * * * *

When I asked my brothers how everyone was doing back home, they always said all was well because they didn't want to worry me. However, in early April, I had a message from my younger brother Job informing me that my father was sick. I knew this was serious because he mentioned it without me asking. I called my elder sister Marie, who is a nurse, and told her to take my father to the hospital. Since Cameroon has a pay-as-you-go healthcare system, I knew money would be essential if my father was to receive treatment as soon as he reached the hospital. Using MoneyGram online service, I sent funds home right from my research computer. As the only family member abroad, it is imperative to always have enough money saved for emergencies like this one.

My father improved and was discharged from the hospital after less than a week, which worried me. He was suffering from some kind of heart condition, but the doctors never explained it. By early May, I learned that his heart problem had become serious and he was back in Bamenda for treatment. I kept up with his situation and my brothers told me he was improving. For a family-oriented person like me, it was painful to be in America and hear about my father's declining health while unable to be with him.

On May 11, after finishing my last final exam, I received the unthinkable news from my brother Job: my father had passed away at the age of seventy-two. It may not have come as a surprise to my siblings who were with him during his final days on earth, but for me it was a deep shock. Receiving the news of my father's death was one of the most painful phone conversations I've ever had. Being thousands of miles away from my family and missing his last days made it so much worse. Finding it hard to stay strong and control my emotions, I totally broke down and cried like I have never cried before.

I had received the sad news in the morning, when I was still at home getting ready to go to school. I sent an email to my advisor, informing him about my father's passing and letting him know I planned to travel to Cameroon to be with my family. He was so understanding. I planned to purchase a plane ticket and travel home as soon as possible. When Ellen got home from work and saw the state I was in, she said she was going to accompany me to Cameroon.

"You're my son. How can I let you travel alone?"

It would have been a very long trip alone and grieving, so I deeply appreciated Ellen's unexpected decision to accompany me. That night, we downloaded and completed the necessary paperwork for her visa application. The next morning, we sent the completed application via priority mail to the Cameroonian embassy in Washington, DC. During a follow-up phone call apprising them of the situation, they agreed to expedite processing. In the meantime, we shopped for the most economical airfares and purchased tickets for a May 18 departure on Turkish Airlines.

Nothing was going to stop me from traveling home to pay my last respects to my father. How could I sit in front of a computer doing research, imagining my father being buried in our village compound? Though I'd had a rocky relationship with him during my teenage years, I still considered him my hero. After all, he had managed to raise a bullheaded kid like me.

I asked my brothers to make sure my father's body was kept in the morgue so that the burial service could be delayed until my arrival. Before my father passed away, the Chief of my village, HRH Samkie Elvis Gahnyam II, had prohibited the practice of keeping bodies in the morgue because it prolonged the mourning period and put immense financial pressure on grieving families. However, he made an exception for my father so that I could be at the burial, which I very much appreciated.

It does not matter how old you are: when you lose a beloved parent, it is a deeply felt pain. Part of that pain for me was knowing I would never have another chance to talk with my father. As I waited for our departure date, I did a lot of thinking about what I could have done differently to help prolong my father's life.

One of the problems with living in a third-world country like Cameroon is the lack of health care for the elderly. If there had been a health-care system for the poor, my father might have had periodic checkups, his heart problems might have been detected, and he might have undergone a modern treatment regimen. I kept thinking that he died from a heart condition because we didn't have the financial means to take him to a well-equipped hospital, where he would likely have received much better care. This could have bought him some extra years.

Oddly, I was angry at my father for dying while I was still away at school. He hadn't given me the opportunity to complete my education, get a job, and repay him for making me who I am today. He died without reaping the fruit of what he worked so hard to nurture.

We arrived in Douala on May 19, just before midnight, and were picked up at the airport by Loic Kamwa, who had offered to drive us to the village after he heard about my father's passing. Loic was a Cameroonian student who graduated from SUNY Canton with a business administration degree, and then returned to Cameroon to run his father's businesses. Since his return home, he had also started a big farming and poultry business.

After a seven-hour drive on poor and potholed roads from Douala, we arrived at Loic's family compound in Baham II, in the Western Region. Because it was rainy season, Loic's father gave us

With Loic's Family: Baham, Western Region, Cameroon

his all-wheel-drive vehicle to use for the rest of the journey to my village. So nice, so generous. Judging from the time we spent with his mother and father, it was apparent to me that Loic inherited his humility and generosity from them. They were especially kind in my moment of need.

Although Loic was accompanying me as a friend, his father sent along the family driver free of charge. All we had to do was pay for fuel. From Baham we drove to Mbouda, a small town where my father's body was being held in a mortuary. When we arrived on May 20, we rented rooms in a small hotel to relax after the long, difficult trip. My brother Vincent came from the village to update us on the funeral plans.

Only a few relatives knew that I was going to be at my father's burial. As a student, I didn't have much money to spend, but nobody was going to believe that I was broke, coming from America. I did send some money for purchasing food and beer, but it was best that most people didn't know I was coming. I grew up there. I know my people well.

On May 21, some of my family members and friends traveled from the village to Mbouda for the removal of my father's body from the mortuary. Several cars and motorbikes followed the hearse transporting his remains to the village. A gendarmerie officer stopped us at a control point outside of Mbouda. He wanted drivers to pay (bribe) him for "overloading."

I know it is a common practice for gendarmerie and police officers to extort money from drivers, but I didn't know they would do it during a time of sorrow. If not for the priest who was accompanying us to the village, the officer would have been beaten by some of the young men who had come from cities across the country to attend the funeral.

As required by village tradition, our first stop upon arriving with my father's casket was at the palace so that the Chief could pay his last respects.

"Pa Jean was a good man who believed in educating all children," he said.

A tailor by trade, my father always found a way to sew school uniforms for poor village children. Even though I sometimes resented this generosity because I was left to wear old, patched uniforms, I now understood why he felt the need to help poor children. My father was one of the few parents in the village who always encouraged and supported students in their educational endeavors. Some who appreciated his support said so in writing.

380

I have personally benefited a lot from your wisdom and encouraging attitude. Countless times, you stitched up my school uniform just like that of a handful of Baligham pupils. Your good works can't be enumerated, and we carry them to heart even as you won't be here again.

RIP Pa Jean. Tributes from John Nkuekue. A well-wisher and a village son who has benefited greatly from Pa's wisdom.

John Nkuekue

Papa, I remember the time you used to encourage me, you even offered me a school uniform when I was in Primary school. Ah, vous resterez gravé dans nos mémoires Papa. RIP.

Leo Didas

My father's death wasn't only a loss for my family, but a big loss for the whole village. Rich or poor, the passing of a village elder is a big deal. Two traditional African quotes come to mind: "What an old man sees sitting down, a young man cannot see standing at the top of the tallest tree"; and, "The death of an elderly man is like a burning library." The atmosphere at the palace demonstrated my father's place of respect in the village.

Ellen accompanied us into the palace compound and everywhere else, so she witnessed the entire funeral process. From the palace, we drove very slowly to the family compound, joined along the way by more cars, motorbikes, and foot traffic. Given the size of my family and our many friends, I had warned Ellen to expect about a thousand people at the funeral service. Our family compound was packed, our neighbors' compounds were full, and there was hardly room to move around.

My family belongs to the Bamiléké tribe. We have our own ways of grieving over the loss of a loved one. As soon as we arrived at the family compound, some of the women led us in songs of mourning. These sorrowful compositions, sung in our dialect, mention

Mourning at the family compound in Baligham village

the name of the deceased and some of the things the person accomplished in their lifetime, as well as the community's sense of loss and grief. These songs are very moving, and the singing can be heard for many kilometers.

My father's coffin was set up in his near-collapsing mud-brick house. I had promised on my trip home the previous year to help rebuild the house for him—once I completed my studies—but he had passed before I was able to do so. His coffin was in the middle of the room, and open, with all his children standing alongside as people filed through, circling the casket to say their goodbyes to him. In some cases, special blankets were placed ceremoniously on top of my father by mourners.

After traditional rituals were performed in the house, the casket was brought outside, placed on a stand, and opened again. A prominent religious leader said a prayer, my mother and stepmother said a few words, my eldest half sister and brother spoke, and my father's friends were given an opportunity to bid farewell.

As tradition demands, people were asked to come forward to say whether my father owed them money or if they owed him money. I was happy that I had collaborated with my siblings to make sure that my father's debts were paid off while he was still alive. Considering that I had come from the United States, it would have been embarrassing for me if people had come forward—witnessed by a thousand people—to say that my father owed them money.

My father's casket was then lowered into a prepared spot in front of his old house. Standing there watching his coffin enter the grave, it was so hard to believe this was really happening.

The next requirement of our tradition was to select my father's successor as leader of the family, and to present that person to the public. For some polygamous families, choosing the successor can be very tense, particularly if each wife wants their son to be the chosen one. The writing of wills is uncommon in the village, so people may confide their chosen successor to the Chief or one of their trusted friends. My father had done something a bit out of the ordinary. Years before he died, he had chosen my half brother, Nchinda Benjamin, as his successor, and he had confided this secret decision to my eldest brother, Vincent. In order to avoid any problems, Vincent asked my father's friends and palace notables if he had told any of them about his choice. The answer was no from all of them. Then Vincent revealed that he had the secret. Apparently, my father had trusted Vincent more than the others to keep his secret and avoid the chaos that might result from people knowing his choice before his death.

During a traditional dance, when the funeral attendees surrounded my father's children, Vincent presented Benjamin to everyone as my father's successor. Many people were shocked, assuming I had come all the way from the United States to attend the funeral because I was to be the successor. They were also stunned that my father had chosen the son of one of his wives as a successor, and entrusted that decision with a son from his other wife. I had never wanted to be my father's successor. It comes with a lot of responsibilities, like attending all major family events, which included weddings, meetings, and conflict mediation sessions. As the only one of my father's children who was living abroad, I was already loaded with responsibilities for the family.

The celebration of my father's life continued. One after another, traditional dance groups made their way into the family compound. Since he had been a member of several such groups in the village, they came to dance at his funeral. Each of my siblings was also obliged to bring at least one traditional dance group to the occasion, but not being a member of any, I hired one to perform. A particular assemblage, the children's ballet group, caught everyone's attention, and for good reason: their founder and coordinator was my father, who had brought the children together on Sundays to enjoy themselves through singing and dancing.

We were unable to have the traditional gun salute that usually came after an elderly person's casket was buried. This common practice had been put on hold after the fairly recent tribal wars between Baligham and Awing. The two neighboring villages had reached a mutual agreement to end the practice of gunshots during death celebrations so that people would not be panicked into believing another war had started.

In Cameroon, the funeral celebration for an elder—a respected Bamiléké man like my father—could go on for several weeks. Mourning is particularly intense for the widows. There is a unique, coordinated system for Bamiléké wives to mourn the loss of their husband. One of the moving experiences of the funeral day was watching my mother and stepmother stand up every so often to perform different types of mourning songs. Each time, other women danced along with them, never letting them feel alone in their grief. Young children, especially little girls, imitated my mother and stepmother as they sang and danced. As demanded by tradition, there would be a full month of mourning, during which the widows would never be left alone. If my father had more wives, the official mourning period would have taken much longer.

Spring Semester 2016

The evening after my father's burial, Loic drove Ellen back to the hotel in Mbouda. I stayed in the village to spend the night with my family. There was music through the night, and I made sure there was enough beer to keep everyone happy. To paraphrase Loh Benson, a popular singer from Bamenda, when you are sick, there is never enough money to buy medicine and there is no food to eat, but when you're gone, there is enough money to buy food and drinks for everyone. He was right. From my observation, it is always easier for relatives to come together in the village to mourn the loss of a loved one—and spend a lot of money in the process—than it is for family members to join hands to help a sick sibling in a hospital bed.

On the day following my father's burial, members of my family gathered at our late grandfather's home to honor our ancestors. We brought some symbols of the tradition—palm wine, kola nuts, and a rooster. Prayers were said, asking my grandfather and his two late wives to welcome their son with open arms. My grandfather's successor provided palm wine, while women from this side of the family cooked meals for us.

After two days in the village, Ellen and I took a bus back to Douala so I could see her off at the airport. I was staying on in Cameroon because I needed more time to grieve with my family.

My siblings spent two more weeks of mourning in the village before returning to their homes in various cities. My brothers' wives, however, remained in the village to take care of my mother and stepmother through the intensive mourning rituals. Seeing how well they were taken care of after my father's passing—and knowing that this support system would be there for many months—I was deeply humbled by traditions I hadn't paid attention to as a child.

* * * * *

During my trip the year before, there was not enough time to do everything and see everyone I wanted to, so I was glad now to spend more time in Cameroon after the funeral. First I traveled to Douala, where many of my family members no longer in the village were now living. We gathered every day at one of my brothers' houses, drinking beer and telling stories about our father. Brother Vincent

385

recalled the time when my father had only two children, him and Marie. When our maternal parents went out to work on the farm, my father would be left to watch the young children. He figured out how to keep Marie and Vincent occupied so he could visit around the village or take care of business away from the family compound. My father would put a rock in a cooking pot and top it with water. He then instructed the two children to maintain a fire in the mud-brick fireplace and warned them not to open the pot. This trick worked for my brother and sister, but I think I would have opened the pot if I was in that situation.

I told my family I wished our father had lived longer so he could see what I accomplished after my education. I began sobbing, saying that he passed away without giving me the chance to make him proud, and to have him realize what a positive impact he had on my life. Vincent assured me that our father was very proud of me, and that he used to brag to people in the village about his son in America.

When I was sending money for my father's treatment during his final days, I had told my brothers not to tell him that I was the one paying his hospital bills. I didn't want him to think more of me than he did of my siblings who couldn't provide money for his treatment. When his health took a turn for the worse, Vincent wanted him to know that I was responsible for paying the hospital bills, and said this made my father cry.

"God will protect him for me," my father, Pa Jean, had replied.

I was touched because I couldn't remember ever seeing my father cry. Spending time with my siblings talking about our dad's memories and his legacy helped me overcome my pain.

From Douala I traveled back to the Northwest Region, where I had received most of my early education, and reconnected with some of my middle school and high school friends through Facebook. Some of them were surprised that I was making time to visit with them. I understood this feeling because when most people who are living abroad return home, they only want to spend time with more-prestigious acquaintances rather than connecting with old friends still struggling to make a living in Cameroon. I had thought this way myself when I first left the country, dreaming about being respected and revered as a rich man when I returned home. However, my experiences in America had changed the way I wanted to treat or be treated by other people.

As a student living on campus, I had interacted with professors and administrative staff who were always down-to-earth and accessible to everyone. During the time I spent on the farm, Ellen would bring me to radio station fundraising events and parties where food and drink were served. I had an opportunity to meet some very wealthy people who were unassuming, and didn't hold themselves above people without wealth. Plus, all of them were philanthropic. So, when I returned to Cameroon for the funeral of my father, I was considered a millionaire in terms of village standards, but didn't want to be treated differently just because I had an education and more money than most people I knew. Growing up in poverty and having the golden opportunity to study in the US, including graduate school, without having to borrow money, and enough of a stipend from my assistantship to have money in my pocket, had humbled me and made me deeply grateful rather than superior.

This quote from an unidentified source comes to mind: "Don't feel too proud because you have bread; remember, someone owns the bakery. Your account balance is another person's tithe. Never look down on anyone in life; only God sits that high. We are all something but none of us is everything."

I spent some wonderful days catching up with old friends, and telling them about daily life in America compared to what we had imagined it would be like when we were children. Having the opportunity to live in two very different parts of the world taught me humility. Even some of my relatives couldn't understand how low-key I was when I visited from America. My brother's wife, Bernadette, was surprised that I would help fetch water and peel potatoes.

After a few weeks in Cameroon, I ran out of money and had to ask Ellen to wire some to me, which I would repay when I returned to the United States. I realized it was time to start planning my trip back to the North Country, but doing so was not that easy because getting a visa is a long, arduous process. It took more than a week from the day I submitted my application form to the point where I had an interview at the embassy. This may not seem like a big deal, but if it takes a week or more just to get a visa, that means it is virtually impossible to take a short trip back to Cameroon. I hoped the United States could modify the visa application process for people who have been studying or working in America.

My interview went smoothly and quickly because of my years of study in the US. I am not really complaining about the process because so many people wouldn't mind enduring far worse measures for the opportunity to travel abroad. Still, it is important to be clear that getting a visa requires money, paperwork, and time.

I stayed a little longer in Yaoundé before journeying to the village to say my goodbyes. My mother couldn't travel to Douala for the airport send-off because of Bamiléké tradition, which required that she remain in the village for a full year after the death of her husband. The only exception to staying there would be if she was ill and needed to go to a hospital.

After a month in Cameroon, I returned to the North Country on June 6 and resumed my graduate research. I was very grateful for the support received from so many after my father's passing. People really came through for me. Every Facebook message I received cheered me up, and of course the cards, emails, and calls all helped get me through this sad time.

47

Fall Semester 2016: Part One

During my time in Cameroon, I realized how much my schooling in the United States had changed my family's perspective on education. Both close and distant relatives were now invested in it like never before. When I was in Douala, my younger nieces and nephews told me they were working very hard at school because they wanted to follow in my footsteps. These kids seemed to think I was in every plane flying over their homes. Each time they heard a plane, they'd wave and yell: "Tonton Pierre, acheter nous les yaourts." (Uncle Pierre, buy us yogurts.) This gesture spread past my family so that kids who had never met me were waving at planes, yelling my name, and asking me to buy stuff for them. While I was with my young family members, some of them asked me where my plane was parked. I told them it was at the airport because I didn't want to discourage them by telling them I didn't own a plane. It made me feel good to know that I was giving these children hope for the future.

Through our nonprofit, we had been helping schools in my village, but my second visit home inspired me to do even more. Ellen and I stepped up our fundraising effort and took in almost twice what we'd received the previous year. Our biggest donor was her brother, Ben Zuckerman. I was getting good at asking for donations—people contributed every time I talked about the work we were doing through AAOOL. This was a skill I learned from Ellen.

When we started offering scholarships during the 2015–16 academic year, I sent application forms to my brother Job. During our previous scholarship offers, we had made a special plea to teachers to help identify the students who most needed our support. I thought this would inevitably skew to the benefit of girls, who are often overlooked by parents when money must be paid to send children to school. Though we did our best to select all the girl applicants, about 70 percent of the scholarships went to boys because parents and teachers overwhelming chose them over girls to receive our help.

Before the start of the 2016–17 academic year, I was looking for a new strategy for selecting scholarship recipients. It occurred to me that almost everyone in the village needed our help because subsistence farming leaves very little cash for school fees. Since the practice of class ranking was still normal in primary schools, I decided to make scholarships merit-based, offering them to the top five students in each class at each of the seven primary schools in the village. The ranking system has some positive outcomes, encouraging students to engage in healthy competition with each other.

We were able to offer a total of 180 scholarships to Baligham's primary-school children, doubling the number from the first year.

G.S. Gahdiwala scholarship recipients with some of their teachers and Job

Most surprising? By using the merit-based system, 116 of the 180 scholarships went to girls! There would have been an even higher percentage of girl recipients, but because we allowed headmasters to select some of the financially neediest at their schools, the number of boys was upped to sixty-four. This was great ammunition to use when talking with parents about the learning capacity of girls, who were expected to just get married and run the household.

After scholarships were allocated, Job, our NGO coordinator, went back to each school to develop a list of basic supplies needed for the nursery and primary schools. He sent us the list and we worked out what could be purchased. Job then returned to the village with supplies that included chalk, drinking buckets, books, pens, pencils, and other basic school resources. After delivering everything, he went to Santa, a small town close to Baligham village, and arranged with a carpenter to build a teacher's table and chair for every classroom at every school in the village. Job oversaw this construction process and personally printed our NGO logo on every table and chair, using the knowledge he had acquired through his serigraphy training program. We also arranged to have extra tables and chairs built for every headmaster's office.

Ellen was so impressed by the work Job was doing for AAOOL in Cameroon that she suggested we start paying him. I thought it would be better if he continued giving back to the community through his work for the NGO. His reward was having me pay his fees for both computer school and serigraphy training. Even though Ellen thought this might not be fair to Job, I just wanted to make sure that 100 percent of the donations we received went directly to scholarships and material supplies for the Baligham village schools.

As a person with a disability, Job was often overlooked or underestimated. This changed when I started sponsoring him through computer training and appointed him coordinator of the nonprofit organization in Cameroon. He interacted with headmasters, PTA staff, and the Chief of Baligham village. He thanked me many times for believing in him and making him feel valuable. He is a good example of what a person can accomplish when they're given even a little bit of opportunity. (Once Job's studies were completed, I opened a graphic design and serigraphy workshop for him in Douala. He is now one of a few people in my family with a stable, long-term livelihood.)

The work of AAOOL was made possible through the generosity of our donors, who I thought of as our heroes. I wish I could make sure they understand what a huge impact their gifts have had on the lives of students and families in my village. Contributors to AAOOL should know that every penny they donated was used for the students and schools—something that cannot always be said about larger nonprofits.

* * * * *

Meanwhile, I was on track to graduate by the end of the fall semester, completing my master's program six months early. This meant I had to start thinking about the next chapter of my life's journey. I had ruled out studying for a PhD. The master's degree was already one step higher than I had ever imagined I would go in my education. Some of my school advisors were urging me to continue my studies at the doctorate level, but I felt it was time to find a job. I was already an essential breadwinner for my family in Cameroon, but I did need to earn more. As much as I loved school, I made the difficult decision to look for work.

After six years of studying in the United States, I had established many connections that I didn't want to lose. With my family all in Cameroon, I wanted a job that would allow time for me to visit them as often as possible. My goal had long been to find a job with an international company that would train me in the United States and assign me to work for them somewhere in Africa. This may have been overly optimistic for a new graduate.

During a July 4th party in Saranac Lake, I met with the president and CEO of GE Africa. It was a pleasure to meet someone of his stature who was very down-to-earth, and I had a great discussion with him. "We're always looking for new talent to join our team in Africa," he said, and told me to get in touch with him as soon as I was done with graduate school. A couple of months before my graduation in 2017, I contacted him and he connected me with the supply chain leader of GE Africa (based in South Africa), with whom I had a nice phone conversation. He then sent me a job description for a leadership position that was available in Congo-Brazzaville. I was a little scared about starting my first job in a supervisory role without any post-graduate workplace experience. The supply chain leader assured me I would be trained for the job, and connected me with a Nigeria-based hiring manager who seemed like a typical African bossy boss. During our first conversation, he wouldn't let me stop him to ask a question. "Don't interrupt me, I'm still talking," he said—repeatedly.

This made me angry. I had become accustomed to the American style of interviewing—courteous and helpful. It seemed as though the hiring manager in Nigeria was still a young man and was flexing his muscles during these job interviews. It was not an uncommon attitude among young people in powerful positions in developing countries—or, perhaps, anywhere. After this unpleasant phone conversation, I talked with the supply chain leader in South Africa and asked him if I would be able to travel easily between African countries and the United States. Unfortunately, he told me that the job I was being offered would have a visa good for me to use in Congo-Brazzaville only. This meant any plan to travel to the US wasn't going to be easy.

After telling him the job offer wasn't going to be a good position for me, I also contacted the president and CEO of GE Africa, thanked him for the opportunity, and explained that the job was not a good fit at this point in my career. Actually, I had assumed I'd be hired and trained in the US for about a year or two before being sent to work in Africa. I was sad things didn't work out as hoped.

Despite the situation, I called my brother Vincent and told him I was considering accepting a job offer in Congo-Brazzaville. He laughed and laughed and thought I was out of my mind. "I don't know what you're talking about; my dream has always been to visit you in America—not Congo," he said. He advised me to remain in the United States even if I didn't find a job immediately. As he reminded me, the family status was at its highest as long as I was in the US, and he didn't want that to change.

Throughout my years of study, many people had told me I'd make a great teacher. At some point, I came to realize I was actually good at motivating and teaching students with different learning abilities. Through my powers of persuasion, I have had a lot of positive influence on young students during my academic journey, and most of my outcomes pointed toward the good I might do as a teacher. During my college education, I had positive experiences working as a peer mentor, resident assistant, library manager, and peer tutor, just to name a few. I was always able to find the right ways to motivate and encourage students. During my senior year at SUNY Canton, I tutored physics, French, mathematics, and almost all the electrical engineering courses offered at the college. A substantial number of students and teachers advised me to consider the teaching profession—which made me deliberate seriously on becoming an instructor. As an international student, however, I didn't have the luxury of experimenting with different jobs before making a long-term decision.

I toyed with the idea of returning to Cameroon to find work. When I told friends back home about this possibility, they laughed and told me I was crazy if I thought there were any jobs. Of course, the government always talks about how many new jobs it is creating, but the unemployment statistics never change. Using the knowledge I had acquired in the US to do some kind of good work in Cameroon had its appeal, but at this point in my life it might have been a pipe dream. As one frustrated Cameroonian once said: "Growing up in Cameroon, youths were told education is the key to success; now, being grown up and having acquired that key, I find my friend Mr. Paul Biya [the president] has changed the lock."

Cameroonian students work very hard at their school studies. It is hard to understand why they can't find jobs with their degrees. When these students complain about the lack of opportunities for young people, they are told to use their knowledge to create jobs for themselves. Some graduates are lucky to find private-sector jobs paying less than one hundred dollars per month—but labor laws aren't enforced and people aren't always paid. Those interested in sports also must come from families with money if they ever want to have opportunities based on athletic talent.

While I'm patriotic and love Cameroon, I know that loving one's country does not mean you have to love a corrupt government, or political practices that work against education as a pathway to work and a brighter future. Yes, corruption plays a part in the country's economic challenges and the difficulties young people face in the job market. But it seemed impossible for me to consider going home to work—there were no jobs and I hadn't accumulated any money.

I definitely wanted to get some work experience and save some money before returning to Cameroon. Further, many people advised me to live in the United States for a while as a way to eventually have a more significant impact back home. After my years in America, I believed that this is a country where hard work is usually rewarded.

Once again, I returned to my dream of becoming an electrical engineer. During a career fair held at Clarkson University, I had a good talk with Eric Hesler, Gerard Lindsey, and Steven Fanning, representatives from an engineering and consulting firm, TRC Companies. They asked if I would be interested in interviewing with them the following day, and of course I said yes. Subsequently, I was invited to the TRC office in Liverpool, New York, near Syracuse, for a pre-employment interview. I had a great session with several supervisors and they took me out to lunch. The following day, I received a job offer and accepted it.

The only glitch was that TRC recommended—but did not require—that I take the Fundamentals of Engineering (F.E.) exam, which is the first step in the process of becoming a professional licensed engineer. Despite the stress of needing to complete my thesis by the end of the semester, I gathered all my undergraduate notebooks and textbooks and began preparing for the F.E. exam. Note to undergraduate students: save those materials in the years following graduation—you may need them to prepare for advanced testing.

48

Fall Semester 2016: Part Two

For Americans who may be offended that I stole a job from a citizen of this country, I have to say that even though America is not my nation of birth, no one wants to work hard and earn the right to the American dream more than I do. For everything that has happened to me through school and being hired for my first professional job, I felt like the Lord's chosen one.

On November 23, I checked online and learned that I had passed the F.E. exam, and on December 8, I successfully defended my thesis. I had only eighteen months at Clarkson University, and during that time I was too busy to engage in a lot of social activities, but one interesting thing happened that has stayed with me. Keep in mind, this could have happened at almost any college. I just happened to be at Clarkson.

Before starting my graduate program, I was told that a tuberculosis (TB) screening test was required before the first day of classes. In the process of completing the TB screening form at the Student Health and Counseling Center (SHAC), I came across this question: "In the last five years, have you spent more than one month in any of the following countries?"

This was followed by a long list of countries: Afghanistan, Africa, Algeria, Angola, Bolivia, Cameroon, Cape Verde, Chad, and so on. I explained to a health center staff person that it wasn't right for Africa to be on the list, which even included *countries located in Africa*. Initially, she didn't understand what I was talking about and thought I was trying to avoid having the TB screening test. Before I left the health center, I promised to return to talk to the director after my screening at the local hospital.

During the first week of classes, I was at the Electrical and Computer Engineering Office with my supervisor, Dr. Ortmeyer, completing some paperwork. I showed the TB screening form to everyone in the office and explained the problem. They all were surprised by the mistake.

"Can you help me to get this changed?" I asked Jill LaCross, an administrative assistant.

"No," she laughed. "You have to go back to where you got the form."

Things got busy, but after several weeks I finally had a chance to return to the health center. A different staff person there told me they used a TB screening form acquired from the St. Lawrence County Public Health Department. I asked for the phone number. Back in our research lab, I called the health department and explained the problem to the woman who answered the phone. Her reply: "I was never good at geography."

She politely asked if she could transfer me to another person, and I agreed. I explained the problem once again, but this person didn't understand it either and transferred me to a third person, where I got an answering machine. I decided I would visit the health department offices on my way to school.

However, my schedule got busy and I didn't actually stop by until the following semester. When I showed the staff there the form that Clarkson was using, no one recognized it. They showed me the county form and it was completely different, so I took a copy back to SHAC, explained to the director everything that had transpired, and presented her with the county TB form. Two students waiting in line behind me began laughing when they heard me explaining that it wasn't right to have both Africa and African countries included on a list of countries.

The story doesn't end here. The director took a copy of the form and made the changes I suggested. She promised to raise the issue at the next meeting, but made it clear she couldn't guarantee the changes would be made anytime soon. Several months later, at the beginning of my final semester, I went back to find out if anything had been done, and was happy when a staff person told me the form had been modified. I asked for a printed copy, and was glad to see that the question had been changed to: "In the last five years, have you spent more than one month in any of the following?"

However, I looked at the list and nothing had been changed: Afghanistan, Africa, Algeria, Angola, Cameroon, Cape Verde, and so on. I thanked the staff person for trying to solve the problem, but she looked unhappy when I said they still had to remove Africa from the list in order for it to be correct.

"We can't remove Africa from the list," she said. "The TB rate there is too high."

"Then I'm going to keep coming back here," I replied, a bit bitingly.

I suggested that if they really wanted to keep Africa on the list, then all the individual African countries should be removed from it. But South Africa and perhaps some other of the more than fifty countries in Africa weren't on it, so I retracted my suggestion and said the only good option was to remove Africa from the list. I could tell the staff at the health center was getting really fed up with me.

I tried to clarify the problem by asking why Portugal was on the list but not Europe. Paraguay was on the list but not South America. I went back to the health center several more times, and asked people in the engineering department if they thought I was crazy. Jill assured me that I was doing the right thing and that it was good for the school to pay attention to this.

After successfully defending my thesis, I decided I couldn't leave Clarkson without having the "Africa problem" addressed. Instead of continuing to make life miserable for the health center staff, I scheduled an appointment to meet with Clarkson University President Dr. Tony Collins. When I showed up at the office, we chatted for a little while before I explained exactly why I had wanted to see him, including a summary of my efforts to have the TB form changed.

"This can't be good for Clarkson," Dr. Collins said. "Don't worry, I'll take care of this."

The president made copies of the TB forms I had brought with me. I thanked him and left. If I became very wealthy and made a huge gift to Clarkson University someday, I did not want to be recognized as Pierre Nzuah from Africa. I really don't know why it's difficult for people to understand that Africa is a continent that is home to dozens of individual nations, not a single country.

* * * * *

Saturday, December 17, 2016, was my Clarkson University graduation day, another milestone in my academic journey. I used to believe that my roots in an impoverished family were a curse, but through hard work, resilience, determination, hope, and lots of prayer, God had led me to the right people (the list is very long) who supported my aspirations. Earning a bachelor's degree was a miracle, but obtaining a master's degree was beyond my wildest dreams. These accomplishments may seem ordinary and unexceptional to many people, but they have brought much joy and many blessings to my family and me.

Graduation day was made even more special because of all the people who made it through frigid weather and terrible road conditions to attend the ceremony. The list included: my church pastor, the Rev. Mike Catanzaro, and his wife Linda Potter, who have been like parents to me; Bob and Jackie Sauter of North Country Public Radio; my dear farm neighbors, Uncle Phil Harnden and M. J. Heisey, who were always there for me; and my two Cameroonian compatriots, Larissa Danielle and Vanessa Tchinda—a big shout out to both of them, as well as my good friend Joseph Kasinge from DR Congo.

Before I walked across the stage, Ellen had chatted with President Collins and told him that my family couldn't be there to watch me receive my degree. After the experience with my brothers trying to get visas to attend my undergraduate ceremony, I hadn't bothered to encourage them to try coming to the Clarkson graduation.

(L-R) Vanessa Tchinda, Larissa Danielle, Pierre Nzuah, Ellen Rocco, M. J. Heisey, Joseph Kasinge, Uncle Phil Harnden, Bob Sauter (photo by Jackie Sauter)

Pierre with Canton Presbyterian congregation family: Linda Potter, Barb Brown (who works at SUNY Canton), Pierre Nzuah, Rev. Mike Catanzaro

If getting a congresswoman involved hadn't help them get visas to attend the SUNY Canton graduation, I didn't think there was anything different I could do this time.

President Collins mentioned my name during his speech and told the audience how my siblings in Cameroon couldn't come to my graduation. I was sitting in the front row with other graduate-degree recipients, and the president asked me to stand up. Completely taken aback by the kind gesture, I totally froze and didn't know how to react. I am a big dreamer, but I never imagined that a short man from Baligham village would be standing in front of a big audience in Schuler Indoor Recreation Center on the Clarkson University campus, receiving a huge round of applause. I am embarrassed to boast or blow my own horn, so I will share the very kind post Ellen wrote for the radio station's website after my graduation.

When Your Heart Needs Warming, Read This

Six years ago, Pierre arrived in the North Country for his first semester at Canton College. He had left his remote village in equatorial Cameroon to land in Syracuse, temperature -20F. Like so many people across this globe, he was motivated by a desire to improve his life and the lives of his family members.

The first few years were bumpy. Pierre does not come from a wealthy family, and there is no scholarship money in the US for international undergraduates. But, with the help of friends he made here, and through his own fierce focus and strong work ethic, he made it through Canton College a year and a half ago.

On Saturday, friends joined Pierre to celebrate the most recent chapter in his progress: Pierre was awarded a Masters in Electrical Engineering from Clarkson. Working with advisor Dr. Ortmeyer through a research assistantship, and thanks to financial help from Clarkson University, Pierre is now poised to begin working with an American company here in New York State.

From his first semesters at Canton College to the present time, Pierre has found ways to give back to the communities that have nurtured him. Two years ago, he helped found Against All Odds: Outreach for Learning, an NGO that is providing scholarships and supplies to the six little elementary schools based in his home village of Baligham. Lately, he's been exploring ways to send used textbooks to high schools in Bamenda, a small Cameroonian city near Baligham.

So what warms my heart about Pierre is his instinctive inclination to pay it forward, to take the impact of community generosity beyond himself. We're very proud of you, Pierre.

Ellen Rocco

49

Blessings

Now I am going to count my blessings and thank everyone who helped me climb upward a rung or two on my academic journey. To all who have offered me moral or financial support, may the sources of your happiness and wealth be like an ocean and never run dry. You have helped me to a place where I am capable of providing for myself, my family, and others in need in a way that I never imagined possible. To Rev. Mike Catanzaro and my American mom, Ellen Rocco, I can't and would never be able to find the right words to thank you.

As I wrote this book, I revisited some painful memories in my life. There were times when I got depressed and wanted to stop writing, but I remember something Ellen Grayson from the Presbyterian congregation in Canton once said to me during a summer boat trip on the St. Lawrence River: "You've got to write down your story. Your story can be a source of inspiration for so many young people out there."

So the idea of writing this book wasn't mine. It was people like Ellen Grayson, Johanna Lee, and many others in upstate New York who had come to know my story and encouraged me to write it down. If it can motivate and inspire even one or two people, then it has been worth writing. My advice to anyone who has worked hard for a long time and starts to lose hope is: Que será, será. What will be, will be. No matter how tough life gets, be strong and don't give up because miracles do happen. Today, I am the product of many miracles.

Epilogue

There are people who accomplish great things without public hoopla or recognition. When you read Pierre's book, what emerges is a portrait of a man who has persisted and persevered since he was a small child, overcoming obstacles that would have stopped most of us in our tracks.

I am reminded of the violinist in the old joke who asks, "How do you get to Carnegie Hall?" The answer, "Practice, practice, practice." Starting in a mud hut in a remote Cameroonian village, without running water or electricity and lacking access to a free education, Pierre combined hard work, ingenuity, and a ferocious determination in order to achieve an advanced degree in engineering from an American university. Along the way, he has helped family, friends, and an ever-growing community of people who look to him as a role model and inspiration. This is not a story of glamor and flash; it is a story of what we can be proud of as human beings—a person at his best whose life says to us, this is a path that matters, this is a path that gets you up the mountain—with grace and dignity.

That's the basic thing to say about this book. But it doesn't tell you how I feel about the person—Pierre Nzuah. I have met Pierre's Cameroonian family—and we have embraced each other as part of one family, separated by the Atlantic Ocean and geopolitics, but joined by a shared, beloved son.

Whenever Pierre thanks me for my help, I say back to him, "Thank *you*." This is not an empty gesture. I cannot imagine my life without Pierre. After less than a decade, he is a part of my heart, home, and family—because he has returned so much to all of us. It is a two-way street, my son.

Thank you.

Ellen Rocco
Richville, NY

Acknowledgments

I would like to thank Ellen Grayson for seeing the difference my life story could make to every struggling kid around the world, and for encouraging me to put it down on paper.

For editing and proofreading the early manuscript of this book, I would like to thank my American mother, Ellen Rocco, and my American uncle, Philip Harnden (Uncle Phil).

For several rounds of revisions and insightful suggestions throughout a lengthy process that helped produce a more readable book, I am grateful to Lawrence Gooley and Jill Jones, my editors at Bloated Toe Publishing.

For adopting me as one of their own; for their endless support throughout my undergraduate and graduate education; and for helping me achieve my American dream, I can never find the words to appropriately thank Ellen Rocco and Rev. Michael Catanzaro.

For his tough love, inculcating discipline, and teaching me the importance of reaching for the stars in everything I do, I owe a debt of gratitude to my late father and hero, Pa Mofor Jean.

For bringing me into this complex world and being my number-one supporter in every aspect of my life, I will forever be indebted to my mother, Ma Ngegang Odette, who steered me through the roller-coaster journey that led to this book.

And finally, there are many people whom I can't acknowledge individually because the list is so long. I would, however, like to say many thanks to everyone who has helped me overcome obstacles along the path of my rocky journey to financial freedom. You will forever have a special place in my heart.

About the Author

PIERRE NZUAH was born in Baligham village, Cameroon. He attended primary, secondary, and high school in Cameroon before moving to the United States in 2011 for greener pastures.

He holds a bachelor's degree in Electrical Engineering Technology from SUNY Canton and a Master of Science in Electrical Engineering from Clarkson University. Pierre currently resides in Liverpool, New York, where he works as a Substation Design Engineer for TRC Companies.